MR. DISTRICT ATTORNEY

MR. DISTRICT ATTORNEY

BY BARRY CUNNINGHAM
WITH MIKE PEARL

 MASON / CHARTER · NEW YORK 1977

Library of Congress Cataloging in Publication Data

Cunningham, Barry.
  Mr. District Attorney.

  Includes index.
    1. Hogan, Frank S.   2. Public prosecutors—New York
(City)—Biography.   3. New York (City)—History—1951–
I. Pearl, Mike, joint author. II. Title.
KF373.H56C8   345'.7471'01 [B]   77-879
ISBN 0-88405-465-9

Strand, 1977

FOR LAURA

"The truth is the best swindle."

—F.S.H.

MR. DISTRICT
ATTORNEY

1
ABOVE THE BATTLE

Frank Smithwick Hogan awakened early, as he always did, and watched the first pale shimmers of daybreak across the Hudson River. On this March morning in 1973, sunrise would already be sparkling on East Side windowpanes, but here on the West Side, the rooftops of Riverside Drive were still cast into black relief. Hogan switched on a bedside lamp and reached for a navy wool robe. He showered, shaved, splashed on bay rum and exchanged the robe for a Brooks Brothers pin-stripe. There were two finishing touches: a stickpin in his necktie and a breast-pocket handkerchief carefully folded into three neat points.

Mary Egan Hogan, his wife of thirty-four years, set down a breakfast tray on a livingroom table near the window. Hogan's breakfast was always the same: tea, rye toast and cereal. The view from the livingroom window still bore the gray imprint of winter: skeletal trees, a frosted ground, vapor rising from manhole covers. It would be a few weeks before cherry and dogwood trees blossomed along Riverside Park.

As he always did during breakfast, Hogan snapped open his briefcase and began to tackle the day's important legal papers. This day would probably end exactly like the great majority of his days—in bureaucratic routine. The paperwork was no more than a dry symbol: it represented the raw facts of murder, assault, rape, robbery, arson. Confronted by the daily onslaught of violence in New York City, Hogan found it necessary (now and then exhilarating) to get up at 6:00 A.M. and begin work early—even at the age of seventy-one, and into his thirty-second year as Manhattan's "Mr. District Attorney."

Scanning the material that would become Police Department statistics,

Hogan winced. His stomach ached. He had slept badly the night before, worry keeping his mind alert but reeling. The District Attorney had been depressed lately—unusual for him. Even more unusual, he had several times felt the world literally spin around him; twice, he'd had to grip his desk to keep from falling. This morning's "confidential" crime file did nothing to dispel the growing uneasiness he felt in himself and in the work of the office he'd administered for three decades.

Since the previous suffocating summer, New York City had seemed in the throes of a collective nervous breakdown. In July and August 1972, a muggy temperature inversion had cupped the city like a vacuum jar, sealing in heat and humidity. Thousands of air conditioners had short-circuited the New York power grid, knocking out electricity, igniting subway fires, dimming the lights and music of ghetto life. Violence had incubated in the trapped air mass. There was a record-breaking rash of murders: by year's end, police had counted 1,812 bodies, 661 of the victims slain in Hogan's Manhattan jurisdiction. The rhythms and patterns of murder had peaked on August 22, a sort of homicidal equinox. Within those twenty-four hours, thirteen persons lay murdered in the street, a homicide statistic later recorded in *The Guinness Book of World Records*.

The violence had not subsided over the winter months, as Hogan had hoped. Instead, the homicide rate was now running 10 percent higher than the 1972 record. And the police were reporting a robbery every six minutes and forty seconds. Fear rose in the streets: windows were caged, doorways triple-locked; wary pedestrians glanced over their shoulders as they walked.

Hogan wondered from time to time if fear didn't feed on itself, as local TV newscasters (to Hogan the new "yellow journalists") raised the adrenalin count of dinner-hour viewers with accounts of the day's switchblade murder, or rape, or armed robbery. Actually, among the country's ten largest cities, New York would survive 1973 with the eighth-ranking murder rate—20.7 for each 100,000 residents, less than half the number in "Kill City," Detroit, where the bloody record would be 49.4.

The possibilities of urban terror as a vote-getting subject had not escaped the notice of politicians. On a national level, Richard Nixon had proved in 1968 that a law-and-order campaign could frighten the electorate into voting for "safe streets" candidates. "If we are to restore order and respect for law in this country," Nixon had said, "there's one place we're going to begin: we're going to have a new Attorney General in the

United States of America." So the blame for cities in chaos was dumped onto the bowed shoulders of Ramsey Clark.

In the microcosm of New York politics, eager opportunists began to play the same simplistic game of pin the tail on the donkey. One person should be made to seem culpable for the abstract social injustices that produce crime in urban life. Mayor John V. Lindsay was the first to take the flak. "Soft on crime," ranted the hardliners who wanted his job. Soft on crime or not, Lindsay was short on patience. He had been blamed for every emergency that befell the five boroughs—including a snowstorm. And so he did what any tired, well-to-do man might have: he eliminated himself from a third-term attempt in 1973 and boarded a yacht for the Caribbean.

Lindsay's departure left the law-and-order types casting about for another fall guy—and they found Frank Hogan. He had once described his job as "a mysterious entity—part lawyer, part policeman, part accountant, part prosecutor, part defender of the innocent, part youth counselor, and part community advisor." Now he would be forced to become what he had always avoided being: a political infighter.

Hogan was no politician. He never went on handshaking tours of the Lower East Side, noshing the obligatory ethnic foods. He did not kiss babies, or make speeches. He had no stomach for the wheeling and dealing, the doubletalk, the backstabbing of the political gutter. He was a registered Democrat, but he had seldom breathed the bad air in the smoky back rooms of influence. His "campaigning" had become mere formality. In late spring, he would announce that he was a candidate for reelection. In the autumn, he would read his acceptance speech. His political exercise consisted of a short bow from the podium every election night.

Hogan had long since resolved to keep partisan politics out of the D.A.'s office, and he had succeeded. His reputation in the news media had been a better support than any Madison Avenue hype could have been. The papers dubbed him "Mr. Integrity." Every four years, the multi-party endorsements rolled in: Hogan was returned to office through eight successive elections without serious opposition. (Once, in 1949, an American Labor Party candidate made a slight splash by opposing him, but the fellow posed no real threat.) Hogan had avoided even the formal swearing-in ceremonies of Inauguration Day. Instead, the presiding judge would come to him—straight to the Hogan apartment at 404 Riverside

Drive. There, among the potted philodendra and the leatherbound volumes of Dickens and Thackeray, Hogan would place his hand on the family Bible and take his oath.

But in the anti-Establishment mood of the 1960s, Hogan's ivory tower became a fortress. From the right, he was castigated for dispensing "turnstile justice." It was charged that his system of plea bargaining spun rapists and muggers right back into the street. On the left, there were those who branded Hogan a grudge fighter: a stodgy defender of the past, a vindictive man who wielded retaliatory prosecution against those who opposed his reactionary views. He was dubbed a prude—and a prick. The counter-culture knew him as the man who had washed out Lenny Bruce's mouth with soap. Young people resented him as the paternal despot who slammed down on protesting Columbia students in the Students for a Democratic Society riots of 1968.

Hogan was a Columbia alumnus and trustee. The proudest moment of his life, he once said, was winning the university's prestigious Alexander Hamilton Medal for "distinguished service and accomplishment." Traditionally, the prize had been bestowed only on writer-scholars, like Lionel Trilling and Mark Van Doren, and past presidents of the university, such as Nicholas Murray Butler and Dwight D. Eisenhower.

The SDS rebellion had wounded Hogan almost viscerally. These students were his intellectual heirs, acting suddenly like intractable grandchildren—screaming obscenities at the cops, defecating on admissions records. One night, a group of them gathered at Columbia's main gates and hoisted aloft an effigy labeled "Frank Hogan—Trustee." They doused the dummy with gasoline and set it aflame. In his apartment only a few blocks away, Hogan could hear the mob screaming at "him" in unison, "PIG! PIG!" while their leaders urged them on with bullhorns. The effigy, curiously, was costumed in a Three Musketeers hat and beard; if the "Frank Hogan" nametag hadn't been pinned to its vest, no one would have recognized the swashbuckling dummy as the dapper D.A.

In fact, Hogan looked more like a pink-cheeked leprechaun than he did a flinty-eyed prosecutor. Snowy-white hair and a gold watch chain across his suit vest imparted the image of a successful bureaucrat.

Burned in effigy or not, the District Attorney proved himself a survivor. In 1973, at an age when many of his old Columbia Law School cronies had retired from practice or from judicial benches, or had given up life's struggle altogether, Hogan was about to embark on an unprecedented ninth-term reelection bid. For the first time in his lengthy career, a serious contender had emerged that year to challenge the D.A. in a Democratic primary election.

The man: William vanden Heuvel. A liberal, vanden Heuvel had risen to prominence in the Justice Department under Robert F. Kennedy. A liaison officer, recruiting judicial candidates for the federal bench, vanden Heuvel had also become a Kennedy family aide. Then, a decade later, he had announced, with Kennedy vitality, "It's time for a change." Getting Hogan's job for himself was the change vanden Heuvel had in mind.

Frank Hogan was no stranger to Kennedy style. The margins of that family's lives had overlapped his own. John F. Kennedy, always respectful of Hogan's influence on the American legal establishment, showed a measure of that respect in 1960, just before the President-elect announced his brother's appointment as U.S. Attorney General. Rumors of the pending announcement had been greeted by howls of nepotism around Washington. The new President was forewarned that the prestigious New York *Times* was particularly bitter; the newspaper planned an editorial attacking the nomination. Tipped off to the *Times* position in advance, J.F.K. turned to the one lawyer's lawyer whose endorsement he felt might silence the criticism.

The White House call came through an intermediary, John G. Bonomi, then chief counsel to the Senate's Kefauver Crime Committee and formerly an assistant D.A. under Hogan. Hogan acceded to Kennedy's wishes and made his R.F.K. endorsement public, thus neutralizing the *Times* attack. Hogan had known Bobby well when the latter was chief counsel to the McClellan Committee. In the late 1950s, Bobby had spent more time in Hogan's office than in his own. Bobby was absorbed in a pet project: the controversial "Get Jimmy Hoffa" campaign.

Bobby got Jimmy Hoffa, and lost Frank Hogan. When federal indictments were handed down in the case, Hogan was miffed. Not because the Teamsters' boss was being railroaded into prison, as some critics charged—Hogan was happy to wave him goodbye. But because Bobby had claimed all the credit for the send-off, while virtually every scrap of evidence that sent Hoffa to jail had been gleaned from Hogan's wiretap investigations. And Bobby never said thank you in public—he *did* send a personal note of thanks.

Hogan carried no lasting grudge, however, and in those Camelot summers, with the undertow of fate still years away, he knew all the Kennedys socially. He and Mary rented a vacation cottage on Martha's Vineyard and joined the Chappaquiddick Beach Club.

By 1969, Hogan knew the Chappaquiddick bridge all too well. And he soon made it known among friends that had *he* been the Massachusetts prosecutor, Senator Edward M. Kennedy might have had a lot more explaining to do. Although the D.A. never commented officially on the Kopechne tragedy, his closest aides knew his distinct opinion of Teddy's "blackout" alibi: "Totally unbelievable . . . nonsense."

"Morally and ethically," Hogan said in confidence, "Teddy should have run down that beach knocking on every door for help, not worrying about his political future."

After Chappaquiddick, the Kennedy name lost its luster for Hogan, and he came to mistrust even the Kennedy hangers-on. Vanden Heuvel was an amiable and articulate fellow, Hogan thought, but a fellow who had also learned all the armtwists and strangleholds of Kennedy-style political infighting.

Throughout this first week of March 1973, Hogan had been in an emotional limbo. Was it indeed time for a change? Should he put himself out to pasture? Or continue to do what he did best? Vanden Heuvel had been publicly criticizing him ever since the '68 Columbia bust. There were charges that Hogan had become "remote and unresponsive" to the social revolution convulsing the city and nation. In the shifting climate of changing sexual and political mores, rumors about Frank Hogan were being whispered even among lawyers and judges who lived off the criminal-justice system. Had Hogan really fallen out of touch with social reality? Was he—even this accusation was leveled—becoming senile?

In the 1940s and '50s, America had come to know Frank Hogan through a fictional "Mr. District Attorney" on radio. The program's famous introduction was delivered by an announcer whose weekly incantation thrilled millions of listeners: "Mis-s-s-ter District Attorney! Champion of the People! Defender of Truth! Guardian of our fundamental rights to life, liberty and the pursuit of happiness!" Now it seemed only a voice in a time tunnel—a far-off echo in the minds of those old enough to remember when Hogan had *been* that image.

The doorman buzzed upstairs at 404 Riverside Drive: the District Attorney's official limousine had arrived. Hogan kissed his wife and rode

down in the elevator to greet his official chauffeur-bodyguard. Detective
Tobias Fennell brought the word "bodyguard" to life. He was built like a
fireplug. Shorter than Hogan, Toby had a bull neck and an Irish face; he
looked like what he was, a New York City cop. His distinction from other
men on the precinct beat was that he'd been a driver for both Roosevelt
and Truman. (In some surviving World War II newsreels, it is Toby who
can be glimpsed chauffeuring Winston Churchill around town in a bulletproof sedan.)

Twenty years separated them in age, but Hogan and Toby Fennell had
much in common. They shared a sense of Irish loyalty, and they kept
each other's secrets. If Hogan wanted to blow off steam in the gray
cocoon of his limousine, he knew it would go no further.

This morning, he had no sooner snapped open a copy of the *New York
Law Journal* than his limousine was stuck in traffic. When Hogan looked
up, he couldn't miss the message pasted to the rump of the Transit Authority bus ahead of them: "Time for a Change" read Bill vanden Heu-
ven's black-and-white campaign poster.

Hogan muttered an expletive and Toby was quick to commiserate.

"I heard him on the radio again."

"What now?"

"He said you're an old man who's been around too long . . . since
Pearl Harbor."

"I think," said Hogan, "he feels I'm *responsible* for Pearl Harbor."

Toby grinned into the rear-view mirror as he was finally able to swerve
the limousine around the bus and accelerate onto an entrance ramp of
the West Side Highway.

Hogan appreciated his driver's aplomb behind the steering wheel. If
Toby had one fault, Hogan said, it was that he made "too much of a
fuss" over the repeated bomb threats and "assassination plots" against the
D.A. Toby accepted it as his solemn duty to be paranoid on behalf of
Frank Hogan—suspicion stayed with the bodyguard throughout his working hours. Driving down the West Side Highway, he was ready for grenade attack, a planned "accident," or somebody's ramming a shotgun
through a window. His contingency plans for disaster were what he called
"evasive-action plans."

Each morning Toby drove his own car to a secret location—usually a
precinct garage. There, he unlocked Hogan's big Cadillac. Toby examined the limousine hood for fingerprints and checked under the chassis
for traces of dynamite or evidence of tampering with electrical wires. He

tested the car's special-frequency police radio—it might be needed to warn headquarters of a suspicious tail.

Once Toby was behind the wheel, his head swiveled constantly, his eye roving and keen. Every ten seconds, he checked the rear-view mirror; no car was allowed to stay close behind for more than three blocks. In traffic, his eyes darted from one license plate to another; suspicious numbers were kept in the back of his mind. He drove with his left hand, his right kept free to grab the snub-nosed service revolver in his belt, or blast the emergency siren, or flick on the flashing red lights concealed behind the front grille of the limousine.

What must have frustrated Toby was that he never got a chance to use any of these doomsday devices—not even to break out of traffic jams. Each time Toby wanted to "lean on the siren a bit," Hogan forbade him to. The boss said he'd rather have walked to work than contribute to noise pollution. Besides, Hogan said, elected officials who raced around with sirens screaming set a bad example. He himself had long since scrapped his official "DA-1" license plates and substituted the anonymous "2200."

Heading downtown, Hogan's limousine banked off Foley Square, the legal acropolis of Manhattan, and drove just north to the Criminal Courts Building at 100 Centre Street. The Romanesque "Temple of Justice" architecture of the Federal Courthouse on Foley Square contrasted sharply with the sixteen-story granite monolith that was the Criminal Courts Building—Hogan's official home for more than a quarter-century. When he moved into the building in 1942, it had just been completed. Hailed then as "modernistic," "futuristic," "streamlined," the building now seemed a gimlet-eyed tombstone, stained by thirty years of sooty air and the droppings of a million disease-bearing pigeons. The Courthouse and Hogan had grown old together.

To many of his critics, the gloomy edifice had become suggestive of Hogan himself—once proud, if monolithic, but now worn-out and unprogressive. From the north end jutted the "Bridge of Sighs" that connected the courthouse to the twelve-story Manhattan Men's House of Detention, the jailhouse known as the Tombs. The ominous name was appropriate. Within the skyscraper dungeon, the dank monotony of prison routine—wash up, shave, urinate, eat, masturbate—would be broken almost once a month with the cry of "Hang-up!"—another inmate found dangling from a knotted bedsheet.

The D.A.'s limousine cruised around the opposite corner of the Courthouse and deposited Hogan in the Art Nouveau entranceway to the New

York County District Attorney's Office at 155 Leonard Street. Hogan felt it improper for the District Attorney to enter the Criminal Courts Building through the public entrance around the corner. That lobby was a sordid setting for justice. Through its glass revolving doors passed generations of New York's outcasts—the human refuse of alcohol and heroin addiction; muggers; knife-wielders; pickpockets; drifters; whores still wearing the previous evening's cocktail dresses, looking for their pimps; pimps looking for their hundred-dollar lawyers; legal hacks hanging out in the press room, playing card games with bail bondsmen.

There were a few perfunctory touches of Art Moderne in the radiator grillwork of the lobby. A Byzantine pattern tiled the floor. One of ten granite inscriptions over the building's portals declared, "Impartiality is the life of justice as justice is of good government." But this vaunted presumption of innocence seemed a cruel hoax once a prospective juror stepped inside the Courthouse. To many people, the building signified a treacherous demilitarized zone between the drug-crazed armies of the criminal underworld and the police. Despite a heavy concentration of policemen in the building, crime flourished.

A faceless succession of young thugs loitered around the candy-and-chewing-gum counter, waiting for the blind newsdealer to get distracted so they could filch coins from his change dish. Thievery was rampant in the courtrooms: typewriters were stolen, judges were robbed of their black robes. Disgruntled defendants would storm out of the courtrooms, slashing the leather door upholstery with switchblades. Warring husbands and wives threw bottles at each other in the corridors. Hispanic mugging victims stabbed the people accused of robbing them—seeking *machismo* revenge. Gunfire had more than once echoed through the cavernous courtrooms. (A judge once admitted to concealing his own loaded revolver under his black robes.)

Reputable citizens reporting for jury duty sensed that they were entering a vast marketplace for the exchange of weapons, stolen wallets, heroin sold in glassine envelopes, and brown-bag wine bottles passed mouth to mouth among the colony of derelicts who lived in the lobby. Vagrants dozed on window ledges or the floor, depositing body lice wherever they lodged. Public phone booths were used as urinals.

A circular information counter in the lobby hadn't been staffed in years. On rainy days, winos positioned themselves behind the counter— while their shoes and socks hung out to dry—offering spaced-out directions to addicts looking for narcotics court, drifters looking to mooch cigarettes, pimps waiting for prostitutes to come out of court. By the close of any day, the lobby was a pigsty, the floor encrusted with spilled food, ground-out cigar butts, candy wrappers, an occasional trace of human excrement. In the early morning, the disinfectant odor of ammonia stung the eyes. Janitors didn't even try to disguise the stench of sweat and vomit in the elevators.

Hogan ruled this "Temple of Justice" from the Olympian detachment of an eighth-floor office suite, a clean and quiet place carpeted with nearly a half-acre of red-and-gold broadloom. Hogan's desk and swivel chair had originally belonged to his idol, Thomas E. Dewey. But Hogan had been behind the desk for so many years that people forgot, or never knew, that Dewey, the former Governor and Presidential aspirant, had been Hogan's immediate predecessor as Manhattan District Attorney.

No one in the history of New York City had ever held an elective office as long as Frank Hogan. He seemed to be a permanent resident of the office that former District Attorney William Travers Jerome once called "the mouth of Hell."

For thirty years, Hogan had been the conscience of the city. His power could not be underestimated. If he decided you were guilty of a crime, you probably were. Cellblocks were crammed with prisoners whose lawyers had convinced them they had a chance of acquittal against Hogan and his stable of young Ivy League assistants. Over the decades, the scandal-ridden office inherited by Dewey had been transformed by Hogan into a quality showcase for American law enforcement. Although there were four other District Attorneys of equal authority in the surrounding boroughs of New York, only Hogan had raised his office above partisan politics. Gone were the days when a Tammany district leader could walk in the door, put his feet up on the desk and get things fixed that only "the D.A." could fix.

"A fresh—if somewhat collegiate—atmosphere replaced the existing moldy odor of city politics," a deputy prosecutor of the Prohibition era noted of the Dewey-Hogan transformation. "The old habitués of the Criminal Court were left without their stock-in-trade. In their days, a fellow could use his pull; now, to get anything, you have to hold up your hand and yell, HAH-VARD, HA-AH-VARD, HAH-VARD!"

Hogan's freedom to hire young legal assistants without political connections, and his nonpartisan pursuit of corrupt politicians, had gained him the stature of a "living monument" in the legal profession—he was the acknowledged dean of public prosecutors. The monastic young academics who trained under him became members of a semi-religious cult that canonized Hogan. They praised him as a man *sui generis,* in a class by himself.

"Hogan" had become a kind of trademark. People spoke of the "Queens D.A." or the "Brooklyn D.A.," because these offices often turned over after each new election. But in Manhattan, they spoke only of "Hogan's office."

Remarkably, it was an office Frank Hogan had never sought for himself. Dewey and Tammany Hall had jointly arranged his nomination, almost as an afterthought, in 1941. The quadrennial multi-party endorsements that rolled in automatically year after year reaffirmed the Utopian dream of Plato's *Republic*—only those who do not seek power should wield it.

There are many reasons to curb the power of the prosecutor from the political arena. Political espionage, dirty-tricks campaigning, the prosecution of dissenters, shoot-the-looters rhetoric, the intimidation of the news media, the misuse of wiretapping, the witchhunts and inflated "crime wave" reporting of the U.S. Justice Department during the White House crime wave of Watergate have taught us the distinctions between honest prosecution and almost totalitarian harassment.

Any prosecutor's prerogatives are almost beyond scrutiny. He can issue subpoenas and obtain search warrants. He can tap wires, plant bugs, and give grants of immunity. Most important, he can determine who gets prosecuted and who gets off. The strict value judgments of Frank Hogan provided models that most big-city D.A.s imitated. The Hogan office was constructed on the quasi-judicial theory of a "ministry of justice," an idea believed to have originated with Jeremy Bentham, the eighteenth-century English philosopher. In the United States, the subject was first broached by Roscoe Pound, Dean of the Harvard Law School, in 1917. The premise, Hogan held, was to give poor and ignorant defendants the same Constitutional protections that well-to-do defendants were traditionally able to purchase with expensive defense lawyers.

Hogan's approach to justice was both objective and humane. He demanded that his assistants fight harder to prove a man innocent than to establish his legal guilt. Hogan held that the fair application of the law should be extended to defendants across the board—to policemen, prosecutors, judges and politicians as well as to poor blacks and other minorities. "Hogan's office," said a former assistant, "is the first place I'd want to go if I were innocent. And the last place I'd want to go if I were guilty."

"The office" had built-in contradictions. Philosophically, Hogan was opposed to capital punishment. Yet he sent more men to the electric chair than any other single individual in U.S. history. He was not a judge, yet over the years he decided the guilt or innocence of more than two million persons accused of crime in New York City. He was not a politician, yet in his relentless pursuit of corrupt officials of whatever party, he wielded absolute power within the political Establishment of his city and state. Hogan had become the most feared man in New York.

Since first elected to office in November 1941, four weeks before Pearl Harbor, Hogan had waged a private thirty-year war against the New York underworld. He had come of age in the heyday of the Prohibition gangs, when union and industrial racketeering was at its zenith. His image, like that of Dewey before him, was of the crusading racket-buster, locked in mortal combat with the "enemies of the people."

Hogan had pitted himself against the lieutenants of Louis "Lepke" Buchalter and his Murder, Inc.; Jacob "Gurrah" Shapiro, Lepke's satanic "management consultant"; glamorous gangsters like Dutch Schultz, Lucky Luciano, Socks Lanza, and Johnny Dio; Frankie Carbo, the fight fixer; gambler Frank Erickson; Frank Costello, the real-life Godfather, and a host of others in organized crime.

Hogan's appeals briefs, and the body of case law that emanated from his office, became important reference works in law schools and law libraries across the land. Congressional crime committees counted on him to provide much of the evidence that exposed organized racketeering in America. Foreign prosecutors—from England, France, Germany, Japan—came to New York to study his methods.

Los Angeles and Chicago, with larger catchment areas, gave their respective D.A.s vaster land jurisdiction. But within the twenty-two square miles of Manhattan Island—less than 7 percent of the total area of New York City—lived nearly two million people. They were joined every day by an additional three million persons who traveled from within a fifty-mile radius of the Big Apple to work and play.

New York County contained one-tenth of the entire wealth of the United States. It also contained some of the most crushing poverty and scabrous living conditions of any metropolis on earth. The congested living space bred short tempers, jealousies, racial vengeance and the natural enmity of those on opposite ends of the social ladder. Nowhere did crime assume so many violent and contagious forms.

Amid the wartime distractions of the early 1940s, the volume of official business in Hogan's office amounted to forty thousand complaints, investigations and arrests each year. Then came the postwar influx of minority groups, their earning power unable to keep pace with the cost of Manhattan's scarcest commodity: living space. By the 1970s, the only war that concerned them was the battlefield of their own lives. Hogan's office had to deal with the most concentrated glut of cases in the world. More than 120,000 criminal matters ground through the legal machinery of the Manhattan D.A.'s office each year. In 1972, for instance, a staggering number of arrests—33,285—had been listed by police as serious felonies. Among them were 439 rapes, 3,957 felonious assaults, 7,159 robberies, and 353 cases involving the taking of a human life. Bringing all those defendants to justice was an administrative nightmare that the D.A. awakened to every day.

Bypassing the Marat/Sade scene in the Courthouse lobby that March morning, Hogan went through the Leonard Street doorway, at which a uniformed policeman stood sentry duty. The officer escorted Hogan past the waiting elevators to a special door in the rear. From there, a private judges' elevator whisked the D.A. up to his three-room office suite on the eighth floor.

The world's busiest prosecutor's office extended beyond these three rooms. In 1973, the legal work was handled by a staff of 171 assistant district attorneys, working within eight bureaus, who occupied most of the sixth through ninth floors of the building. In terms of manpower, Hogan ran the biggest law firm in the city.

Almost $2.5 million of his yearly budget went into maintaining a legal and secretarial staff, civilian investigators, accountants and clerks: 260 positions in all. Hogan surrounded this office complex with security measures that might have done credit to an atomic-energy plant. Two uniformed patrolmen sealed off the entrance corridor to Hogan's private chambers and kept out the strays: ambulance chasers, cranks, ward heelers and people with minor, noncriminal complaints. One needed an appointment even to approach Hogan's confidential secretary, Ida Delaney.

Ida was noticeable around the office as much for her flamboyant good looks (her clothes were the only dash of color in a blue-serge world) as for her sober dedication to Frank Hogan. She was not only his secretary but his all-round office wife, setting out black tie and tuxedo for banquet appearances and preparing the same lunch for him every day—chicken sandwich, coffee and an apple. Ida herself ate a hurried sandwich at her desk, as did Hogan's men, instead of going out for lunch. She stayed at her typewriter many evenings until nine, and often worked overtime without pay on Saturdays and Sundays. Privy to countless shreds of unproved evidence and tantalizing hints of corruption in the body politic, her confidential secretary's motto was "File and forget."

It was Ida who announced each visitor to the District Attorney's office. The visitor in turn made his way down a narrow marble corridor, a panel of accusatory faces following every footstep. The faces were museum portraits—a gallery of all the forgotten District Attorneys of New York's past. Hogan knew every name and family history.

The visitor seeking an audience with the D.A. next passed through the office of executive assistant David S. Worgan, a mild, erudite lawyer who was the closest thing to a press secretary in the office. If Hogan's rule was sovereign over the fiefdom of Manhattan, then Dave Worgan acted as his viceroy. Only one other man—Chief Assistant Alfred J. Scotti—outranked Worgan on the organizational pyramid. Few others in the office had lasted as many years. Hogan's highest praise for an assistant was that he could stay in the office "as long as Dave and Al"—meaning forever. The D.A. wished all his men would resist the blandishments of higher-paying Wall Street law firms and remain loyal to the "Hogan tradition."

Dave Worgan had been with Hogan since the old Dewey days of the 1930s. He was now an office fixture, scurrying between the Chief and his top aides, attending to myriad matters: budget allocations, official correspondence, grand-jury investigations, personnel problems, phone calls from the Mayor, press releases. Bald, squinty-eyed, slightly deaf, Worgan was usually the first person to see Frank Hogan each morning. All day long, running in and out of the office, he adjusted his hearing aid to the varying levels of the boss's angry or gentle tones.

On this particular morning, Worgan waited outside with a visitor as Hogan strode through. Like a Marine drill instructor, he ran his index finger across a glossy display case that contained his treasured athletic memorabilia. Worgan, a Latin scholar like the man he served, called these keepsakes *lares* and *penates*, symbols of the household gods in ancient Rome. The favorites: a baseball autographed by Mickey Mantle, a New York Mets World Series bat, signed by all the players, and silver trophies won by "Hogan's Hooligans," the office softball team.

Once at his desk, the District Attorney settled down in a big swivel chair to read the day's mail. Every morning, the mailroom brought him two folders. The smaller folder was Hogan's mail. The larger one was everybody else's. Hogan read it all. This was his way of keeping up with the office, he told people; he did it to keep from wasting time in discussing things with junior assistants. Some of these younger men regarded the policy as a monstrous invasion of privacy. Others dismissed it as an unimportant idiosyncrasy. The mailbag ritual, they explained, was simply Hogan's way of enforcing office etiquette—every letter must get answered; no form letters allowed. Incoming mail that tipped Hogan off to possible trouble got passed down the chain of command, from Worgan to the respective bureau chiefs to the assistants working on individual cases. They dreaded a "See me about this" or "Telephone me" scrawled in red ink in the margins. Ordinarily, only bureau chiefs were summoned directly to Hogan's office. More often, they were consulted by telephone. The Chief seldom emerged from the isolation of his eighth-floor inner sanctum. He remained a stranger to most of his staff except at Christmas and New Year's parties.

It was said that a new assistant district attorney could spend years in the office and see Hogan only twice—the day he was hired and the day Ida said to Hogan: "He wants to see you on a personal matter." "Personal matter" meant that one more apprentice had fulfilled his four-year commitment and this was Graduation Day; the young man was moving on to a more lucrative job with a big firm.

The brisk turnover accelerated office promotions, so that relatively inexperienced prosecutors could try major cases within four or five years of law-school graduation. That opportunity made the D.A.'s office an attractive proving ground for bold young lawyers. A few hopeful young men were waiting in Hogan's outer office this morning when the author heard his own name announced: "Mr. Cunningham."

I was there as a reporter for the New York *Post*, hoping for an exclusive interview. Worgan escorted me past the anxious assistant D.A.s in the waiting room. Unavoidable eavesdropping had confirmed the old Tammany prosecutor's assessment of Hogan's men: "HAH-VARD, HA-AH-VARD, HAH-VARD!" I knew that a bright future beckoned them. The Hogan alumni roster listed many illustrious names in the nation's legal, business and educational fraternity: former Attorney General and Secretary of State William P. Rogers; Chief Judge Stanley Fuld and Associate Judge Charles D. Breitel of the Court of Appeals; Charles Tillinghast, president of TWA; Harvard Professor David Riesman, author of *The*

Lonely Crowd and the nation's best-known sociologist; novelist Eleazar Lipsky, a prosecutor turned Hollywood screenwriter with *The Kiss of Death*; Presiding Appellate Judge Bernard Botein, also a novelist; and Family Court Judge Florence Kelley, the first woman admitted to the American Bar Association.

Worgan said, "Good morning, Mr. Hogan," and stood by until the District Attorney offered me a seat. The D.A. was always addressed as "Mr. Hogan," never "Frank." Hogan insisted on this himself. It was said that only two people had ever been heard calling him "Frank": Tom Dewey and Hogan's wife.

Anyone else who called him by his first name committed a breach of courtesy, as Hogan saw it. The office rule was spelled out in inch-high Gothic letters on a ceramic plaque over his desk: "Courtesy is the golden key that opens every door."

The courtesy motto had been pointed out to me once before, on a visit to Hogan's private domain two years earlier. I had interviewed Hogan then on "moonlighting," the controversial practice of many American prosecutors who work both sides of the street: a private shingle on the door and the People's business part-time. The conflict of interest is still something of a national scandal, especially when a D.A.'s law partners are permitted to handle criminal cases. Hogan himself had long before abolished the practice. His legal staff of career prosecutors was forbidden to handle even a will or a real-estate closing. As with most of Hogan's ethical judgments, this office policy was gradually being adopted in other D.A.'s offices across the land, an example of Hogan's influence as the conscience of the legal profession.

My own visit to Hogan-land had begun with Worgan's standard lecture on the meaning of the courtesy motto:

"Courtesy means more to him than holding a door open for someone. It's an appreciation that this is a public office and the public is entitled to be served. Not as a matter of grace or condescension, but because of a man's or woman's basic human worth. You have to know what a shattering experience it is to come into this office, either as a crime victim or a defendant.

"The courtliness Mr. Hogan embodies in his conduct must be shown to every defendant, every victim, every judge, every court clerk. We let every person tell his story. We answer every letter, every phone call. We're never late for an appointment. We represent Mr. Hogan and Mr. Hogan represents the People of New York."

His disciples considered him a living legend in the annals of jurisprudence. For such a legend, he seemed shy, almost bashful. I had trouble connecting this meek little man with the trumpeted "Mr. District Attorney." He averted his eyes as I reached out to shake hands, grasping a pipe cleaner as an excuse to busy his fingers. Each time I tried to make eye contact, Hogan looked not at me, but past me—over my shoulder. I swiveled around finally to see what he was looking at, only to find myself gazing at Hogan's familiar view of his own office.

Two years hadn't changed the décor as I remembered it: the walls were framed with aquatints of Hudson River scenes, on permanent loan from the Museum of the City of New York. The windows looked out on a lower Manhattan neighborhood rich in criminal history. One could see the infamous Five Points, a five-street junction where the Bowery and East Side gangs slugged and knifed it out over boundary rights in the nineteenth century. An Albany legislative report once located five churches and 237 saloons in the six-by-seven-block area. Every one of these saloons had been the site of much boozing and bloodletting before the passage of the Sullivan Law, when the Third Avenue "sheenies" and the "wops" of Little Italy openly wore six-shooters strapped to their belts. Now, English-speaking children from nearby Chinatown played basketball in the tiny triangle of asphalt playground where crawling tenements once spawned the worst of the Mafia's killers.

My peripheral vision picked up other details of the office: a conference table large enough for a board meeting at General Motors; Ben Franklin's "Healthy, Wealthy & Wise" almanac on the same table as a miniature Columbia football pennant; a model of the luxury liner *Queen Mary*; a lithograph of the old Woolworth Building, Dewey and Hogan's original headquarters.

I noticed that Hogan's white hair had receded slightly on top, exposing a forehead dotted with liver spots. His nose, slightly varicosed, gave a quizzical twitch as he sucked on an unlit pipe and said:

"Shoot."

I resisted firing off my first question and exchanged some ritual pleasantries instead, remarking that his courtesy plaque had cracked since our last visit. Hogan nodded, yes, the courtesy rule harked back to the Depression days, when he was struggling along in private practice. "I was making the rounds of the big law firms and it seemed I was treated . . . *rudely* . . . wherever I went. I resolved that in this position, I would never make the same mistake. Very few of us are cruelly wronged in life.

It's the small blows to our self-esteem and the little jolts to our vanity that cause half the heartaches in the world."

Now I explained the official purpose of my visit: I had been assigned by the *Post* to write a series of articles on the growing problem of mugging. I had already interviewed the Police Commissioner, the Mayor, precinct cops, criminologists, parole officers, prison wardens, robbery victims. To hear the other side, I went behind bars at Riker's Island, the city penitentiary, and talked to the muggers.

Hogan, a good listener, wanted to know what the muggers had had to say for themselves. I told him. One young thug, nabbed by police after he had stomped an elderly man near the Coney Island boardwalk, said he *had* to get the money—for heroin: "If Jesus Christ had been walking down the boardwalk that night, I'd have ripped Him off." The attack had netted the assailant five dollars and his victim a skull fracture—"I didn't expect to see all that blood."

Another mugger confided to me: "This may sound sick to you, but there's such a feeling of power to a knife, or a gun. I've been afraid of that feeling in myself. It's sick, I know, but when you stick a knife or a gun in somebody's face, it gives you this fantastic sense of power. You see people actually gagging with fear. It's like—I've been afraid of people all my life and now I see other people in fear of me. I am God for the moment. If I want to, I can erase this man or this woman."

This convict estimated he had "earned" over $70,000 during his career as a mugger; he had gotten away with about thirty attacks for every one of his twenty-three arrests. As I recounted these figures, Hogan flinched.

First of all, he told me, the slang term "mugging" was too ambiguous to have any official status in police reports or court records. People used the term to describe purse-snatches as well as armed holdups. The word was only useful, Hogan said, because it satisfied the public's need for generic labels. The *modus operandi* generally meant lunging at a victim from behind and using a stranglehold or a knife to the throat.

Originally, Hogan explained, the word for the crime was "garrote." An armlock or a knife to the throat had been the favorite technique of criminals since the nineteenth century, when Sir Robert Peel stood before the English Parliament and deplored "an army of trained and hardened robbers" that terrorized respectable members of the upper class. Today, the crime had different names in different places. In Chicago, it was called "strong-arming"; in Washington, D.C., muggers were known as "yokers"; in Montreal, the crime was "jack-rolling."

Narcotics addicts, Hogan went on, were to blame for most of the assaults. He gave me a capsule history of society's ambivalence toward the treatment of addicts: "Twenty years ago, this office threw up its hands at law enforcement as the remedy for addiction. We decided to treat addicts as Typhoid Marys, carriers of a communicable disease, sick persons in need of treatment. We said we didn't need prisons, we needed treatment centers. We talked about heroin therapy modeled on the British system. We tried methadone. We tried the State Narcotics Control Commission, until the state couldn't finance it any longer. Governor Rockefeller couldn't conclude the '71 Legislature without showing action. So he set up special addiction courts. And now we're right back where we were twenty years ago—we're back to law enforcement as the answer."

Over and over, Hogan spoke of "dispositions," his term for clearing the court calendar. To dispose of cases, he felt forced to rely on plea bargaining—"conviction without trial," as he preferred to call it. Ninety percent of his convictions were obtained by offering defendants a pre-trial opportunity to plead guilty to a lesser offense in exchange for a reduced sentence. Almost eight out of every ten defendants accused of murder in New York were allowed to plead guilty to a reduced charge, then freed on probation or sentenced to less than ten years.

Most prisoners who received a maximum ten-year term were eligible for parole in three years. Hogan worried that trial-court judges might be too lenient. He openly criticized judges as "soft" on defendants who pleaded guilty. Over the years, defense lawyers chafed at Hogan's *ex parte* forays into judges' chambers to complain of the "shockingly low sentences" meted out by the court. (In the mid 1950s, Judge Jacob Gould Schurman, a Harvard Law grad, had fought back. He blasted Hogan's tactics in narcotics cases: "Too close to the rack-and-screw to be permitted to stand." Dissension climaxed when Hogan tried to pressure Schurman into imposing a stiff sentence on a pusher. The judge angrily put Hogan himself on the witness stand and called the D.A. "an oppressor." Hogan, in turn, denounced the jurist as "a tyrant.")

Hogan described his plea-bargaining practice as a "necessary evil." Evil? An occasionally innocent person *might* be coerced into pleading guilty because the District Attorney allowed him to cop a plea to a lesser charge and get out of jail on "time served." Necessary? Yes, because the technique provided a degree of flexibility and humanity to the sterner application of the law.

Hogan gave me an example of one such humane disposition: a young heroin user and seller who had faced a lengthy prison term if his case went to trial. The D.A. allowed the addict to plead guilty to a misdemeanor and enter a treatment program after it was shown the boy had become addicted to morphine as a painkiller while his war wounds were being treated in Vietnam. That story was touching, but most "plea bargains" were not—just as most addicts were not luckless GIs. Closer to the truth was the fact that plea bargaining was *practical*.

Consider, Hogan suggested, what would happen in 1973 if the New York State Supreme Court swept aside all its other criminal and civil matters and, starting from scratch, decided to bring every one of the 384 pending murder and manslaughter cases to trial. It would take two years to clear the calendar. During that time, a backlog of 90,000 other cases would "engulf the system," Hogan said, virtually assuring that none of the defendants would ever be brought to justice.

Even with dispositions rolling along, the District Attorney said, the backlog swelled. In addition to the guilty, Hogan was haunted by the innocent—or, at least, those unwilling to plead guilty. Many of the men sitting in the Tombs for lack of bail money had lengthy prison pasts. But they had not been convicted of the crime presently charged. The machinery of "due process" was so clogged that some of the inmates had been caged in the detention pens for over a year while waiting their day in court.

The pre-trial confinement of prisoners bothered Hogan's conscience as well as his sense of efficiency. Why weren't these cases being moved along to trial? Was it because defense lawyers deliberately postponed the finality of judgment, keeping their clients locked up in hopes that the cases would eventually get dismissed in the backlog? Why did the accused felons themselves request adjournment after adjournment, getting cold feet whenever it was time to face the jury?

"The last thing in the world a guilty man wants is a speedy trial," Hogan remarked with irony.

Perhaps his advancing age was making him philosophical, Hogan added, since he found himself meditating a great deal lately over "metaphysical" guilt and innocence. This glimpse of the bureaucrat indulging in contemplation startled me. But I was yet to know Hogan as a legal theoretician, historian, criminologist and social philosopher. Later, I would learn from Mike Pearl, the *Post*'s courthouse reporter, that the D.A.'s office was also a law school, and a think tank for intellectual seminars on the sociology of crime. The Aristotelian teacher-pupil rela-

tionship was especially evident in Hogan's affection for Kenneth Conboy, the lean, ascetic assistant D.A. in charge of official corruption cases. Conboy told Pearl that he had given the Chief a book that had ruined his sleep two nights in a row. The book was Tolstoy's last novel, *Resurrection*, that masterpiece about retributive justice meted out by the law courts of nineteenth-century Russia. Tolstoy captured every detail of the criminal-justice system in Czarist days—prisoners with shaven heads, coldblooded judges, crowded courtrooms. The only difference between Tolstoy's time and his own, Hogan told Conboy, was that eyes were no longer gouged or ears amputated. But prisoners still swung from improvised nooses, and the system itself strangled under the pressure of revenge.

As he and I talked that day, Hogan's conversation repeatedly wandered back to his glory years: the 1940s, when society was still the victim of crime. Now in the 1970s, criminals were the victims of society. Today, he told me, Ph.D. theses were being churned out on victimology, which asserted that crime victims set themselves up for mugging attacks and murders. According to certain trendy criminologists, street addicts and muggers were the *real* victims of society, and the people stabbed and robbed were somehow to blame for their own misfortune.

Mass entertainment and the media reflected this reversal of attitudes. In movies like *Superfly* and *Easy Rider*, the heavies became the anti-heroes, glorifying drug peddling and violence. Hogan saw these films as a "dangerous artistic license." He missed the black-and-white certainties of right and wrong. His conscience and career were increasingly mired in the gray area of social values. Hogan found himself no longer a hero. These days, he was more often reviled than revered. He had outlived his glory years. Frank Hogan was an anachronism.

"Sometimes, when he opens his mouth and all those Victorian paragraphs come pouring out, I have to look out the window to make sure there aren't horse-drawn carriages on the street," said Mike Pearl. "Hogan just isn't your twentieth-century type of guy. Here's this poor Irish immigrant's son whose patron saint is Horatio Alger. He got where he is through old-fashioned idealism. Now, he's sitting up there in his tower—King Lear trying to keep the lid on the Age of Aquarius."

2
SALAD DAYS

In 1911, when Frank Hogan was nine years old, his uncle John Smithwick, who lived in Waterbury, Connecticut, would now and then take down from the Hogan mantelpiece a velvet box. Inside was a polished bronze medal. It was the Crimean Campaign Decoration for Bravery, awarded to Frank's grandfather in 1857. This maternal grandfather, whom young Frank had never seen, was John Smithwick, an Englishman who enlisted in the British Army while still in his teens and rose through the ranks to become a sergeant major. According to Uncle Smithwick, the Crimean War decoration had been pinned to his father's tunic by Her Majesty Queen Victoria.

With an affectation of British pomp, Uncle Smithwick would pin the red-ribboned medal on Frank's knicker-blouse. Uncle and nephew would exchange playful, heel-clicking salutes. Then Uncle John would settle into an easy chair and lift his nephew onto the griffin armrests, to hear again the legend of Sergeant Major Smithwick, long in his grave.

As the stories unfolded, the Sergeant Major took physical shape and grew solid before the boy's eyes. After his grandfather had fought in the Crimean War, he had set sail for India in 1857, "in the service of the Crown." Indian voyages of the 1800s involved dangers that would have kept any small boy agog. Pirates. Killer whales. Shipwrecks. Disease—especially cholera; a man would weaken and begin to choke. Within hours, his body shriveled. His lungs drowned. The Sergeant Major had witnessed mass burials at sea, dozens of yellowed corpses flung overboard.

The stories always ended with Grandfather Smithwick landing safely in

Calcutta; a man who had seen bejeweled rajahs, heard the "Ayyyyagghhhs" of blind beggars, and smelled the "untouchables" sprawled on their pallets of cow manure. Uncle John Smithwick's haunted visions of the perils and romance of India were of major importance in shaping the character of his nephew. Frank's adolescent daydreams were colored by tales of the Khyber Pass, the Taj Mahal, the ivory palaces of Kashmir. He went to bed at night in twentieth-century Connecticut with the realization that his own grandfather had ridden in the battle garb of a Bengal Lancer, faced King Cobra, hunted tigers in Jaipur. There was even a strong assertion from Uncle Smithwick that Frank's grandfather had visited the Black Hole of Calcutta, had actually *seen* that narrow prison cell where English prisoners had suffocated overnight.

In actuality, Sergeant Major Smithwick had been assigned to a colonial trading fortress north of Calcutta. His duties were those of a quartermaster: he was in charge of a vast trading warehouse, the Union Jack fluttering from its flagpole. His military mission was to "order and secure" the riches of the East for their faraway island destination. An Anglican, he converted to Catholicism in order to marry an Irish girl who lived with him in India. She died, still a young girl, in a cholera epidemic, leaving behind a daughter, christened Martha.

At convent school in Calcutta, little Martha's hours were strictly disciplined, but at home with her father she enjoyed an enchanted childhood. She was the Sergeant Major's only indulgence; she was even treated to an elephant as a pet.

Frank's mother, Martha's half-sister, loved to tell how the little girl's life was once saved by that elephant. Miss Martha was playing in the garden, it seemed, so preoccupied that she did not see a giant cobra slithering toward her. The serpent coiled, its tongue darting. Martha's pet elephant was standing guard, however, and spotted the snake just in time. The pachyderm's trunk descended, curled around Martha's waist, and scooped her up to safety. Trumpeting victory, the beast carried its mistress back to the veranda unharmed.

By the time his daughter was sixteen, in 1870, Sergeant Major Smithwick was reassigned to a British garrison in Ireland. The widower and his daughter settled in County Limerick. Smithwick married again, this time to one Catherine Bradshaw, who was no older than Martha.

The young wife and stepdaughter evidently did not see eye to eye: Martha soon announced she was going off to join a religious order of nuns. She said goodbye to Ireland, returned to India, and died in a convent there many years later.

In 1873, Frank Hogan's mother, Anne Smithwick, was born. She was the third of thirteen children sired by the Sergeant Major and his wife over the next two decades.

"That gives you an idea of the virility of my stock," District Attorney Hogan was fond of reminding his assistants whenever anyone mentioned his Irish ancestry.

The D.A.'s father, Michael Hogan, was the youngest of five children. Only four years old when his mother died, he worked as a stable boy on his father's horse farm in County Clare. The elder Hogan, a small, compactly built man, owned two racehorses, which he himself rode. Race days were times of gaiety when the isolated farmers of the county drew together for amusement. Frank Hogan's father had the knack of bringing to life again those relationships of the past. He remembered Duffy's Circus pitching its tent outside the racetrack grounds. There were sideshows—and gambling lures: Three Card Monte, Find the Lady, Under and Over Seven. The card hustlers, of course, always took your money.

A racetrack accident ruined Grandfather Hogan financially and was the immediate cause of his emigration to America. He had entered both his thoroughbreds in the same race. In the stretch run, the lead horse, bunched against the rail, threw its rider into the dust. Other horses collided. The two Hogan thoroughbreds staggered and fell, snapping their fine narrow legs.

Michael Hogan was only eight years old when the accident occurred, but he always remembered watching his father walk out on the track with a rifle. "The animals had to be put down, y'see," Michael Hogan would explain to his son Frank in later years.

Bankrupt soon after the incident, grandfather Hogan was forced to sell his house and stable. Unable to provide for his children, he sent young Michael and one brother to live with a neighbor named Carthy, then booked passage to New York with his three oldest children in tow. That was in 1870, the same year Sergeant Major Southwick returned to Ireland.

To go to school, young Michael, after milking cows, walked six miles from his adopted home each day, carrying a pocketful of crackers for lunch. Three years passed before enough money arrived for him to join his father where he had settled: in Waterbury, Connecticut.

Destitute as he had been before he crossed the Atlantic, Frank Hogan's grandfather found the deprivations of a New England immigrant life even worse. His high hopes of becoming a Connecticut tobacco farmer quickly dissolved: the supply of free land had already been exhausted. For every man who was lucky enough to become a farmer, two men descended into the darkness of coal mines and factories.

Factory pay scales averaged ten dollars for a fifty-nine-hour week, and in the Waterbury sweatshops an eighty-four-hour week was not unheard of. People dreaded Christmas and Easter because holidays meant no work and no pay.

Grandfather Hogan and his sons geared their lives to the sound of factory whistles. Even the courtship of Frank's father and mother began on the assembly line. Mike Hogan met Anne Smithwick in 1899, the year she came to work at the Waterville Pin Company, where he was a machine operator. Annie introduced herself as the daughter of a former British sergeant major in India. She explained that she had recently emigrated from County Limerick with her widowed mother and twelve brothers and sisters (including three sets of twins). Mike and Annie were married in 1900, and two years later, Annie gave birth to a son. The boy was christened Frank Smithwick Hogan—a fact that he later had trouble communicating to the nuns in parochial school. Assuming "Frank" to be a nickname, they insisted he sign all his homework papers "Francis."

While his wife was pregnant with her second child, Mike Hogan suffered a serious accident. He caught his left hand in the grinding teeth of a milling machine, and before he could shut off the motor, his forearm was splintered and his fingers and knuckles were mangled. At the small hospital where he was taken by horse-drawn ambulance, he overheard the surgeon say something about an amputation from the shoulder.

"I'm not going to have this arm taken off!" Mike Hogan vowed to an intern.

"Then you'd better get out of here and go over to New Haven Hospital," the young medic advised.

Frank's father "escaped," as he later put it, to New Haven, and the arm stayed intact. But the hand was useless, an atrophied claw. When he went to get his old job back at the factory, the response was, "Sorry."

These were the days before workmen's compensation. The labor movement hadn't achieved medical benefits yet. Overnight, Frank's father had become an out-of-work cripple with a family to support. His wife saved the day by opening a small grocery store.

By turns, Mike Hogan was able to find work as a tea salesman, an insurance man, a high-school janitor. He ended up as a buffer for the Ingersoll Watch Company. Almost every working man in those days wore an "Ingersoll," the famous one-dollar pocketwatch that put "Waterbury, Conn." on the map.

Mrs. Hogan became a heavy-set, matriarchal figure behind the grocery counter. She kept the store open from eight in the morning until ten at night. Frank helped out whenever he could, struggling with a peck of potatoes, filling customers' oil cans, or presiding over the penny-candy counter.

Play and games were "too frivolous" for her children, Annie Hogan believed. She felt that praising a child undermined self-confidence in later life. She also frowned on "superficial" signs of affection.

Frank's sister Martha recalled: "My mother never touched or kissed any of us. I would hear other little girls' mothers say, 'Oh, you look beautiful today!' But my mother never said anything like that. Frank got good grades in school, but my mother never complimented him on his report card. She thought that it would make him feel proud, and pride was a sin in our house."

Frank's mother disapproved of gambling, whiskey, lipstick, headache powders, and women who kept poodles. Her vehemence was directed particularly against gambling because of a poker-playing relative whose betting obsession was a standard subject of family gossip. Gambling was a disease, Annie said, that sapped a man of his industry and drove his family to the poorhouse.

Frank's lifelong work habits were formed by early conditioning. His mother insisted that her sons take after-school jobs. Frank started out at ten, delivering the Waterbury *Republican*. His customers were factory folk, up for breakfast by five o'clock; Frank was up by four.

A sadistically loud Waterbury Clock Co. alarm—the kind with two brass bells on top—jangled Frank and his younger brother Joe awake. The boys shared a bed, and Joe still recalls Frank's wake-up routine: he would stagger out from under the covers, grab the alarm clock and smash the damned thing against a wall. This was before the days of planned obsolescence, and despite the punishment Frank inflicted on it, the dented, twisted, lopsided alarm clock stubbornly persisted in getting him up on time morning after morning.

Punctuality eventually became a passion. Judge Sol Gelb, once a prosecutor under both Dewey and Hogan, said by way of contrasting the two men: "Dewey thought in terms of a totality of achievement. If he had five thousand men under his command, he'd wonder how much he could accomplish with all of them. Hogan would be worried about whether the five thousandth man showed up late for work in the morning."

Another Dewey prosecutor, who went off to join the Navy after Pearl Harbor, returned to Hogan's office in 1945: "There wasn't the eagerness to get to work that there had been in the Dewey days." The deputy remembered that even on Thanksgiving Day, Dewey's men reported to work, rushed home to eat turkey in the afternoon, then went back to the office. "I arrived back at work at nine o'clock in the morning and there was Hogan standing in the Leonard Street lobby, marking down the time each assistant came in. He started off a staff meeting with a temper: a number of assistants were 'trickling in whenever it pleased them,' he said, and told us: 'The woods are full of lawyers who are anxious to come into this office . . . anybody who doesn't get to work on time can go elsewhere.' "

In his teens, Frank Hogan was painfully bashful with girls. His shyness may have stemmed from physical problems. He frequently broke out with neck boils and knuckle warts. He had also been quite chubby during his altar-boy days, and his neighborhood nickname was "Fats."

Perhaps as a consequence, Frank became a reader, addicted to boys' periodicals such as *Youth's Companion* and series novels such as "The Prescott Boys at Annapolis." Most of all, he loved Horatio Alger books—there was something in the poor-boy formula that Frank found irresistible. He also liked H. G. Wells' *Outline of History*, despite the big words, and he was developing a lifelong infatuation with Charles Dickens.

After high-school graduation in 1919, Frank went to work in a brassrod foundry in Waterbury. Manual labor was not new to him: from the time he was thirteen, he had held a flabbergasting variety of summer and after-school jobs.

"At one time or other I worked for just about every factory in Waterbury," Hogan reminisced in later years. His first summer job was at the New England Watch Co., where he earned fifteen cents an hour dipping watch backs in an acid bath. The next three summers, he sawed wood for a carpenter, sold rubber goods door-to-door, and wore a green eyeshade as timekeeper for the watch factory. At a munitions plant, he banged crates together to hold guns and dynamite.

And one summer he worked as a bill collector for a "One Dollar Down—One Dollar a Week" clothing company. This job paid him the highest salary ($23 a week) but was his least favorite. On one occasion, his assignment was to retrieve a tuxedo from a Naugatuck man who had proved a poor credit risk. There had been trouble locating the delinquent customer, but Frank finally found him—at home, laid out in a coffin.

The man's widow answered Frank's knock on the door and invited him into the living room, where several mourners were seated in the midst of an Irish wake.

"I've come to take back the tuxedo," Frank whispered.

"He's wearing it," she whispered back, pointing to the corpse in its financed finery.

Frank wanted to go on to college after his summer in the brass-rod factory, but his father opposed the plan, declaring that Frank should be out earning a living rather than eating into family finances with school expenses.

Annie Hogan, however, had secretly squirreled away all of Frank's summer-job earnings. With the $700 she gave back to him, Frank Hogan was able to afford tuition at Columbia, which a family friend had recommended. Thinking he might like to write as much as he liked to read, he enrolled in the Pulitzer School of Journalism.

Frank had no sooner signed up for a dormitory room in Hartley Hall than he went back to work—in the student cafeteria. He washed dishes all through his freshman year. Summer vacation was no relaxation for him either: he spent it selling something called *The People's Home Library* to upstate farmers.

"I'd get my foot in the door," he recalled, "and say, 'Mrs. Jones, this is *not* a *book*. It's a complete *library*—three books in one, for ten-fifty—containing thousands of simple remedies for colic and all other afflictions of the animal world.' "

He sold 150 books and also won a $250 scholarship. The combined income enabled him to go back to Columbia for his sophomore year. By then he had given up on the idea of becoming a newspaperman. Most of the reporters you heard about—even the well-known ones—were $25-a-week wrecks with alcohol problems. A legal career seemed to offer a brighter earning potential, so he switched from journalism to an undergraduate pre-law course.

It didn't take long for him to turn into Joe College: he won a spot as left halfback on the second-string varsity football team, swam for the Columbia squad and was an oarsman in eight-man scull regattas. He pledged Beta Theta Pi, sported a raccoon coat and joined in ukulele songfests. By his senior year, he was class president, managing editor of the yearbook and president of the fraternity chapter.

Academically, however, Hogan was a bored and mediocre student. (At Columbia Law School, the student destined to become the nation's most famous prosecutor almost flunked the course in criminal law.)

"The law didn't interest me at all then," he told an alumni meeting in 1954. "I regret to say that in those youthful days a varsity C was just a little more important to me than a degree. More deplorable, it still is."

Frank helped win his C by playing in Columbia's first game at Baker Field, a 13-0 triumph over Ursinus in 1923. He substituted as left halfback for a top player who had been sidelined with injuries.

Hogan never protested in later life when old school buddies exaggerated his actual accomplishments on the gridiron. For years, Federal Judge Frederick Van Pelt Bryan, a Columbia trustee, was a loyal Hogan rooter—telling people that Hogan scored the only touchdown in Columbia's 7-to-10 loss to Pennsylvania in 1924.

If that was true, Hogan must have been playing under an alias. Keven De Marrais, the curator of Columbia's athletic archives, blew the dust off some long-forgotten score books recently and set the record straight: Frank never scored at all during his Columbia career. Indeed, his total playing time on the field added up to thirty-six minutes. Nine of those minutes were played in the Ursinus game, the other twenty-seven in a game against Pennsylvania later that year.

Hogan used to say that Coach Percy Haughton had put him in the Penn game just so Frank could qualify for his varsity letter. Reenacting the game for a testimonial dinner in 1971, Hogan said: "Desperate and unnerved, Haughton paced up and down the sidelines. He stopped in front of me, looked me squarely in the eye, and uttered the immortal words, 'You! Hogan! Get in there!' Many, many years later, I'm still amazed. Penn promptly ripped our line to pieces. They scored twice. But the blur in the coach's eye persisted and I played the rest of the game."

Picking up on the story, a younger assistant kidded Hogan: "Hey, Chief—is it true you spent so much time on the bench they called you 'Judge'?"

Everybody laughed—except Hogan. He gave a phony stage smile, but the blood drained from his face. He blinked in disbelief, stricken by this gentle mockery of those precious thirty-six minutes of remembered glory. Voices in the room dropped off, like a phonograph when somebody pulls the plug. Hogan just stood there, eyes lowered, a product of the whole yearning American male psyche—the Jack Armstrong heart cut out of him.

Countless Saturday afternoons of his adult life were spent rooting for the Columbia team. Hogan always bought a season ticket and kept a regular bleacher seat on the 45-yard line at Baker Field. He seldom missed a game.

One bleacher buddy was Court of Appeals Justice Myles J. Lane, himself a former ice-hockey star at Dartmouth. (Lane was also one of the federal prosecutors who convicted Julius and Ethel Rosenberg in the notorious "atom spy" case of the 1950s.)

It amused the judge to watch his friend regress from the dignified "Mr. District Attorney" to an exuberant freshman fan all over again. Hogan yelled and cheered and groaned, and if his team got behind, he chewed on his hat brim. On one occasion, Lane recalled, Hogan threw his expensive fedora to the ground and jumped up and down on it like a frazzled Mr. Magoo. Win, lose or draw, Hogan would diagnose himself as "emotionally dehydrated" after a game and insist on a "bracing libation" (usually a Scotch and water) at his Riverside Drive apartment.

As he had been the ultimate Joe College, Hogan became the ultimate alumni rooter. When a hurricane nearly swept the players off the field in a 1947 game with Holy Cross, *Columbia Spectator* sports editor Irving Lang noted that Hogan was one of seven fans who kept their seats while thousands of other rain-soaked spectators headed for the exits.

Hogan's loyalty to Columbia was matched by the honor he himself reflected on the university by his prominence in New York City. For years, his name would appear three or four times a week, alongside news of the Nazis in France; U.S. troops in Japan and Korea; the Kennedy and King assassinations; American footprints on the moon as well as in My Lai; and, of course, Watergate. He would be the Manhattan D.A. longer than people were able to remember, a constant of the city.

But in 1924, when Hogan was graduated, the future that would be his, and the city's, was still a free-form daydream. He spent his first summer out of college in an unorthodox way. To earn his tuition money for law school, Hogan took a job as an "advance man" for a Russian baron, one Eugene Fersen. A physicist who spoke eight or ten languages, Fersen wanted to deliver a psychic message.

"The Baron came over here with Kerensky, began to give lectures, and founded the International Order of Light Bearers, which disseminated what he called the Science of Being," Hogan recalled. "He contended that civilized man had lost the ability to contact universal life energy."

The Baron strove to renew this psychic energy in the dispossessed—for a fee. He brought Frank up to his headquarters in Maine to learn the "Science of Being." Headquarters was a beautiful chateau on Deer Island that once belonged to Frederick Law Olmsted, the designer of Central Park.

Fersen's disciples gathered there in a sylvan setting and listened to their spiritual leader dispense a blend of faith healing, yoga, meditation, and the occult. The first day, Hogan joined the other barefoot disciples out on the lawn. The Baron directed them to assume a physical position which he called "The Five-Pointed Star." Frank spread-eagled himself as the Baron directed, legs wide apart, arms straight out, head thrown back so he was squinting into the sun, fingers and toes straining to stretch his frame as far as his muscles would allow. From his upright position, the Baron intoned, and his disciples repeated after him: "I am one with universal life energy! It is flowing through me now! I feel it!"

After about twelve minutes of this, concentric sun-circles started whirling in Frank's eyes. A tingle of "universal life energy" reached his solar plexus. He felt a warm rush of nausea, and then his body writhed in a muscle spasm.

The gimmick for inducing "universal life energy" was succeeding with other disciples too—bodies all around him were contorted. But the job paid $150 a month, plus keep. Hogan signed on.

"We toured various New England cities, including Boston. For fifty dollars a head, the Baron lectured and gave seven-lesson courses in his Science," Hogan recalled. "I helped him prepare pamphlets, passed the hat at lectures, and sold his book, *Science of Being*, which was bound in lizardskin and fetched fifteen dollars. After a couple months, I resigned. The Baron was a con man and I was afraid I might be on my way to becoming a junior con man."

Youthful wanderlust set in, so Frank set off for Guatemala, where he found a job keeping the books of the Guatemala Gold Dredging Company in Las Quebradas. For ten months, Frank looked after the payroll records in the mornings and in the afternoons gave English lessons. In return, he picked up some Spanish and enough money to enable him to enter Columbia Law School in the fall.

If there is an Irish gene for politicking, it skipped a generation in the case of Frank's father—a registered Democrat who voted independent and never joined a clubhouse. But the gene surfaced in his son. Hogan's

Class of '24 yearbook provides us with a glimpse of his earliest political yearnings:

"Frank has risen steadily in the esteem of his classmates by his earnest work for his Class and College. Quiet, with reserve and dignity he is. It is suspected that he is going into law and looks forward to the mayorship of his native Waterbury, with perhaps a couple of terms in the Legislature."

As managing editor of the yearbook, Frank approved that write-up for himself, backward syntax and all. His first serious exposure to organized politics, however, didn't come until 1927.

A few bad experiences that year created in Frank Hogan a lifelong aversion to campaign "dirty tricks" as well as a permanent love-hate relationship with the electoral process itself. It was the year before law-school graduation, and Hogan was again short of tuition money. Through his friend George Pease, Columbia star quarterback of 1924, Frank wangled an introduction to Jimmy Hines, the powerful captain of the James J. Hines Association. The Tammany clubhouse at Columbus Avenue and 116th Street was a familiar fixture in Hogan's neighborhood. Pease set up the meeting through one of Jimmy's five sons, a football player at Harvard.

The meeting took place. In exchange for a promise to ring doorbells for him at election time, Hines pulled a few strings and got Frank Hogan his first decent-paying job in New York—as a plumber's helper on the Columbia Hospital construction site. The Hines clubhouse next found Frank part-time work as a playground instructor, and later landed him a job as an appliance demonstrator in a Consolidated Edison display room. While there, Frank brought his younger brother Joe down from Waterbury and got him a Con Ed showroom job; in the evenings Joey studied law at Fordham night school.

All in all, young Hogan profited from Jimmy Hines, and worked for him in return. Frank marched in the torchlight parades Jimmy led through the streets of his district at election time. Hogan ran errands. He rang doorbells. And he retained a peculiar affection for this genial, paternal gent.

Jimmy Hines was an old-time political fixer. His dealings with bootleggers had been rumored about for years. In fact, Prohibition had enabled him to rise from being a common blacksmith to the iron-handed district leadership of Tammany Hall. Such was his rule of the Tammany roost that he continued to direct the inner councils of the Democratic organization even after Dewey put him behind bars in 1939 as protector of Dutch Schultz's racket enterprises.

There was double irony in the situation because Frank Hogan, then Dewey's chief investigator, researched most of the evidence that sent his one-time mentor to Sing Sing.

Some of that evidence concerned the poor people in Hines' district who could always count on Jimmy for free turkeys at Thanksgiving. Hogan knew how and why. In November 1927, he had been the clubhouse gofer. As Thanksgiving approached, Frank was given the address of a poultry warehouse under the Williamsburg Bridge and sent by subway to pick up a supply of turkeys. Nothing could have prepared Hogan, however, for the nauseating stench of meat that greeted him at the front door of the building.

It was a kosher slaughterhouse. Inside, Frank found a grizzled Hassidic Jew who held a squawking rooster. The man slashed its gullet with a straight-edge and dumped the bird upside down in a funnel so its blood could drain into a rusty barrel. This was no different from the way poultry was butchered in gentile slaughterhouses. But the city's two million orthodox Jews were paying extra money to have their poultry dressed in a sanitary ritual manner by rabbinical slaughterers called *Shochtim*. What Frank was seeing was typical of the fly-infested, health-hazardous conditions inside many of the city's meatpacking warehouses—which bred violations he would endlessly prosecute after becoming Manhattan D.A.

When Frank reached out to pay for the turkeys, the slaughterer wiped a handful of bloody feathers off on his apron and offered to shake hands instead.

"It's been taken care of," the man winked, and offered no explanation. Frank went back to the clubhouse with the turkeys. The "taken care of" bothered him; he smelled another kind of stench in the deal—corruption. In disgust, he quit the Hines club.

Ten years later, Jimmy Hines was still riding high in Democratic politics. And Frank Hogan found it almost unbelievable that this man who took tainted money had risen to power through the highest mansion of politics, the White House. At the 1932 Democratic Convention in Chicago, Jimmy shared a room at the Drake Hotel with mob boss Frank Costello. Hines switched his support from Al Smith, the Tammany favorite, to Franklin D. Roosevelt. When F.D.R. won, he repaid Jimmy by making him federal patronage dispenser in Manhattan.

In 1938, while investigating Hines' patronage—"protection" might have been a better word—of Dutch Schultz's policy-racket kingdom, Hogan discovered that Jimmy's friend "Tootsie" Herbert had controlled racketeering in the poultry industry. Those free Thanksgiving turkeys that had been "taken care of" were a gift to Jimmy from Joey Wiener, a convicted safecracker and ex-con whom Herbert hired as a strong-arm enforcer to take over the *Shochtim* union.

This first exposure to the guttermuck of politics didn't completely kill Frank Hogan's interest in local elections. After his law-school graduation in 1928, he landed a $26-a-week job doing insurance investigating for the law firm of Gleason, McLanahan, Merritt and Ingraham. A year later, a lawyer friend in the firm interested him in working after-hours for Patrick S. Dowd, an insurgent trying to take over as Tammany district leader from Andrew B. Keating, incumbent in the 13th Assembly District.

Hogan went back to ringing doorbells again. When the polls closed that November, Dowd apparently had a substantial plurality. But—according to witnesses—Jimmy Hines came bursting on the scene, accompanied by Dutch Schultz and his goon squad. They ordered the polling place reopened, then proceeded to stuff the ballot boxes with enough votes to elect Keating. Hogan tried to argue with Hines, the witnesses said, and was shouldered aside. Hogan was reported to have taken a vow then and there to "get Hines if it takes me the rest of my life."

3
GANGBUSTERS

Frank Hogan couldn't sleep. He lay motionless atop his Murphy bed, sweating out a Manhattan heat-wave. The night of July 30, 1935, was unbearably humid, worse than anything he remembered in Guatemala. Wearing only undershorts—he never felt comfortable naked—he got out of bed and padded over to the kitchenette. The room was pitch dark. He stood before the faint light of the open Frigidaire and fixed another glass of ice water. To help himself through the long night, Frank switched on the radio—a treasured old Philco. There was little enough to treasure in his one-room "efficiency" apartment in Tudor City. The best of the few sticks of furniture was the coffee table he had obtained by saving Kool cigarette coupons. There was not space enough for beds—the twin Murphy beds (his brother Joe used the second) unfolded from the wall at night. Still in night school, Joe had taken over his brother's job as an insurance investigator, earning $26 a week. Frank earned slightly more than that as a practicing attorney. He had long since left Gleason, McLanahan to strike out with Anthony Liebler, a young colleague in the firm. The Depression had exerted its downward pull and their partnership was barely surviving as a business.

Between Frank and Joey, the brothers barely scraped together enough for food and their $47-a-month rent. The partnership with Liebler, the son of a Yorkville realtor, was one of countless two-member law firms that sprang up after the Crash of '29. The firm of Hogan & Liebler was luckier than most of these Depression duos because the partners had been able to hang on for six years, specializing in seamen's negligence, federal employees' liability cases and landlord-tenant disputes. Neither partner averaged more than $50 a week in fees, and troubles developed with their own landlord. The bulk of their earnings went for rent on their office in the old Lincoln Building on East 42nd Street.

It was a shabby, threadbare existence, and Hogan felt his shoulders bowed by a mountain of debt. The Depression was squeezing the youth and optimism from him. On nights like this one, the physical oppression of the heat added to his growing malaise of the spirit.

Outside, neighbors exchanged desultory talk across the fire escapes, mopping their faces, fanning themselves with newspapers. Hogan was listening now to the sound of a rich baritone coming from the Philco—the voice of a radio orator, a man addressing the city with an urgent message. In spite of the heat and his own torpor, Hogan began to pay sharp attention. This compelling voice was to set the tone of moral indignation that would carry the young lawyer through his entire life.

"There is today scarcely a business in New York which does not somehow pay its tribute to the underworld—a tribute levied by force and collected by fears. . . . In some industries in New York, organized crime has actually been invited by certain groups of businessmen to 'organize,' as they call it, the industry. . . . If a businessman does not join promptly, his windows are broken, and his employees are assaulted. Stink bombs ruin his goods and drive away his customers. If he surrenders and joins the association, as he almost always does, from then on he pays and pays. . . ."

The stinging voice and grandiloquent delivery belonged to Thomas Edmund Dewey.

The radio speech that midsummer night was Dewey's inaugural address to the people of New York after having been sworn in the previous evening as Special Prosecutor of Manhattan. The thirty-three-year-old prosecutor's rise to celebrity status contained many stock ingredients of the American success story. Dewey came of solid WASP background and solid Midwestern patriotism. In a virtuous youth he had been a Boy Scout and a member of the church choir. He had also peddled newspapers in his hometown of Owosso, Michigan. A graduate of the University of Michigan, he came to New York City with magisterial ambitions.

Although he and Hogan were the same age, Dewey was just a year away from finishing law school at Columbia (Class of '25) when Hogan was still an undergraduate there; the two had never met. In the intervening years, Dewey had become the acting U.S. Attorney for the Southern

District of New York, and his precocious career was chronicled almost daily in the press.

Hogan had read every word. On the day of Dewey's appointment as Special Prosecutor, superseding then District Attorney William Copeland Dodge, political cartoonists ridiculed Dewey as Jack the Giant Killer—a young David against the Gang Goliaths. But on the editorial pages, Hogan noted, "the man from Owosso" was hailed as a young conquistador, a bona-fide champion of the people.

When Dewey first set foot on New York City pavement, Prohibition had just begun. The man who would soon make "gangbusters" a household word would be thirty-one before he could legally buy a drink at any bar in the United States. Gangsterism as a result of the unpopular amendment was just burgeoning into the bonanza it would eventually become.

The intense melodrama of the twenties accustomed people to the idea that a navy of bootleggers prowled the seas. An illicit land fleet of rumrunning trucks zoomed the highways. Policemen were either bought or shot. Politicians' pockets were lined with graft money. Ordinary men and women had to rub elbows in speakeasies with thieves and murderers. Dewey's inaugural radio speech did little to dissuade people from feeling that they were taking part in a Hollywood gangster movie. There was a warning tremor in the baritone voice now as the new Special Prosecutor declared:

"Your businesses, your safety, and your daily lives are affected by criminal conditions in this city. There is certainly not a family in the City of New York which does not pay its toll to racketeers."

Hogan listened attentively as Dewey argued that Repeal, having taken the profit out of illicit booze, had diverted mob interests to other industries:

"Every barrel of flour consumed in New York City now pays its toll to racketeers, which goes right into the price of a loaf of bread," Dewey declared with solemn hyperbole. "Every chicken shipped into the City of New York pays its tribute to the poultry racket, out of the pockets of the public. There are few vegetable or fish markets in the City of New York where merchants are not forced by sluggings, destruction of goods, threats, and stink bombs to pay heavy tolls."

Praised as a man of his times, Dewey was fortunate in the times that produced him. Just as Prohibition conditioned people to the menace of the underworld, it also got the city and nation ready for the coming of Dewey. The public yearning for a crime-busting hero had grown increasingly since the "little tin box" disclosures of Judge Samuel Seabury's investigation into the crooked politics of Tammany Hall.

People were fed up with the gangs, and the gangsters. Unlike Seabury, who lacked prosecutorial power to put people in jail, Dewey came on like . . . well, like gangbusters. His designation as a "super" District Attorney gave him vast discretionary powers to subpoena and browbeat witnesses, to use wiretaps, bugging and grants of immunity. Mayor Fiorello La Guardia might be able to go on radio and order numbers racketeer Dutch Schultz to "stay out of town!" but Dewey could—and would—put the Dutchman's political protector, Jimmy Hines, in Sing Sing. Even the manner in which Dewey came to office provided one of the most dramatic appointments of a Special Prosecutor in U.S. history.

The rising public protest over corruption in Democratic-controlled New York City had grown to a roar earlier that year. Abruptly, on May 13, word leaked out of the Criminal Courts Building that a grand jury had declared war on the District Attorney and was indicting everyone in sight. It was the classic case of a "runaway" grand jury. The panel chased District Attorney Dodge and his staff out of the jury room, rebelling against his "cold water tactics." Jury foreman Lee Thompson Smith startled the city by a declaration of independence: "We have labored under the most difficult handicaps. Every conceivable obstacle has been put in our path."

The jury called upon Governor Herbert H. Lehman to appoint a new man to investigate vice and racketeering. To remove all suspicion of partisanship, the Governor suggested four Republicans. None of the four was willing to accept, but one of them, former U.S. Attorney George Z. Medalie, recommended that his protégé, Tom Dewey, an ardent and lifelong Republican, be appointed instead. The Governor reluctantly agreed. He named Dewey "Deputy Assistant" to Democratic Attorney Dodge, who was in turn a devoted member of the very Tammany Hall that Dewey was supposed to assail. The newspapers called the arrangement "fusion" politics. The cynics laughed aloud.

There had been many such special investigations in the past. Each time a new probe was announced, the only response from the fugitives was an enormous collective yawn. Other investigations had proved futile, and Dewey's probe seemed headed for the same fate. His theatrical radio appeal for shakedown victims to come forward in secrecy ("We will respect your confidence. We will protect you") was a fizzle. No one showed up.

But applicants for positions on Dewey's staff *did* show up—especially when they heard he had set his own annual salary at $16,695. That was high pay for low times, and the day after the radio address, two hundred people telephoned to ask for work. Three thousand others wrote to him for a job. One of the three thousand was Frank S. Hogan.

It was once said of Dewey that the only time he picked up a pen was to sign an indictment. By contrast, Hogan was a longhand letter-writer of consummate skill and craftsmanship. He drafted several painstaking versions of any letter—crossing out, erasing, endlessly rewriting. After Dewey signed off the air that night, Frank Hogan switched on the lights and sat down to write him a letter. He worked until four in the morning, polishing every sentence. Mailed out in the first morning post, the letter struck paydirt: it was selected as one of thirty applications to be given consideration by the Special Prosecutor for the twenty vacancies on his staff. Hogan was invited down to Dewey's law office at 120 Broadway, where anxious applicants waited to be screened in interview.

Hogan was seen by Murray I. Gurfein, a Columbia graduate (Phi Bete) and *Harvard Law Review* editor already chosen by Dewey to help with his cleanup. Gurfein had been a prizewinning essayist at Columbia and was impressed with the clarity and frankness of Hogan's letter. "He didn't pretend to have any trial experience and admitted that, financially, he was having a hard time," recalled Gurfein, now a U.S. District Court judge.

"Frank was a big man on campus when I was wearing a freshman beanie," Gurfein remembers further. "When he came to Dewey's office, we had a preponderance of Republicans applying for jobs, but Dewey really wanted to take a nonpartisan stance, so that gave Frank a leg up."

Gurfein was so impressed at the initial interview that he wanted Dewey to meet Hogan as soon as possible.

"Well, I have to tell you something first," Hogan warned. "I'm a Democrat. I've even been a member of Jimmy Hines' club." He described how he used to "walk downtown with Hines and the other hangers-on to see if we could get a little patronage for the club." However, Hogan insisted forthrightly: "I'm completely independent. No man living could ever boss me."

On that note, Hogan started uptown, with a promise that he would hear from the office later. It was thirty minutes later, as it turned out.

Gurfein had gone straight to Dewey and announced, "Have I got a man for *you*."

Hogan had no sooner gotten back to his midtown office than Gurfein telephoned him to come back downtown again: "Mr. Dewey wants to see you." Hogan rushed back—and it was an unforgettable meeting.

Reflected Hogan later: "Now, I had been examined by prospective employers since I was thirteen. But this meeting proved to be something else again. In less than an hour, he raked me fore and aft with questions, held me up to the light, put me under a microscope, and turned me inside out. He rooted out facts deeply buried in my subconscious mind, and put together an inventory of my physical, mental and spiritual condition and its possible development. Not only did he put it together, he never forgot it."

Dewey hired Hogan immediately, offering him a starting salary of $3,700, provided the office expense budget was officially approved. It was. And Hogan obtained a co-signer to settle all his debts.

The first week in August 1935, he moved with the rest of Dewey's staff to offices in the Woolworth Building, across from City Hall. Dewey set up elaborate defenses against the "sinister forces" that opposed him. The windows were sealed. A twenty-four-hour police guard was assigned to the front door. There were frosted glass partitions in the waiting room, and secret entrances and exits. Special locks replaced the standard ones on the filing cabinets. An untappable phone cable connected Dewey with the main office of the Telephone Company.

The Special Rackets Investigation concentrated first on loan-sharking operations in the city. The loan-shark probe was a difficult job, because so many of the broken-spirited witnesses were afraid to come forward and testify. The bloodsuckers chose their victims carefully, extorting money from the neediest—people hard up for cash to pay rent, doctor's bills, grocery bills. The loan-sharking raids gave Hogan his first exposure to the Dewey technique of investigating rackets independently, rather than waiting for cases to be brought to him by the police. He made bold use of such controversial police methods as wiretaps and bugging. Detectives assigned to Dewey's office were regularly out posing as gas-meter readers or telephone repairmen in order to gain access to the basement, where the pairs of proper phone wires could be tapped with alligator plugs. Through court-ordered taps planted on the premises of various bars and hotels during the loan-shark problem, Dewey's eavesdroppers grimly noted evidence of another flourishing racket in the city—prostitution. The top man, referred to as "the Boss," was not identified until Dave Marcus, a booker of prostitutes, turned state's evidence. Dewey learned from Marcus that "the Boss" was Lucky Luciano.

Luciano, born Salvidore Lucania, was said to have gotten his nickname during an early Prohibition gang war, in which he was purportedly stabbed and left for dead on Staten Island. The story may be apocryphal. Mob insiders who told the tale could never explain how Lucky survived the "one-way ride." If the story was true, Lucky's return trip led him back to command the so-called Unione Siciliana, later called Cosa Nostra.

During his lengthy tenure as Boss, Luciano ruled, virtually immune from arrest, from his suite in the Waldorf-Astoria, where he was known by the debonaire alias "Charles Ross." Although police suspected him as the versatile monopolist not only of gambling clubs but of narcotics and numbers operations, they had nothing they could pin on him. With his secure position and power, it seemed difficult to imagine Lucky's stooping to something as petty as the coercion of prostitutes.

But in Dewey's crusade, any method of penetrating the layers of insulation that protected Luciano from the crimes of his subordinates seemed justified. Traditionally, police arrested the small-time addict, numbers runner or pimp, rather than zero in on syndicate bosses. Indictments were required to be confined to a charge of one crime. With a stroke of political genius, Dewey changed all that. He secured passage of a state law that would adapt several tactics already used in the federal courts. The so-called "Dewey law" authorized the joinder of connected offenses in a single indictment, punishable by an appropriate sentence. This device enabled Dewey to use that ancient body the grand jury as an investigating tool.

Whatever else it may have accomplished, the Luciano case established the concept of calling witnesses before the grand jury, then granting them immunity from prosecution if they talked against higher-ups in the organization. Those who refused to testify were jailed in contempt of court until they decided to talk. This technique of turning suspects into witnesses was Dewey's major contribution to criminal law. (Its effectiveness was dramatized in the most famous and high-reaching criminal prosecution of U.S. history: Watergate.)

The system had many built-in perils, however, some of which stayed on Hogan's conscience over the years. It was remarkable, Hogan thought when he looked back on it, how the crosscurrents of public opinion, as well as his own social attitudes, had changed since Luciano's conviction in 1936. There were those, even among his enemies, who claimed that Luciano never got a dollar from prostitution in his life, and was in fact doing nothing more culpable than making book at a racetrack when he was surprised to hear that Dewey had crowned him Public Enemy Number One. More than thirty years later, Hogan doubted that Luciano could have been tried on the same evidence in 1972 that convicted him in 1936. Hogan even suggested that Luciano had some basis for insisting he was innocent of the charge of compulsory prostitution:

"He didn't come within miles of the operation, but those who were running it had received his approval. So in *fact* he was part of the conspiracy," Hogan told Mike Pearl. "He wasn't getting any money out of it, but this was their territory [the bookers'] so he was guilty, although I'm sure he went to his grave thinking he wasn't involved at all."

The nine volumes of official transcripts in the Luciano case amounted to two million words on seven thousand pages of testimony from dozens of hookers, pimps, madams and panderers. Yet only the evidence of four witnesses was considered important by Justice Philip J. McCook, who tried the case in less than a month. The witnesses: Joe Bendix, a convicted hotel safecracker; and Nancy Presser, Mildred Harris Bulitzer and a drug addict called Cokey Flo Brown, three prostitutes being held as material witnesses at the Women's House of Detention.

The three hookers had been rounded up on a crisp February evening in 1936, during a vice raid unprecedented in the city's history: more than seventy-five prostitutes and a dozen pimps were hauled up in the freight elevator to Dewey's fourteenth-floor office in the Woolworth Building. This surprise party brought in a few sleek harlots, but most were the usual peroxided blondes, many of them old and diseased.

The girls turned Luciano's trial into one of the most flamboyant public spectacles of the years between Prohibition and Pearl Harbor. Part of the entertainment value lay in the names the hookers had dreamed up for themselves: Gashouse Lil, Nigger Ruth, Silver-Tongued Elsie, Jennie the Factory. Before the trial began, Dewey assigned Hogan to set the girls up in various hotels around town, where they were wined and dined, taken to movies and night clubs, escorted on shopping trips. Dewey even sent two of them abroad on all-expense-paid trips. When the money stopped coming in, however, the witnesses began to get rough and demand bonuses to tell Dewey what he wanted to hear—that Luciano had directly or indirectly profited from the skin trade. On the witness stand, most of the girls told their stories poorly, contradicting themselves or giving worthless testimony. The three who were able to pin Luciano to the racket said they had been won over not by money but by Deputy Assistant Hogan's exceptional tenderness and chivalry when he came to visit them at the House of Detention.

When he first entered the cellblock, the smells and sounds engulfed Hogan. All around him, women shouted, their perspiration and cheap perfume suffusing the stale air. They were an odd lot. Some had the expected exaggerated sexuality of prostitutes: wicked red lipstick and large breasts that spilled out of their prison-gray cottons. Many of the women lacquered their hair into upswept coiffeurs, and painted their toenails. Others, to make themselves as tough-looking and masculine as possible, had deliberately slashed off their hair in butch cuts. Sexual roles in women's prison were reversed, exaggerated, warped beyond straight imagination. An astonished Frank Hogan told his brother Joe, when he got home that night, how some women behind bars played the husband, the mother, or even the child, in a grotesque imitation of the outside world.

Hogan became so involved with the hookers held in the Luciano case that the heavyset matron who greeted him at the door every day called that row of cells "Hogan's Alley." The girls themselves, taken by his pious manner and black Homburg, nicknamed him "Father Hogan."

As he walked briskly down the prison corridor, Hogan could hear the high-pitched caterwauling all around him. "You git away from her, tha's my ole lady." "Keep yo' hands off ma letters—they's from my husband!" "She took mah lipstick and busted it!"

Some women inmates tried to attract Hogan himself: "Whoooeee, Daddy, look what I got for you! You be good to me and I'll be good to you." Saddest of all, and often repeated: "I don't belong here! I didn' do nuthin' " and "My babies need me! Nobody's takin' care of 'em at home!"

No civilian male ever went through this prison without being shaken to the core. Hogan was especially vulnerable to the women's cries, pleas and taunts. He had grown up revering women, had been taught to put them on pedestals. To see them now—see their nakedness and degradation—moved him in a way that the plight of the imprisoned male could not have.

The prettiest of the three prostitutes in his charge was Cokey Flo, who before her arrest had been leading a triple life as mistress to three men. None of her three paramours sent money or bothered to visit her when she was in jail, sick and broke. She blamed one of the men, a reputed Luciano sidekick, for starting her on dope.

Hogan, when he came to visit, brought her Kool cigarettes to help try to satisfy her craving for cocaine, and lent a helpful shoulder upon which she could sob out her story of thrice-unrequited love. That early experience in the House of Dee, as the girls called it, hinted at one of the paradoxes in Frank Hogan's character. Despite an almost eccentric capacity for moral indignation, Hogan had no surface characteristics of the aggressive, Jim Garrison-style prosecutor. The Hogan quality that shone through the bars of the sordid detention pen was one of ingratiating warmth—a compassion that would win him notable successes in his later years as District Attorney.

The Luciano case ended happily for Dewey: Justice McCook put Lucky away for from thirty to fifty years, with the warning that he would serve the maximum if any of the witnesses against him came to harm. The girls slunk back to their regular doorways as soon as the heat was off. Some time later, Frank's look-alike brother Joe was walking past the Hotel Commodore, on 42nd Street, on his way to work. Cokey Flo and Mildred ran up and kissed him on the cheek, mistaking Joe for "Father Hogan." Still plying their trade, as Joe remembers, they were excited that *Liberty* magazine was selling their lifestories to Warner Brothers for a movie. When the deal later fell through, the girls blamed Dewey and repudiated their previous confessions. The Luciano conviction was in danger of being upset. Only the word of Bendix, the hotel thief, now linked Luciano with the case. Moreover, during the Luciano trial, the defense had impressively submitted a letter that Bendix had written to his wife, asking her to "think up some real clever story to tell" in exchange for a lighter sentence than the fifteen years to life he was serving as a fourth felony offender up at Sing Sing.

Bendix may have perjured himself, but he stuck to his story. Motions for a retrial were denied.

Was Luciano framed? There was no doubt in the mind of Governor Lehman that Lucky was guilty of much—but not of compulsory prostitution. When Dewey went to the Governor to try to have Bendix paroled for his cooperation in the case, Lehman refused. He feared, "When a man is in prison for thirty years, he is under tremendous temptation to find any way out—he is under a strong temptation to deviate from the truth." The Governor's refusal to accommodate Dewey may have reflected his disapproval of the Special Prosecutor's tactics, especially the "we're having a crime wave" atmosphere he had created.

"We are passing through a cycle of hysteria," outgoing District Attorney Dodge had declared on the day Dewey replaced him as D.A. Despite

Dewey's denials, there was some truth to the charge that he was inciting mass hysteria. Public concern over crime had mounted higher than ever. There were bills sponsored in Congress that would forbid known criminals to consort together, thus making a *prima facie* case of guilt out of a bad reputation. There were public demands for the death penalty to be meted out to gangleaders, and mandatory life sentences for fourth offenders accused of felonies. Lehman's apprehensions about all of this led to an open break with Dewey over the question of Joe Bendix, who had already served five years for burglary. Dewey had enticed Joe into giving evidence against the accused Luciano by the suggestion, if not the definite promise, of a mitigation of sentence. Accordingly, Joe was the only witness who hadn't recanted his testimony. Motions for a new trial were denied as a result, and Luciano's conviction was upheld.

As the years went by, and Frank Hogan became entrenched as Manhattan District Attorney, he was reminded of Joe Bendix by a letter from the safecracker in prison, noting that he was again applying for parole. Dewey had become Governor in 1946. Bearing in mind all that Bendix had done to help Dewey make it to the state capitol, Hogan figured Dewey might want to make good his broken promise of 1936. This was the wrong assumption. When Hogan reminded his old boss that Bendix was still languishing up in Sing Sing, Dewey—like Lehman—refused to grant parole. Frank Hogan was upset. A man is only as good as his word, he reasoned, ordering his house intellectual, Stanley H. Fuld, chief of the Appeals Bureau, to get up to the law library and find something with which to spring Joe Bendix.

The result was a fascinating landmark in the field of criminal law. Perhaps no enumeration of appeals briefs submitted by Hogan's office over the years does more than suggest the immensity of his ideological influence on the criminal-justice system. But a quick look at the Joe Bendix case conveys a sense of Hogan's enormous involvement in the evolution of modern American penal law.

In those early days, Hogan, like the rest of Dewey's bright young lawyers, was totally unfamiliar with the state's criminal law. Assistants looked up the law as they went along and played it by ear, making trial-and-error decisions. Then Stanley Fuld arrived on the scene. A Kent scholar and one of the top five men in his 1926 graduating class at Columbia Law School, Fuld was a perfectionist who was endlessly fascinated with the complexities, logic, symmetry and finer points of the law. Some of his more aggressive associates dismissed him as an intellectual robot, possessed of a computer brain and elephant's memory. But Hogan saw a creative intelligence in Fuld's intellectual gifts and assigned him a massive undertaking: to read and digest every Court of Appeals decision on criminal law since 1847, the first year records were kept. Fuld began his painstaking research with the help of a number of dollar-a-year law graduates. Eventually, he was put in charge of all applications served upon the District Attorney.

The scrupulous operation of Fuld's Appeals Bureau was a rare contribution to civic life. We get a sense of the bureau's workings in the world of criminal justice as it then existed through the recollections of David Riesman, then an office underling, now professor of sociology at Harvard and perhaps the nation's best-known student of society.

"Some of this work was baroque, overdone in terms of the importance of the case and the triviality—and often disingenuousness—of the opposition," Professor Riesman recalled for me. "Still, it held a high standard and provided a model. . . . The judges seemed to me, under the canons of restraints on them, imposed by an egalitarian society, to be handicapped in conducting trials with any semblance of dignity—long before there were the kind of political trials we have seen in recent years. There was no sanction to prevent defense lawyers from showing off to their clients by every manner of rudeness and abuse of witnesses, generally to no avail, except the prolongation of the trial and the disgrace of the behavior itself. In the federal courts, counsel could not put on the same kind of circus with impunity."

In Riesman's estimation, prosecutors under Frank Hogan's aegis behaved a good deal better than Dewey's. When one of his assistants lost a case, he complained to Dewey that the defense lawyer had cried in front of the jury during summation. Dewey thundered, "Well, can't you cry, too?"

Hogan's scrupulousness implied an overriding sense of fair play and a willingness to confess error. It is necessary to keep this in mind when considering Bendix's claim that he had been doublecrossed not by Dewey, but by a former assistant under District Attorney Dodge during the original prosecution. Bendix said the assistant fraudulently promised him a lighter sentence if he pleaded guilty.

Fuld scoured law books and his own memory until he dug up a remedy long dead in the annals of common law. It was called the writ of error *coram nobis*. Conceived by the judiciary of sixteenth-century England and obsolete in Great Britain even before the age of Blackstone, the forgotten remedy was disinterred by Fuld from its grave in antiquity and came back to haunt Frank Hogan for the rest of his life.

Beyond the immediate goal of granting Joe Bendix his freedom—which it succeeded in doing—the writ became an emergency measure that was absorbed by legal osmosis through almost every state in the union, becoming, as one jurist termed it, "the wild ass of the law which the courts cannot control."

Coram nobis (from *quae coram nobis residant*, "Let the record remain before us") referred chiefly to guilty pleas entered after duplicitous promises made off the record by the District Attorney. It soon became an innocent man's last chance to escape injustice when all other avenues of appeal were closed to him. Although fewer than one out of a thousand applications are ever granted, hardly a day has gone by since 1943, when Stanley Fuld and Frank Hogan first made use of the ancient writ, that prisoners haven't clamored at the gates, *all* claiming they were defrauded into pleading guilty.

Hogan's office was flooded with *coram nobis* applications, all of them costly and time-consuming, adding an extra burden to the seemingly inexhaustible opportunities for other review and reexamination of trial proceedings. The all-time *coram nobis* champion was Charley Glinton, a murderer who narrowly escaped the death penalty in 1959 after he was convicted in a classic "double indemnity" case. If ever a man had proved himself guilty of murder in the first degree, that man was Charles Glinton.

In May 1959, he reported to his insurance company that his brother had accidentally fallen to his death from a fifth-floor apartment window. Glinton arranged for an elaborate funeral in a Staten Island cemetery, complete with floral tributes and an expensive tombstone. Four months later, acting on an insurance investigator's tip, Hogan ordered a background check on Glinton's family history. The D.A. made two interesting discoveries. One, Glinton was homosexual. Two, he didn't have a brother.

Hogan ordered the D.A.'s squad to go over to Staten Island and dig up the body of Glinton's dead "brother." An autopsy confirmed what Hogan already suspected. The dead man had been Glinton's homosexual roommate. The suspect went on trial for murder.

Hogan's proof: Glinton had taken out a $14,000 double-indemnity insurance policy on the life of his roommate before the "accident," after getting the fellow drunk enough to sign a statement representing that they were brothers. On the night of the murder, Glinton got the roommate drunk again, further weakened him with judo holds and finally threw him out a window in order to collect the money.

Glinton was convicted and sentenced to death. Were it not for the abolition of the death penalty in 1959, he would have died in the electric chair. Instead, he got a new lease on life—albeit life in prison.

Behind bars, Glinton settled down to the life of a jailhouse lawyer. He did his homework regularly in the prison law library. One day, he discovered a chapter on *coram nobis* applications. Glinton was delighted. He decided to devote the rest of his life, if need be, to the search for some minor legal technicality that would set him free. Despite the overwhelming murder evidence against him, Glinton found new ways to appeal the guilty verdict month after month, year after year, always with the help of licensed defense attorneys paid by the state. The amount of time and tax money wasted on answering the convict's frivolous appeals from year to year convinced Hogan that "maybe we should have a special Glinton Bureau."

Charley Glinton was the subject of a speech District Attorney Hogan made to the New York Commerce and Industry Association in August 1965, a speech vivifying the failure of the appellate courts to arrive at any finality of judgment in criminal cases:

"We can say that the case is over only if the verdict is 'not guilty.' The People have no appeal from an acquittal. If, however, the jury convicts the defendant, as they often do, our task has just begun. Years of litigation lie ahead as the case winds its way through an elaborate structure of review. Every conceivable aspect of the case, including things that were never thought of at the trial, will be argued and reargued to panels of state and federal appellate judges whose appetite for reexamination seems inexhaustible. Indeed, it is possible to say that there is virtually no such thing as finality in a judgment of conviction. One of my associates has calculated that a convicted defendant, with only moderate diligence and small imagination, can get a single, well-devised legal point reviewed by no fewer than fifty-seven judges.

"Back in May of 1959, one Charles Glinton was convicted of murder in the first degree and sentenced to death. The proof at his trial was that he had taken out an insurance policy on the life of his roommate, after falsely representing that they were brothers. Our highest New York court, the Court of Appeals, affirmed the conviction on April 21, 1960. Five years later, Mr. Glinton is still very much with us. With the help, successively, of several attorneys, he has presented his claims of perjury, coercion, fraud and newly discovered evidence to five courts in sixteen proceedings: three times in the New York Supreme Court, twice in our Court of Appeals, five times in the U.S. District Court, three times in the U.S. Court of Appeals, and three times in the U.S. Supreme Court. Convicted in 1959 for a murder committed in 1957, Mr. Glinton is still litigating the issue of his guilt, and his appellate remedies, I assure you, are far from exhausted." (Update: as of April 24, 1974, four motions for reargument had been denied by the N.Y. Court of Appeals. Six writs of *habeas corpus* had been brought in the Federal District Court and denied. Several *coram nobis* applications had been brought unsuccessfully. Moreover, none of this cost Mr. Glinton a nickel.)

"As a result of this excessive fullness of review," Hogan concluded, ". . . our old cases come back in a great wave, threatening to engulf the gasping trial courts . . ."

Impatient with his own role as the architect of civil liberties that would later break the back of the overworked court system, Hogan in the 1970s seemed to express a greater willingness to take shortcuts with the Bill of Rights. Conversely, whenever he was charged in later years with manufacturing "political" cases—the Panther 21 and Lenny Bruce were examples—the District Attorney always coupled his strong denials with a candid comparison of office policies in the 1930s. Back in those days, he'd say, we *did* go after Fritz Kuhn and the "communist sympathizers." Now *that* was political. *This* isn't.

Hogan was referring to the rest of Dewey's term as Special Prosecutor. Union racketeers in the restaurant, poultry and baking empires were overthrown, but not until December 31, 1937, when Dewey took office as District Attorney, did the real fireworks begin. World War II was just around the corner, and the office had to deal with an American fascist, Fritz Kuhn, the Fuehrer of the German-American Bund, who swaggered about the country extolling the benefits of National Socialism.

At his carefully staged rallies in Madison Square Garden, the cardboard dictator goose-stepped down the aisle, followed by bodyguards and surrounded by bellicose supporters. He would mount the stage under a solitary searchlight, to the roar of Nazi songs. One night, Hogan went up to the Garden to take notes, listening to Kuhn's threats against the Jews and Catholics. Hogan reported back to Dewey: "A sickening spectacle."

"Let's do some work on Kuhn and see what we can come up with," said Dewey. Hogan promptly ordered his investigators to infiltrate the Bund.

Disguised in Storm Trooper uniforms with swastika armbands, the

D.A.'s men were soon swilling beer in Yorkville taverns and heiling Kuhn at his rallies. The pursuit of Kuhn was an admittedly political prosecution, although the only person willing to make that charge was Kuhn himself. Dewey persuaded a Manhattan jury to convict the Fuehrer on grand-larceny charges, although Dewey had to stretch the law quite a bit to make that accusation. Dewey charged Kuhn with making false bookkeeping entries for the Bund while collecting money from German sympathizers.

Hogan's mention of "communist sympathizers" referred to editor Clarence Hathaway of the *Daily Worker*. Dewey had Hathaway convicted on "criminal libel" charges that would be laughed out of court today. The libelous remark? Pure rhetoric. Hathaway charged that the widow of a rival editor, machine-gunned by Midwestern gangsters, was "selling his corpse limb by limb to the highest bidder." All Hathaway had been guilty of was purple prose, hysterical hyperbole. But Dewey had him jailed on the strength of the prosecutor's uncontested power.

Dewey seemed to have become dictatorial even in his attitude toward the bench. "A lot of judges stood in awe of Dewey," recalls U.S. District Judge Arnold Bauman, a former Dewey-Hogan associate. "If Dewey told them today was Friday, it was Friday. They canonized him, or lived in terror of him—and he regarded them as not much better than senior district attorneys."

It is easy to understand how the cult of personality that embraced Dewey carried over to his successor, Frank Hogan. Before the war years, Dewey's "crusaders" were riding high in public prestige and personal adoration. Politicians kow-towed to them. Defense lawyers fawned over them. The press used every rhetorical device it could think of to magnify Dewey's successes. The underworld was so frightened that the syndicates began relocating policy and gambling operations across the river in New Jersey. With a straight face, official biographer Rupert Hughes likened Dewey to Alexander the Great, Emperor Napoleon, and Chancellor of the Exchequer William Pitt. (Woolcott Gibbs later wrote that Hughes' campaign biography "compares very favorably with some of Albert Payson Terhune's hymns to the collie.") But such witty zingers were aimed only from outside Dewey's office. Inside, the mood bordered on cathedral.

To be a member of Dewey's staff carried with it a presumption of ability that was the envy of the legal world. Looking back, one veteran of the Dewey crusade likened the office in the mid-thirties to "the Watergate prosecution staff without the controversy of the Nixon-lovers. We were national heroes in those days. People were deferential to us wherever we went."

A half-dozen Dewey assistants lunched every day at the Antica Roma, a small Italian restaurant near the Courthouse where the food was good and the wine inexpensive. The headwaiter always reserved the best table for the young prosecutors, whose names were on the front pages every day: Nick Atlas, a boisterous deputy assistant with a waxed handlebar mustache, a gold watch fob, and a tendency to sound like Colonel Hoople; William P. Rogers, the suave, handsome lawyer-diplomat destined to become U.S. Attorney General and Secretary of State; Arnold Bauman, who was Jewish and came to work with Dewey because the high-powered Wall Street firms in those days always wanted to know, "To what church do you belong, Mr. Bauman?"

Dewey's administrative assistants Paul Lockwood and Frank Hogan were the quietest members of the clique. Hogan always retained a nostalgic affection for the group. The man who presided over the checkered-cloth luncheon table was Assistant D.A. Sol Gelb, "the Gertrude Stein of the pithy, common-sense remark," as Bauman called him. Gelb transformed the Antica Roma into a legal version of a Paris literary salon, electric with wit and charm. Hogan listened eagerly as Gelb held forth daily on a range of topics as diverse as Restoration drama, prizefighting and the Chinese philosophy of prosecution.

The D.A.'s men worked in the superfluous splendor of the old Manhattan Courthouse at 137 Centre Street, where Dewey had moved his staff after his election as Manhattan District Attorney. It was there, in an atmosphere of carved walnut furniture and birdcage elevators, that Frank Hogan tried his first minor cases, becoming, in one judge's opinion, "a master of the gentle art of cross-examination." The wainscoted courtrooms were connected to each other by an immense corridor called the "cave of the winds" because of the political gossip that echoed back and forth. Hogan loved the old edifice. When WPA workers demolished it and replaced it with the modernistic Criminal Courts Building in 1942, Hogan saved one of the old jury-box adornments—a bare-breasted mahogany sphinx—as a desk ornament for his private office. As sentimental as he was about the old Courthouse, Hogan couldn't have cared less about the adjoining D.A.'s office—a dilapidated barracks originally built as a laundry. In the dusty setting of green lamp shades and lazy overhead fans, Frank had trouble keeping clean his white, wide-lapeled Gatsby suit and his straw boater. When his back was turned, the secretaries playfully skimmed his hat around the office, like a forerunner of the Frisbee. In this rather picturesque setting, Frank did much of the background work that helped Dewey reach his peak in the Jimmy Hines investigation—the first case in which an alliance between politics and the underworld was ever established in a court of law.

The Hines prosecution offered publicity value for Dewey in its Runyonesque cast of characters—gangster hero Dutch Schultz (born Arthur Flegenheimer) and his lawyer J. Richard (Dixie) Davis, the first of many "mouthpiece" attorneys Hogan would learn to deal with; the bikini beauty Hope Dare, who, before becoming Dixie's companion, had been a star bronco rider in Wild West rodeos; the fantastic Otto (Abbadabba) Berman, a horse player who got his nickname because he could do complicated applications of the binomial theorem in his head; and underworld accountant George Weinberg, who had succeeded his brother Abe (Bo) Weinberg as the financial brains of Schultz's empire.

Bo had reputedly sold out to rivals while the boss was indisposed because of legal problems. At any rate, he vanished without a trace one night, and by some accounts, it was Schultz who personally took Weinberg on the traditional one-way ride. It was even rumored that the Dutchman conceived of an interesting way to dispose of the evidence: according to the underworld grapevine, Bo was rowed out to the middle of the East River and forced to sit down in a barrel of cement until it hardened into a concrete overcoat. Sealed in cement, he was tossed overboard and sank—presumably forever.

At the Hines trial, the evidence proved that policy money was carried up the criminal pyramid step by step and passed to progressively higher-ranking collectors, comptrollers, bankers, accountants and lawyers before it reached Schultz. Operating a $20-million-a-year numbers-racket monopoly out of temporary headquarters in Newark, where he was under indictment on federal tax-evasion charges, Schultz blabbermouthed about finding somebody to knock off Dewey, his old nemesis in the U.S. Attorney's office in New York. Somebody got to the Dutchman first.

Schultz and three associates were massacred on October 23, 1935, in a Newark saloon. The Dutchman was relieving himself at a urinal in the men's room when a gunman kicked open the door and raked his body with gunfire. Simultaneously, the ambush party riddled his bodyguards, who had been counting receipts in a back room.

Schultz lingered, semi-conscious, in a hospital emergency room for

twenty hours, delirious with a fever of 106 degrees. "A boy has never wept nor dashed a thousand kim . . ." he jabbered cryptically at one moment, but nobody ever deciphered the message. At the end, he embraced Catholicism and died whimpering, "Mama, mama . . ."

In his 1970 book *Kill The Dutchman*, Paul Sann, executive editor of the New York *Post*, makes a compelling case that Schultz was silenced by his own hoodlum empire. Mafia informer Joe Valachi has given credence to Sann's assertion that Schultz ordered Bo Weinberg killed because Weinberg had been "brooding about the way the policy racket's proceeds were being drained off to defray the Dutchman's legal expenses, had been talking to Lucky Luciano about retiring his old buddy to some other field, possibly even a field of lilies."

With the aid of underworld informants and a confidential police report, Sann reconstructed the saloon massacre to show how Luciano may have provided the inspiration, but Murder, Inc.'s Louis (Lepke) Buchalter supplied the firepower—a paid assassin named Charlie (The Bug) Workman, a New Jersey ex-convict. Today, the whole subject of Schultz's murder is distasteful to Workman, who is now a ladies'-garment salesman in Manhattan. "Talk to me in fifteen years" is his standard rejoinder to questions about events on the night of October 23, 1935.

At any rate, Dewey drew a posthumous prosecution from Schultz when it was discovered in 1936 that the Dutchman had paid $1,000 a week to Tammany district leader Hines under the useful heading of "ice." It was proved that police who arrested Schultz's men were transferred at Jimmy's request; that in 1933, District Attorney Dodge was elected with the help of campaign funds contributed by the Dutchman; and that Hines was putting in the fix with certain judicial officers. In short, he was the political guardian angel of the numbers combination.

The first trial of Jimmy Hines in 1938 ended in a disaster for Dewey, and for Frank Hogan, who had spent three years developing the evidence. The mistrial was Dewey's fault. At one point in his cross-examination, he not only linked Hines with the numbers racket—for which he was on trial—but also insinuated that Hines was mixed up with the poultry racket. There are thousands of students just out of law school each year who would not have made that fundamental mistake. Dewey's blunder was more than just a mental lapse. It violated the deeply rooted rule of law that a man on trial for one crime cannot be faced in the courtroom with evidence showing he has committed another. Justice Ferdinand Pecora had no choice but to grant Hines a mistrial.

The second trial was also a near disaster. While being held under indictment in the Tombs, Dixie Davis and George Weinberg, whose brother Bo had already been disposed of, were shipped out to a Long Island cottage, where they learned to play badminton under round-the-clock police protection. This protective custody turned into something of an embarrassment when Weinberg ungratefully shot himself dead with a bodyguard's gun. Frank Hogan never forgot that day: January 29, 1939.

Hogan reflected on the event in an emotional tribute to Dewey on the day Dewey died, March 17, 1971. Judge Myles Lane was sitting in Part XXX, the arraignment part of State Supreme Court, when District Attorney Hogan made one of his rare appearances. With the court's permission, he eulogized his former boss in an emotional voice:

"In discussing moral courage Napoleon once said, 'I have never met with the two-o'clock-in-the-morning-kind' . . . I shall not forget a Sunday afternoon during the second trial of James Hines. . . . A few of us were hurriedly summoned to the office. We found District Attorney Dewey absorbed in the composition of a letter. As we entered the room, he looked up and said, 'Glad you came. There's plenty to do. I have just had word that George Weinberg has shot and killed himself.' I reached for a chair. The other assistants needed support also. Weinberg was our most important witness next to Dixie Davis. Our case! But Mr. Dewey brought us to with a snap, gave precise and detailed instructions as to what we were to do, and then calmly returned to his letter—a letter to the House Judiciary Committee, which resulted in the removal and prosecution and conviction of Martin Manton, Presiding Judge of the Circuit Court of Appeals." *

Hogan modestly omitted from his tribute that he himself saved the Hines case by eventually locating an equestrian academy up in Connecticut where Hines and Schultz had gone horseback riding together. The connection proved crucial to a conviction in the case.

The public's obsession with the Hines case was such that radio stations across the country interrupted their programming on February 25, 1939,

---

* Manton had been accused by Dewey of taking $435,000 in bribes to fix cases involving such corporate giants as the American Tobacco Co. and the Schick Electric Razor Co. (There was never a suggestion that the companies knew the purpose of various insurance "loans" that had found their way—through middlemen—into Manton's bank account.) Dewey's letter kicked off an impeachment stampede in the House, and Manton, unlike Richard Nixon in later years, grasped an immediate sense of the inevitable. The highest-ranking jurist in the United States next to the Supreme Court resigned from the bench to face criminal charges.

to announce that a New York grand jury had brought in a verdict of guilty on all thirteen counts. Hines was sentenced to a term of four to eight years in Sing Sing.

The downfall of Hines and Manton catapulted Dewey into the national consciousness. And he was determined to make the most of it. Undeterred by the fact that he had been narrowly defeated by Herbert Lehman in the 1938 gubernatorial race, Dewey, the mustachioed Sir Galahad of political cartoons, sallied forth anew in a somewhat egomaniacal bid for higher office. He announced on December 1, 1939, that he was a candidate for the Republican nomination for President of the United States. Although the Hines case inflated his prestige, it was remarkable that it got Dewey as far as it did. The two trials were the only ones he argued in person while District Attorney—and he lost the first one in a blunder so thick-headed that he became the laughingstock of the legal fraternity. But as District Attorney, his was now a hard act to follow. As for those who wondered who his successor might be, well, Dewey was really looking too far ahead even to give a damn. He submitted the names of three men he felt would make suitable successors, all Republicans: executive aide Paul Lockwood, Rackets Bureau chief Murray Gurfein, and Assistant D.A. Robert Thayer. Since Lockwood seemed to have the inside track with Dewey, the possibility of Frank Hogan's becoming District Attorney seemed little more than a joke when his only friend at Tammany Hall, Judge John Mullen, mentioned it over dinner one night. Hogan laughed out loud, and then said soberly that he wouldn't dream of taking this chance away from Paul Lockwood. Lockwood was an old friend and fraternity brother from Columbia. Most significantly, in 1936, Lockwood had introduced Frank Hogan to a pretty Irish-American colleen named Mary Egan.

Mary Egan, like Hogan, was the product of a strict Catholic upbringing. They met for the first time at a party in Brooklyn. She was working as a secretary at Barclay's Bank in New York. A few months after Frank introduced Mary to his parents at a July outing in Indian Head, on the Connecticut shore, the couple announced their engagement. Hogan framed Mary's photograph on a wall of the cobwebby loft building that served as D.A.'s quarters. And in November they were wed.

Lockwood lent his silk hat to Hogan for the ceremony at St. Saviour Church in Brooklyn. When the groom returned it, he told Lockwood, "You'll have to keep this so you'll look dignified when you're District Attorney." Now, five years later, Tammany boss Christy Sullivan was still smarting over the Hines conviction. And when Judge Mullen suggested that Tammany ought to change its image by endorsing an anti-Tammany reformer as District Attorney, Sullivan opened his eyes wide.

The ways of politics being deep and devious, this seemed a devilish way to confound the opposition do-gooders. Only in the role of repentant sinner, Sullivan realized, could Tammany Hall have a chance of getting its candidates elected again. Sullivan agreed to sponsor a Dewey man— provided he was a Democrat. Mullen then convinced Dewey to add Hogan's name to the list. The Republican and Fusion parties were left looking foolishly at each other. With Dewey's help, they finally agreed to tag along with the deal. And to Frank Hogan's surprise, he was nominated on March 7.

"I'll be goddamned," he blurted out when his secretary, Miss Anna Berson, rushed in with the news and kissed him. Hogan called up his wife and told her. Mary was stunned. "What?" she said. "District Attorney!" he said. "Say it again!" she demanded.

Later, over wine and escargots at Charles à la Pomme Soufflé, an East Side restaurant, Dewey persuaded Hogan to accept the nomination.

Hogan was very solicitous. "Don't think about me. Think about what's best for yourself," he said.

Dewey looked him straight in the eye: "I always do."

When Hogan returned to work next morning, there was Lockwood, waiting to shake his hand. "The silk hat's still in good shape," Lockwood said in barely disguised disappointment. "I took it down and dusted it off. It's ready to ride again."

Swept into office without opposition, Frank S. Hogan was sworn in as District Attorney of New York County on December 29, 1941, three weeks after the Japanese sneak attack on Pearl Harbor.

Solemn-faced, Hogan began his first full working day walking between aisles of packing crates and filing cabinets barricading his old office. The D.A.'s staff was in the process of moving down the block to new offices at 155 Leonard Street.

That first day on the job set the tone of moral rectitude that carried Hogan through eight consecutive terms of office. From his old office, he performed his first official act—calling his brother Joe, by then a practicing attorney, and requesting a special favor: "Please, Joe, never take a criminal case while I'm District Attorney." Joe said sure, it would mean some financial hardships, but he'd drop his criminal clients and stay in civil practice to avoid even the appearance of conflict of interest.

Hogan next called in the press to announce that he was retaining sixty-eight members of Dewey's staff of seventy-four, and naming Paul Lockwood his chief assistant. Then, for the first time, Hogan walked into his ex-boss's office without knocking. He sat down in Dewey's big upholstered swivel chair. At $28,000 a year, with his official limousine waiting outside, Frank Hogan had "arrived."

Hogan's first work day also brought his first conviction, that of John (Cockeye) Dunne, a legendary power on the New York waterfront. An ex-convict with a sixteen-year record in Sing Sing, Dunne was boss stevedore on the West Side docks. His enemies frequently wound up in the quicklime of New Jersey. He decided who was hired and who was not included in the shape-up. He had his own union, the Inland Checkers and Platform Workers Union (AFL), and his own title: "Business Agent."

The particular crime of which Dunne and his lieutenants were convicted involved the tying up of a British ship, the *Essex Lancer*, for over a week. As a result, the ship missed two convoys for Britain with vital war matériel. Hogan's feeling was that waterfront racketeering was menacing the nation's war effort.

The D.A. declared that any crime taking advantage of wartime conditions amounted to sabotage, and he included pickpockets, prowlers and looters who skulked around during air-raid blackouts. Hogan was concerned about a new era of bootlegging in Manhattan and predicted a black market of commodities limited by price controls. He began prosecuting food-stamp "fences." He staged the first of hundreds of Times Square cleanups—the frustrating, always unsuccessful vice raids to rid the tourist mecca of pimps and prostitutes. In later years, he would attribute Times Square degradation to heroin. But back in the 1940s, he blamed "the emotional effects of war" for the sorry spectacle of runaway high-school girls becoming the prey of panders.

During this period, Hogan and his wife shared a weekend cottage in Smithtown, Long Island, with Assistant D.A. Whitman Knapp and his family. Knapp, who years later turned into a thorn in Hogan's side as chairman of the 1970 Knapp Commission on police corruption, recalled Hogan's obsession with war-related crimes in those early days:

"Anybody who wasn't in the Armed Forces, including Hogan, felt guilty about not being in uniform. It was inevitable that a man who felt guilty about it would want to interpret his present work as patriotic. Of course, in Hogan's case, it would have been asinine to leave his job to take a desk job as a colonel—but that didn't alter the fact that he was out and everybody else was in."

Hogan interpreted his own patriotic duty to mean constant vigilance around New York's bustling piers and shipping terminals, busy with the loading and offloading of weapons and ammunition cargo destined for Europe and the Pacific.

National security worried him, and in February 1942, Hogan's fear of sabotage peaked: for the first time since the war had begun, there was a major ship disaster in his home port. The $60-million superliner *Normandie*, second-largest ship in the world, had just been taken over by the U.S. Navy and rechristened the *Lafayette*. The ship caught fire with two hundred officers and men aboard and keeled over, sizzling, in its Hudson River berth. The men abandoned ship in time. No one died. But arson was suspected. Standing over the blackened, sodden ruin, Frank Hogan was caught in the first public controversy of his career—*he* almost went down with the ship.

The D.A. had arrived at the cold, windswept pier shed, with his Chesterfield collar up around his ears, and strode through the mob of newspaper reporters on the scene. The burned-out ship lay helpless on her port side. "Christ, it looks like the Empire State Building toppled into the water," one of the reporters exclaimed. Hogan and his men herded seventy witnesses into the pier shed and questioned them into the pre-dawn hours. Bleary-eyed, Hogan finally emerged from the shed to meet the press and disappoint them with his assessment: "one little spark" from a welder's acetylene torch had ignited the vessel. The reporters were accusing: "Not arson, Mr. District Attorney?"

"No," Hogan said, shaking his head, "but carelessness has served the enemy with equal effectiveness as sabotage."

Eliminating sabotage as a possibility was disagreeable to editorial writers, who began demanding a civilian inquiry into the fire. Hogan was even blitzed by newspaper cartoons; one showed grotesque, swastika-tattooed snakes chuckling over the smoking hull of the ship. Hogan stuck with his convictions, sensing what wartime hysteria could do to the city. The rumor-mongering finally halted when a U.S. Navy inquiry affirmed Hogan's assessment of the cause. Years passed before the D.A.'s word was seriously challenged again.

Those first heady months in office brought Hogan as close as he ever came to being a visible public figure. He performed protocol chores for the Mayor, such as escorting Lord Halifax, the British Ambassador, and Lady Halifax to a police lineup. (The D.A. had to act as interpreter when one of the prisoners kicked the King's English into "I didn't have no rod, boss.") His favorite social lion was the Duke of Windsor, a crime buff who more than once squired his duchess around Hogan's fascinating premises. ("Those, my dear, are the interrogation rooms. Frightfully interesting . . . ") Wallis Simpson, who thrived on an atmosphere of danger and power, would agree—her ice-blue eyes sparkling into Hogan's.

The new District Attorney seemed to be everywhere at once, hurtling from Times Square, where patrol wagons were rounding up hookers and pinball racketeers, to the scene of a Harlem crap game where two black gamblers had been shot to death. "Where were the police?" Hogan demanded of one of the crapshooters. The witness flashed a gold-toothed grin: "They was in the game, boss. But they took off over the roof when the shootin' started."

Hogan came to grips gradually with the surface sensationalism of the American press during the war years. The first case of his to warrant headlines was the fevered trial of Madeline Webb. If it demonstrated nothing else, the trial proved that it's easier for people to grasp a single death than the death of millions. While the bodies of U.S. troops rotted on the battlefields of the Dnieper and Volturno, many Americans at home reserved their morbid interest for the corpse of a middle-aged heiress found murdered in her New York City hotel room.

Hogan charged Madeline, a G-string dancer, with luring a well-to-do Polish refugee, Mrs. Susan Flora Reich, to the hotel suite. There, Hogan charged, Madeline's lover, Eli Shonbrun, a petty thief, strangled Mrs. Reich and stole $2,000 worth of jewelry. During the trial, virtually every word from Madeline's mouth ballooned into a tabloid headline. "THEY CAN'T DO THIS TO ME!" she screamed at her arraignment, her mouth a smear of scarlet lipstick. "I had nothing to do with it!"

Her steamy reputation raised everyone's body temperature in the usually sedate courtroom. To this day, Judge Jacob Grumet, the former Hogan assistant who tried the case, refuses to release the "scorching" diary in which Madeline listed her boudoir conquests. ("One of her paramours is still on the bench and I wouldn't want to embarrass him," Judge Grumet confides.)

Before the trial opened in February 1942, Grumet warned Hogan: "Madeline has the sexiest walk of any girl I've ever seen."

"Then get her seated before they bring in the jury," Hogan advised.

Every morning, hundreds of women spectators set up a clamor at the courtroom door, straining for a glimpse of Madeline cuddling and making kissy-face with Eli Shonbrun at the defense table. Madeline, a stage-struck girl from the Oklahoma dustbowl, auditioned for the court with her ladylike sniffles. Whenever Grumet called her a "murder decoy," she gave a pout worthy of Brigitte Bardot.

But her acting talent stretched no further in court than it had at Broadway theater auditions. Trying to be demure on the witness stand, she cracked and became a vulgar, shrieking bitch—"a Hepburn gone haywire," according to one spectator. Digressing, she hissed that her failure as an actress was caused by a car accident that had knocked her teeth crooked. At one point, she framed her pouting lips into an X-rated epithet for Hogan and then yelled at Grumet: "You filthy, no-good son of a bitch!"

A tough act to follow, Madeline was nevertheless upstaged by her lover. Shonbrun took the stand and blurted out a confession that absolved his girl of the murder: "'As God is my judge, Madeline is innocent!" Madeline's lawyer, in his defense summation, pleaded to the jury (with a straight face): "Send her back to her mother to bind up the threads of a broken heart and begin life over again." The jury did indeed give her a new life—in prison.

After the verdict, District Attorney Hogan standardized his policy of interviewing jurors. It was an interesting footnote to the prevailing morality of the 1940s—Madeline's jurors said they had considered acquitting her at first, but the day she cursed out the prosecutor, "We decided that no innocent girl would talk like that in public."

Shonbrun, who listed his occupation as "murderer" after the verdict, had another distinction: he became the first famous defendant, under District Attorney Frank Hogan, sentenced to die in the electric chair. There would be others.

4

DEATH HOUSE CALLS

etween 1942 and 1965, when the death penalty was effectively abolished by the New York State Legislature, fifty-seven murderers were hooded and strapped into the electric chair for capital crimes committed in Frank Hogan's Manhattan jurisdiction. Commutation hearings were regularly held by the Governor's office to determine whether or not the District Attorney had any new evidence to show why any of the condemned men should be spared the ultimate penalty.

In Hogan's view, prosecuting a first-degree murder case to verdict and then recommending clemency suggested moral inconsistency. He seldom made the recommendation, and then only in special cases, such as that of Salvatore (Cape Man) Agron. Cape Man was the boy who, in Dracula costume, stabbed two teen-age boys to death in a playground gang battle one summer night. What moved Hogan toward clemency was his discovery of Agron's grotesquely deprived background. (Before his arrest, the homeless boy had slept in hallways and foraged for food in garbage pails.) The District Attorney debated the matter with his staff. Appeals Chief Richard Uviller suggested that the double homicide might have been "a case of teen-age bravado that went too far." Hogan concluded that the sixteen-year-old Cape Man should not die for his crime, and his life was spared.

The fifty-seven killers who did die caused Hogan some anguish. While some men in the Homicide Bureau could enjoy a seven-course Italian meal on the night that State Executioner Joseph Francel threw the switch in Sing Sing's Death House, Frank Hogan couldn't have joined them. On those dark nights, he could neither eat nor sleep. He would stay late at the office and pace the floor. Philosophically, morally, Hogan was tormented by capital punishment; but he was also certain of its deterrent effect.

Because no one ever questioned Hogan's neutral function as an instrument of the law in capital cases, people in the office always assumed that the District Attorney was in favor of the death penalty. It came as a surprise to Dick Uviller when Hogan said to him one day, "I know if I cut off the arms of a thief it would stop him from stealing, but who could condone such a thing?" Uviller seemed perplexed. Did that mean the Chief was against capital punishment? Hogan nodded. "Of course."

Hogan could never absorb the weight of officially premeditated death without thinking the unthinkable: a mistaken execution. There was never a documented case in which an innocent man was put to death in Hogan's term of office. But the possibility was always there. As the clock's second hand ticked nearer to the appointed hour of doom in each case, Hogan experienced a debilitating anxiety. Sometimes, the Chief would summon his Homicide Bureau chief, Al Herman, into the office "just to hold hands with me." Herman was flatly oppposed to the death penalty, and a mere news photo of the empty electric chair unsettled him. On the eve of an execution, Herman and Hogan reviewed each item of evidence, read over every word of testimony, grappled with even the remotest possibility of error—up until there was no longer need for any "word from the Governor."

Hogan's role in capital cases must be viewed in the context of official vengeance perpetrated by government, the press, and the courts during World War II and the postwar years. Those were days of harsh punishment, stipulated by the state's unrevised penal law. Punishment sometimes seemed too harsh for the crime. Among several "glass jaw" cases Hogan had to try in the 1940s was that of a youngster who, in horseplay, slapped a friend on the head with a rolled-up newspaper. The blow killed the boy. Under the old penal code, that tap on the head was second-degree manslaughter, and the youngster received a maximum fifteen-year prison sentence. Under revised law today, the severest charge possible would be third-degree assault, carrying a one-year maximum prison term. Realistically, the same youth committing the same unintentional offense today would probably get a ninety-day suspended sentence and would walk out of the courtroom on his own recognizance.

The postwar decade also featured hard-nosed jurists. General Sessions Judge James Wallace was the last of the city's 'hanging judges.' Known as a terror on the bench, Wallace insisted that it was better to throw the switch on lifers in prison than to waste taxpayers' money on rehabilitation programs "which see only the good in everybody—not the bad."

Abolition of the death penalty in 1965 (except for cop killers and prison inmates who commit murder while serving life sentences) drained the suspense and drama from newspaper reporting, too.

Executions sold papers—and city desks sent their best men to cover the deathwatch. The reporters' eyewitness accounts are classics of rhetorical glibness in the face of officially sanctioned murder. Hogan cringed every time he read how a condemned gangster "rode the lightning" or how the state executioner "had a good night last night," executing "five murderers at $150 a head."

The Death House vigil for Lepke Buchalter was as close as Frank Hogan ever got to becoming personally involved with an execution at Sing Sing. The emotional fallout of that face-to-face encounter in the shadow of the death chamber was so strong that Hogan refused to discuss the meeting, except as a family confidence, for years afterward.

The story must be prefaced by a few words about Louis (Lepke was his mother's name for him) Buchalter. Lepke had the style not of a bruising gangster gorilla, but of the corporate business executive, secure in his economic power and in his managerial ability to keep underlings in place. Asked once to describe the warped dimensions of the "criminal mentality," District Attorney Hogan paused for thought and then said, "I once knew a punk whose greatest ambition in life was to shake hands with Lepke."

That was Hogan's way of delineating the caste system, the aristocracy of crime that Lepke helped create in the United States. The notorious Murder, Inc. was the terrorist arm of his enterprise. Mention of recourse to its operation became the final cincher in any business contract, the "offer you can't refuse." In 1941, Murder, Inc. went out of business when the little man who ordered his enemies shot, stabbed, garroted, buried in quicklime and burned in gasoline was finally convicted for the murder of a Brooklyn shopkeeper. Lepke was sentenced to die.

Given every last doubt of the law he had belittled for so long, his appeals exhausted down to the wire by March 3, 1944, Lepke sent word to Albany: "Tell that son of a bitch Hogan I'm ready to talk to him." Governor Dewey granted a forty-eight-hour stay of execution. Then he called Hogan and asked the D.A. to meet Lepke on Death Row. Hogan agreed to make the trip upstate.

Lepke's life now depended on whether the information he gave Hogan would be good enough to corroborate in court. If cases could be made, there might be reason to recommend commutation of the death sentence to Dewey. Hogan doubted the possibility. The urge to break the underworld code of silence had overtaken Lepke a few months before, while a prisoner in the Federal House of Detention. At the time, FBI Director J. Edgar Hoover was subpoenaing bank records all over town trying to get something on certain "prominent New Dealers" rumored to have ties with Lepke. The gang leader had reputedly been active during the 1944 Presidential campaign.

While in the federal pen, Lepke had spent several weeks with Hogan's Rackets Bureau, unfolding the "political connections" of Murder, Inc. Lepke had talked a blue streak, but he hadn't said anything. Not anything of substance, at any rate, and Hogan had given up trying.

The word this trip was that Lepke had new evidence on his accomplices. He vowed he could produce witnesses against them in court. Without witnesses, Lepke's word alone was worthless—particularly since he was under death sentence. The afternoon of the scheduled execution, Hogan and two of his top assistants, Sol Gelb and Joseph Sarafite, piled into the D.A.'s limousine and drove through a snowstorm to Ossining. Riding north along the Hudson River, the three men discussed the near certainty that Lepke was a doomed man. "He's scared silly," said Hogan. "He just can't face the music," said Gelb.

Sarafite, now a State Supreme Court judge, recalls that he sensed another storm brewing that day: a massive struggle of conscience within Frank Hogan. Sarafite began to reminisce, "You remember Little Benny?" Hogan and Gelb nodded. How could they forget Benjamin (Little Benny) Ertel, a kill-crazy thug who in 1937 had gunned down a detective in a Second Avenue coffeeshop?

For Hogan, the case seemed to buttress his theory of capital punishment as a deterrent. Ertel was one of seventeen cop-killers convicted during the Dewey days of 1939–40 for the murders of five policemen. Sixteen of those defendants went to the chair. The salutary effect, as Hogan saw it, was that after Dewey announced a show-no-mercy crackdown on cop-killers in 1938, four years went by before another police officer was murdered in Manhattan. In the preceding twenty-year period, at least one policeman, and often more, were assassinated every twelve months in New York County.

Little Benny was Joe Sarafite's first murder conviction. Sarafite had asked a jury recommendation of 'no mercy.' As a result, Ertel died in the electric chair. Thinking about it now, on the way to the Death House, the assistant D.A. confided something to Hogan and Gelb that he had not been able to admit before: "I really had a tussle with myself about that case. I even consulted a priest."

Hogan gazed into the swirling blindness of the snowstorm and didn't speak. Sarafite proceeded to enumerate each point of the rationalization he had worked out with his priest: "One, I took an oath as Assistant District Attorney to enforce the law. Two, the law says the penalty for felony murder is death. Three, this is the public policy of the state. Four, my obligation is to get the truth of the case and present this honestly to the jury. Five, I would be bound by the verdict of the jury."

Hogan continued gazing into the storm. "Joe," he sighed, "I'm afraid the mass of humanity isn't prepared to abolish capital punishment right now. They're not enlightened . . . not understanding enough."

Sarafite still shudders, recalling that Death House ride: "It was a different world in those days. We did what we saw according to our own lights; but in all fairness, if I were still an assistant D.A., I don't know what I'd do today. I might have begged off a case like Little Benny's and said I'd rather not try it. I think Frank's psychological makeup was different. He had a sense of absolute integrity to fulfilling his oath of office."

As Hogan's official car cruised through the big iron gate of the fortress penitentiary on the Hudson, the chauffeur asked a sentry for directions to the Death House. "Turn right for the Dance Hall," the guard cracked, and Hogan winced. "I'm going to need a drink after this," he told Gelb. The car pulled into the parking lot and the three men glanced over at a macabre detail: a hearse was backed up to the rear exit of the death chamber. The tailgate yawned open expectantly. "Make that two drinks," said Gelb.

Inside, tables and wooden chairs were arranged on opposite sides of prison bars. Hogan and Lepke sat face to face. The latter's lips were ashen but set in fierce disdain, his face mottled but not perspiring.

"He was funny," Hogan told his friend Richard Rovere of *The New Yorker* in later years. "Outwardly he didn't show much; he was hysterical all right, but the hysteria was inside. He sat there talking to us calmly enough. If you'd been standing twenty feet away, you'd have thought he was trying to sell insurance. But inside he was all jelly. If he hadn't been, he wouldn't have called for us. That afternoon, he even squealed against one of the punks who'd worked for him, some kid who'd committed a murder several years back. As a matter of fact, that was one case where he could have got us all the evidence we needed. That proves he'd sunk about as low as he could go, you know. It's one thing to turn against somebody your own size or bigger, but to tell on a kid who was taking your orders—well, you just couldn't go any lower. We had to tell him it was no dice—that we weren't baiting minnows with whales.

"He talked on an hour or more, but still everything was on his say-so. No witnesses. He'd always made his deals by himself, so he didn't have anyone to back him up when he needed it."

In the late 1960s, two other journalists managed to draw Hogan out on the subjects he had discussed during that tense interrogation a quarter-century earlier. "We reeled off one name after another and just drew blanks," the District Attorney told Paul Sann, executive editor of the New York *Post*. "He did mention two or three cases, but they were typical Lepke cases. All we could say was that Lepke talked about these cases but there was no corroboration and no accomplices."

At a cocktail party some time later, the D.A. was buttonholed by one of Sann's former cityside reporters, Paul Hoffman. Hoffman, too, had become something of a Frank Hogan scholar during his days on the courthouse beat, and in answer to the big question about the Lepke session, Hogan rattled the ice in his glass and shrugged:

"Oh, well, he mentioned some common gossip about Sidney Hillman."

This had been during the "Clear it with Sidney" days of labor leader Hillman, co-director of President Roosevelt's wartime Office of Production Management.

The press innuendo might have been political dynamite had Hogan let the cat out of the bag in 1945. But in 1969, Hillman was long dead, and besides, nobody in the press was anxious to "do a job" on Sidney any more. As Sarafite reminded, "It was a different world in those days."

The final scene with Lepke was recounted by Hogan for Richard Rovere in 1947:

"Before we left, we shook hands all around and told him we were sorry we couldn't do anything for him. He said very calmly and very quietly, 'Well, I'm sorry, too, but that's the way these things work out a lot of the time.' It was as if we hadn't been able to get together on a weekend date. But I knew how he felt. We drove down the parkway through the snow and then stopped off at my house for a few drinks. There are a lot of things on this job that call for a drink, but that night I wanted more than one."

The execution of Lepke and his accomplices fit the pattern of routine death administered by the State of New York during the Hogan years. There was sepulchral silence in the whitewashed vault. Thirty legal witnesses in a glassed-in gallery watched the oak door swing inward. A priest in prayer robes accompanied Lepke's Catholic accomplices; a rabbi chanted for Lepke himself.

A leather mask was dipped in salt water to facilitate passage of electrical current. The trouser leg was bunched where an electrode was snapped to the knee. Then the searing fury of 2,200 volts jolted the doomed man from his seat. Once, twice—the straps strained. A third time: a crackle as hair and flesh burned. The hand became a bluish-red talon with each fuse. Arteries bulged at the neck. Smoke furled, feathery, up from the hood. Then the prison doctor, stethoscope against the victim's chest, intoned formally: "This man is dead."

The electric chair remains in good working order, although dusty with disuse, in upstate New York today. The last of 695 murderers executed by the state was Eddie Lee Mays, jolted out of mortality in March 1961. Since then, abolition of the death penalty hasn't affected the conviction rate in murder cases one iota. From 1942 to 1972, the conviction rate in Hogan's office remained constant. However, the police "clearance rate" for solving murder cases dipped considerably. There were 170 reported killings in 1942 and 110 arrests, compared with the 1972 figures of 661 homicide complaints and 353 arrests. (Murder is the most reliably reported crime anywhere, because it is virtually impossible to "lose" a dead body.) Hogan attributed the decreased clearance rate partly to the wide-open sale of handguns, and partly to the guidelines written into the Supreme Court's 1966 ruling in *Miranda v. Arizona*, which circumscribed police methods of obtaining stationhouse confessions.

The death penalty may have disappeared, but murder hasn't. Hardly a day went by after Hogan took office that Manhattan's Homicide Bureau experts weren't consulted by prosecutors all over the country, asking how to proceed with a murder case in their own domain. The Homicide Bureau is a repository of thousands of confessions, sordid or tangled tales, absurd alibis, and the actual weapons used in Manhattan's two-a-day killings. The arsenal collected from all this bloodletting was once dramatized when Hogan donated the storekeeper's thirty-year inventory of murder weapons to a scrap-metal drive. The mountain of bloodstained butcher knives, rifles, pistols, switchblades, ice picks, candlesticks, meat cleavers, crowbars, axes and assorted blunt instruments weighed a ton and a half.

Hogan organized an office uniquely suited to cope with grand-scale crime. His procedures and innovations are still in effect today, and widely imitated elsewhere. At each report of death with suspicion of foul play, the Manhattan Homicide Bureau and a "D.A.'s Squad" detective "roll" rush to the scene. Often they reach the corpse before policemen get there.

Members of the Homicide Bureau are on call for this purpose night and day. During the investigation, they warn suspects of their rights, assist police in interrogations, and dam up any legal loopholes in the statements of suspects and witnesses. Hogan used to insist: "Quick response!" Which meant getting to the crime scene in under fifteen minutes. Lose time, and you lose eyewitnesses and others with possible information about the killing. Hogan knew, of course, that the victim himself is the best witness. If still alive and able to speak to police, the victim's posthumous testimony can be heard in court.

For a dying declaration to stand up in court, the "last gasp" must fit certain legal standards. Should the victim name his killer, then call, "Get me a doctor!" the victim's accusation might be ruled inadmissable evidence—given, as it was, in the hope of recovery. If he doesn't believe he's dying, he may be motivated to name someone other than the actual killer. If, however, his final words are "Get me a priest!" the law is likely to honor his credibility as a witness to his own death.

The most famous dying declaration of Hogan's career involved boss stevedore John (Cockeye) Dunn. In 1947, Dunn was back on the waterfront, having served time in Hogan's first racketeering conviction. Soon after Dunn's homecoming, a hiring stevedore named Anthony Hintz was found in a bloody heap in Greenwich Village, five bullets in his body, but still alive. "Johnny Dunn shot me," Hintz gasped to his wife.

Four days later, hovering near death in a hospital, Hintz, talking to detectives, again accused Dunn and named two accomplices. Then doctors surprised Hintz by telling him he had a good chance of making a full recovery. He doubtless got to thinking about his life expectancy on the waterfront, now that he had blabbed about Dunn and his trigger-happy sidekicks. And so he called in the cops and recanted his previous statement.

The detectives were crestfallen. Then a surgeon appeared, reporting to them that the patient's condition had again taken a critical nosedive. The plainclothesmen rushed back to Hintz's bedside, where the gunshot victim repeated in a croaking whisper that the two accomplices chased him up a stairway and Dunn opened fire.

But it was not long before Hintz again appeared to be gaining ground. The doctors again reassured him of another full recovery. This sudden new luck produced a second change of heart. Hintz called in the detectives for another game of musical statements, recanting his testimony once more.

Hintz died before regaining enough vocal stamina to squeal again. The accumulated weight of his admissions, however—thrice given, twice repudiated—was enough to convince the jury. Cockeye Dunn, Andrew (Squint) Sheridan ("Killing's easy," he said in court, "like ordering a cup of coffee") and Danny Gentile 'rode the lightning' in Sing Sing on July 7, 1949. The case became something of a judicial landmark as well: the first murder conviction in legal history based solely on a "dying declaration."

In none of the thousands of homicide cases brought to his attention did Frank Hogan ever make a determination of guilt on his own. A consensus of all members of the bureau was reached first. Only then would Hogan form a decision to seek an indictment on various degrees of murder and manslaughter. The D.A. would rely, as did his friend Dwight D. Eisenhower, on a staff system for doing the People's business. When mistakes happened—as they were bound to, given the fallibility of human judgment—only one person was held accountable: Hogan.

Hogan made mistakes. When he did, he usually erred in being too rigid. Hogan's errors were illustrative of his personal moral code, the sternness of which was often called into question by members of the bench. Federal Judge Murray Gurfein, looking back on his days as a defense lawyer fighting Hogan indictments, makes an Eisenhower-era comparison of Hogan's perspective as viewed from the other side of the bench:

"He represented the kind of moralistic rigidity that John Foster Dulles showed in foreign affairs," says Gurfein, remembering a case in which he had represented an artist who went up to Cape Cod one summer to paint. A nautical buff liked one seascape, but didn't have the money to buy it. He offered instead to swap the picture for a souvenir flare gun—the kind used for sea rescue. Gurfein's client accepted the trade, came back to New York with the gun, and mounted it on his wall as a collector's item. When the artist went away again the following summer, a burglar broke into the apartment. Finding it vacant, the burglar camped out there for a couple of weeks, until a neighbor saw a light and summoned police. Gurfein recalled what happened next:

"This guy had already taken the flare gun and chiseled the bore to make a shell fit. When the cops came to the door, he killed one of them. With my client's gun! Now there was a case in which I expected Hogan to show a little heart, a little feeling. What did he do? He went ahead and indicted the artist for violating the Sullivan Law. I told Frank it was an unfair prosecution. I'll never forget his answer: 'A cop was killed. I've got to do something about it.'

"Now I'm not saying I was right and he was wrong," Gurfein rushed to explain. "He really believed it was a moral matter. A cop was dead, so somebody had to pay for it. When Frank Hogan decided somebody goes to jail, somebody goes."

The D.A.'s rigidity, his dogged pursuit of the difficult, led to some fascinating prosecutions—cases that have not only filled criminology textbooks but have also provided suspense plots for novelists and Hollywood producers.

Attempted murder, for example, is an extremely uncommon charge, difficult to sustain in court. Hogan found a way to do it, though, in the case of a dressmaker named Alfred Wilson. Enraged during a lover's quarrel, Wilson flattened his sweetheart, Evangeline Garcia, with a knockout punch. He picked her up off the floor, carried her to an open window, and dropped her. Evangeline fell thirteen floors to the roof of an adjoining building. Seeing her sprawled out like a rag doll on the roof, and certain that every bone in her body must be broken, Wilson left her for dead.

A neighbor spotted the body, and an ambulance rushed Evangeline to the hospital. She lingered in extremis, stubbornly refusing to die. She was propped up in a body cast for five months with only eye slits and a ragged mouth hole for liquid feeding. Hogan's men visited her, and Evangeline eventually agreed to testify against her would-be murderer.

Two months later, Alfred Wilson nearly collapsed in the courtroom he'd been brought to when the doors opened and there, miraculously, stood Evangeline. Her limbs, torso and neck encased in braces, she hobbled down the aisle on orthopedic crutches to identify the man who had wronged her. Wilson received twenty-five to fifty years in state prison.

Resurrecting a "murder victim" created a sensation because it was so rare. Most people thrown from windows and rooftops do not live to tell the tale. Actual murder cases, then, constitute the classic "mystery." The main witness can't talk and the only person who can—the killer—has every reason to keep silent.

Hogan's strong suit was his belief that circumstantial evidence (fingerprints, bloodstains, murder weapons, etc.) can provide "proof beyond a reasonable doubt." And putting together the facts, solving the mystery, challenged his staff:

"To me, a circumstantial case is fun to try, because you're building brick by brick," says John F. Keenan, who was Chief Assistant D.A. and Homicide Bureau chief in 1972, and then became the state's Special Prosecutor in 1976. "The objective evidence can't be mistaken, whereas an eyewitness can be *honestly* mistaken. It's what Mr. Hogan called an 'exclusive opportunity' case—you've got to prove that the defendant had the exclusive opportunity to perform the act that resulted in death.

"You've got to exclude every other human being on the face of the earth from that opportunity. That's pretty hard to do without a statement from the defendant inculpating himself. Since *Miranda*, most people when warned that they have a right to a lawyer and a right to remain silent are not going to talk. Because most people don't want to go to jail. The police used to break nine out of ten homicides. Now they break one out of two."

Dealing with whatever the detectives found—hair, teeth, perfume stains, secretions—Hogan's experts made advances in forensic chemistry, anthropometry, toxicology, ballistics, analysis of semen and blood types. Sometimes, an almost invisible clue could pinpoint a killer.

A few grass seeds in the pants cuffs of a party-loving rhumba dancer named Anibal Almodovar marked the entry of spectroscopic analysis into crime detection. Hogan charged the dancer with strangling his wife in Central Park one autumn evening because she interfered too much in his dates with other women. Several of the caballero's sexy dance partners provided him with an alibi for the night of the murder. They swore he had been with them, whispering moist propositions as he swirled them around the dance floor of a taco-and-tequila joint called the Rhumba Palace.

Under cross-examination, Almodovar was asked: "When was the last time you visited Central Park?"

"Not in two years!" he protested.

The prosecution then introduced into evidence a suit Almodovar had pawned, and a few pinches of dirt taken from the trouser cuffs. Next Hogan's men showed the jury magnified microphotos of the grass seed *Dicot milleflorium,* a wild, matted growth peculiar to the tangled underbrush of a thicket in Central Park called Harlem Meer. A botanist appeared as an expert witness for the prosecution and testified that the seeds do not detach until a five-day period in October—the approximate time of the murder. The dancer flew into a rage when confronted with the evidence and tried to run from the courtroom. He was subdued. The jury was unanimous: "Murder in the first degree."

Solving another not-so-perfect crime, Hogan's office pioneered advances in forensic serology. An unidentified woman had been found strangled outside a rooming house on Manhattan's West Side. Police later identified the victim as Mrs. Alice Persico. Then the investigative work ran into a wall. There were twenty-two boarders in the rooming house at the time of the slaying. Every one had an alibi. Questioning of the tenants revealed nothing. They had heard no noises. No screams. Nothing.

Then detectives lucked onto a trashcan loaded with evidence: Mrs. Persico's shredded nylon stockings, her purse, and a man's T-shirt. This should have been a bonanza; but forensic science was not very advanced in 1943. Today, a solitary bloodstain—or telltale droplets of semen, saliva, or sweat, as well as microscopic bits of flesh torn by fingernails, pulled hair follicles and so on—can explain volumes to a medical examiner. In 1943, no one even knew about the existence of the Rh factor.

But Hogan was intrigued by advances in European forensic science: there was much more known by Scotland Yard, the German police, and the French Sûreté than by the N.Y.P.D. Hogan crammed into his studies as much as he could learn at the time. His tutor in the principles of European forensic pathology was Assistant District Attorney Louis Pagnucco.

Educated in Italy, Pagnucco was something of a Renaissance scholar. In addition to having his law degree, he was an expert in forensic criminology and held a Ph.D. in philology from Columbia University. He spoke fourteen languages, including Chinese, and even practiced calligraphy with a bamboo brush.

To help crack the Persico case, Pagnucco brought in Dr. Alexander Wiener, a pioneer in forensic serology. Wiener became known as the "blood detective" in the New York Medical Examiner's office.

The T-shirt (could it have been worn by the man who killed Mrs. Persico?) bore no obvious signs of violence, but Hogan sent it to Dr. Wiener, who was able to make some crucial analyses. Invisible stains on the front of the shirt, he said, were the residue of a bilious fluid that foams from the mouth of a strangulation victim. When a person dies by strangulation, pulmonary edema discharges a pinkish froth that mixes with air in the nostrils and mouth and becomes a white foam. In medical detective argot, this is called *mousse blanche*. Without the complex subgroupings and factors known today, the *mousse* on the T-shirt was isolated as belonging to someone with Type A blood. The yellowed semicircles under the armpits of the shirt were tested with serum extracts and traced to a Type B person.

Meanwhile, Pagnucco had grown suspicious of a swarthy Greek immigrant boarder in the rooming house, John Manos, although Manos insisted he had never met Mrs. Persico and never allowed visitors to his room. When Pagnucco and detectives searched the room, they found a shiny red spot on the linoleum floor. Manos, a restaurant chef, said he'd spilled some wine and wiped it up with his handkerchief. The handkerchief was immediately sent to Wiener's laboratory. The suspect also consented to having a blood test. Results: the red stains on the handkerchief *were* wine; but Wiener also discovered traces of another fluid—Type A edema. John Manos, as his test showed, was Type B.

Over and over, Hogan explained the principles of the blood grouping to the rather dim-bulbed Manos. Pagnucco, the linguist, served as Greek interpreter. Simplifying things finally, he shouted at Manos across the room, "She left her calling card on your floor!"

At last Manos realized his alibi had caved in. He hung his head and confessed. He had picked up Mrs. Persico and taken her to his room, hoping that she would sleep with him. She had refused and started to cry, "Rape!" Trying to silence her, Manos found his hands sliding around her throat, then squeezing tighter. He pleaded guilty to manslaughter, and received ten to twenty years.

Pagnucco's linguistic skills played a role in another bizarre murder, the Green Parrot Mystery, a case that became part of the office folklore. The

Green Parrot Restaurant in Harlem was, at that time, popular among out-of-town sightseers. The restaurant's main draw was a foul-tempered eighty-year-old parrot. The bird perched by the cash register and waited for unsuspecting tourists to step up and offer it a cracker. The words "Polly want a cracker" outraged the bird.

"Stick it up your ass!" it would scream out, and if the shocked stranger tried to talk back, the bird would flap its wings and squawk, "Fuck you. Fuck you. Fuck you . . ." One of the bird's favorite tricks was to announce the arrival of regular customers at the bar, sometimes getting their names mixed up, but always flavoring the greeting with, "You ugly bastard!"

Pleased at any disturbance in the restaurant—especially the sound of dishware crashing to the floor—the parrot would screech, "It's murder!" in a voice that frequently had dinner guests jumping up from their chairs in panic. The tourists would then laugh, call for more drinks, and await the parrot's next victim.

Shortly after six o'clock on a busy July evening in 1942, the bird was spewing sunflower seeds and obscenities at the guests when a loud shot rang out near the cash register. "It's murder . . . murder!" the parrot screeched, strutting excitedly up and down on its perch. Restaurateur Max Geller, the parrot's owner, slumped on the floor in front of the perch. A bullet had shattered his vocal cords and lodged in his spine. Geller lost consciousness. A police ambulance was summoned, but the Green Parrot owner died three weeks later, still in a coma.

Most of the customers in the restaurant that night—all of them under investigation by Hogan's office—insisted that they knew nothing about the shooting. They claimed to have been so engrossed in their food and drink that all they heard was a shot fired and the parrot squawking.

One bar patron gave a little more information. He swore he heard the parrot scream, "Robber . . . robber . . ." just as Geller dropped to the floor. Harlem detectives dutifully recorded this information, and one of them hurried into Pagnucco's office. "I think the parrot has been naming the killer for us," he said. The detective explained the bird's habit of identifying regular customers by name when they arrived at the bar. It might be a silly hunch, Pagnucco told Hogan, but he had ordered the detective to make a quick check of all the men named Robert who drank at the Green Parrot.

"I hope you don't catch this guy on the parrot's say-so," Hogan said with a smile. "If you do, the bird will be our grand-jury witness, and with *that* language, it'll be cited for contempt."

Police eliminated most of the Roberts on the list they had drawn up. But Pagnucco's linguistic ability paid off in an entirely unexpected way. Outside the stationhouse where witnesses from the restaurant were being interrogated, he overheard two frightened women talking in a language that, at first, Pagnucco was unable to understand. Listening intently, he realized they were speaking in a dialect of seventeenth-century French, a quaint patois spoken only in the northernmost region of Quebec.

"Remember, we saw nothing." One of the Canadian women was rehearsing the other in answers she should give to detectives' questions. "If your husband finds out we went up there instead of going to the movies, you know what he'll do to you."

Inside the police station later, one of the Canadians was telling detectives, "We heard a backfiring noise and covered up our eyes and didn't look."

"Ah, yes," Pagnucco interrupted from behind, speaking in French, "and about your girlfriend here, does her husband really beat her up?" Bewildered, both women burst into tears. "And now," said Pagnucco, "suppose you tell me what you really saw." With more coaxing, the whole story came out. The two women were at a table facing the cash register when the fatal shot was fired. They had caught a glimpse of the killer—and they gave Pagnucco a complete physical description.

But more than a year passed without another clue. Then detectives got a lead on their first likely suspect. A black taxi driver who worked in the vicinity of the Green Parrot identified the gunman as a regular customer at the bar. The suspect had operated a taxi stand near the Green Parrot until the night of the murder. Since then, he had disappeared without a trace.

"What's this fellow's name?" Pagnucco asked the cabbie.

"Robert Butler."

For several weeks, Butler couldn't be located. His wife didn't know where he was, but gave the detective her husband's photograph. The photo perfectly matched the description provided by the French-speaking eyewitnesses.

Pagnucco also learned that the missing man's closest friend was a postal clerk. The Post Office agreed to supply tracings of his mail. A few weeks later, an unsigned letter arrived, postmarked from Maryland. Pagnucco and a detective traced it to the Bethlehem Steel plant in Baltimore. They took the train to Baltimore and stationed themselves in front of the main gate at Bethlehem. They waited for the midnight shift to report for duty. Among the hundreds of war workers streaming into the huge plant, the pair spotted the man they were looking for.

"Robert Butler?" the detective inquired.

The man stared sullenly at the officer.

"Yes."

"You're under arrest."

On the train ride back to New York, Robert Butler confessed. He said he had been drinking heavily on the night of the murder. Geller was tending bar and told him he had had enough. Infuriated, the drunken taxi driver pulled out a gun and shot the Green Parrot owner in the throat. On February 10, 1944, Butler was sentenced to Sing Sing.

"Funny coincidence about that defendant's name," Pagnucco twitted Hogan. "What do you think of that parrot now?"

"I don't know, Louis," Hogan deadpanned, "but there was another killing in Harlem this morning and the victim's dog keeps saying, 'Ralph . . . Ralph . . .' Think we ought to check it out?"

For many years, Hogan's Homicide Bureau worked closely with the man whose name was to become almost synonymous with forensic pathology in the United States—Dr. Milton Helpern. A jovial, benign man who grew to resemble Father Time, Helpern had a career as intense and fascinating as Frank Hogan's. An assistant medical examiner in the 1930s and '40s, the snowy-haired Helpern was appointed Chief Medical Examiner in 1953, when Hogan was in his prime. Both men were to become patriarchal figures in the city. Both were to serve for decades. And both would be accused of ruling their respective roosts too long.

By 1972, Hogan and Helpern would be battered by press criticism, accusations that they were behind the times. Accustomed to loyalty and respect, the two men would find themselves in great disfavor—shipwrecks on the urban shoals of "relevance." Hogan would be accused of treating crime as Original Sin rather than as a social disease—and being a little too eager to stow people in prisons. Helpern would be rebuked for "burying" his mistakes.

Helpern's lifelong credo was a Latin inscription borrowed from a Roman mortuary and engraved on a marble wall of the New York City morgue: "Let conversation cease, let laughter flee. This is the place where death delights to serve the living." The living indeed benefited from the Medical Examiner's skillful pursuit of the causes of traumatic death. But the longer any administrator stays in office, the greater the opportunity for mediocrity to surface. By 1973, Helpern's reputation had eroded in case after case of carelessness, and he was forced to resign after a series of grisly mistakes came to light. For example, his office once severed the head of an unidentified woman thought to have drowned. A morgue employee decided to keep the skull as a desk ornament, and the unautopsied body was buried in a pauper's grave in Potter's Field. A week later, the skull was found to contain a bullet.

Outraged, the city elders demanded Helpern's ouster. The old man perhaps took solace in his memories of the 1940s and '50s, when retirement, with its sour surprises of senility and impotent rage, seemed light-years away. In their golden days, Hogan and Helpern had worked together wonderfully well.

For years their teamwork unearthed so many corpses that people made jokes: no one buried in Hogan's jurisdiction would stay peacefully in his grave. Hogan kept a keen eye on wills and the settlements of estates. In case after case, he would spot a suspicious aspect to a will and order the corpse exhumed, sometimes years after the deceased had been pronounced dead of "natural causes." From its unsettled grave, the cadaver would be trundled off in a rubber bag to a slab in Dr. Helpern's autopsy chamber. Helpern, who performed over 80,000 autopsies in his career, could whip a corpse inside out in record time: the average autopsy took him just fifteen minutes.

Helpern worked with a hardiness most of us would find unaesthetic. Scorning rubber gloves, he plunged his bare hands into the opened bodies of the recently—and not so recently—dead. He could also keep a ham sandwich going on the side. In his prime, he was peerless: as an expert witness in court, he could reconstruct a human being from a bag of bones—tell you the victim's age, his habits, when he died, and how. What Hogan suspected, Helpern often proved: natural causes became unnatural ones—a broken neck, a squashed larynx, a dose of arsenic, traces of a paralyzing drug, a self-sealing puncture wound. During one grotesque investigation, Helpern turned up evidence of barbituric-acid poisoning in the body of a wealthy spinster who had died alone. Although murder couldn't be proved against the undertaker, Hogan prosecuted him for concocting a will under a fake signature of the deceased. The mortician had named himself as executor of her $285,000 estate.

In one of the last years of their alliance, Hogan and Helpern outdid themselves by proving a "no-hands" murder. The victim, an elderly woman, was literally scared to death. In the past, Hogan could never have convinced the M.E. to say that the shock of finding an intruder in one's home was the direct cause of a lethal stroke or fatal heart attack. But in this case, the old lady had been bound and gagged in her apartment by a burglar. Helpern was able to prove that the exertion and struggle to free herself brought on the coronary: a felony murder had occurred. It was the first such prosecution in New York State since 1870.

If murder without a weapon didn't faze Hogan, neither did murder without a corpse. Many people think of the *corpus delicti* as the actual corpse, and believe that police need the body to prove a murder has been committed. Actually, *corpus delicti* means the body of *evidence* in the crime, and Hogan established this in the case of a foreign medical student who had botched an illegal abortion. His patient hemorrhaged and died. As the story was reconstructed, the student recruited friends from medical school to help him dispose of the evidence. The young men spent many grisly hours dissecting the woman's body in the student's apartment. Then they wrapped the pieces in parcels. The packages were dropped off in various trash receptacles around town when no one was looking—and without a trace of blood showing. Not one of the parcels was recovered before ending up in the city's garbage incinerator. However, a non-accomplice eyewitness presented the *corpus delicti*, testifying in court to the substantial facts that proved a murder had occurred. The young doctor was convicted of manslaughter.

A man of Hogan's nominal Catholic faith and background couldn't be expected to deal sympathetically with an illegal abortionist who dissected his patient afterward. But on the issue of abortion itself, Hogan was extending leniency to abortionists long before the New York State Legislature legalized "on demand" abortions in 1971. One reason was pragmatic. Juries generally did not want to return guilty verdicts on evidence that a medical doctor had performed a single, successful abortion. There was a better than even chance of acquittal. Hogan's policy was to treat isolated abortions as personal tragedies deserving leniency—and to prosecute only the "abortion mill" operations of the medical trade.

Murder held a morbid fascination for many men in the D.A.'s office, but the District Attorney himself couldn't stand the sight of blood. He dismissed detective stories and murder mysteries as vulgar pulp. (Occasionally, the D.A. did dip into the crime-fiction classics of Poe or Dumas, and he enjoyed Dickens' Inspector Bucket in *Bleak House*.)

Hogan *was* intrigued by the real-life detective endeavors of his homicide staff. "The cleverest thing I ever saw," Hogan complimented John F. Keenan in 1966, when the Homicide Bureau assistant cracked a two-year-old murder case involving a myriad of seemingly unrelated factors— a slain nuclear scientist, a missing pistol, the Audubon Society, homosexuality, the Russian KGB, and a weekly newspaper called *The Irish Echo*.

Dr. Charles J. Gallagher, a Columbia University physicist, was found shot to death in the Ramble, a Central Park wildlife sanctuary frequented by birdwatchers during the day and by homosexuals at night. The professor had worked on the cyclotron, the atom smasher, at Columbia. He had just returned from a lecture tour of the Soviet Union in April 1964 when his body was found in a clump of bushes, a .25-caliber slug through the heart. Cloak-and-dagger rumors of a KGB assassination swept the city when it was learned the Gallagher had worked on a semi-secret project for the Atomic Energy Commission.

For weeks, Hogan's men attended meetings of the Audubon Society, interrogating ornithologists and following up on leads that Gallagher was a "birdwatcher." This turned out to be a newspaper euphemism for Gallagher's real interest in the Ramble. Park police identified him as a cruising closet queen—married, with two children—who took his strolls to the gay garden only after midnight. But the .25-caliber pistol was never recovered, and for more than a year, the search for a killer led detectives up blind alleys.

It is a truism of police work that the best detective is only as good as his informants. Tipsters account for 95 percent of the newspaper stories you read praising "intensive detective work" in major investigations. The Gallagher case was no exception. According to an informant, the professor had died a more prosaic death than the titillating aspects of the case suggested. He had been a mugging victim.

A bartender friendly with a twenty-three-year-old drifter named Richard Conroy tipped off the Queens D.A.'s squad one day with the information that he had seen Conroy disassemble a .25-caliber pistol on the night of the murder and deep-six it in filthy Newtown Creek, the site of a city sewage plant. Police scuba divers dredged the cesspool, but couldn't find the gun.

Hogan secured a court-ordered wiretap on Conroy's telephone. Detectives began listening in, but months went by without the suspect's uttering a single incriminating word. Obviously a way had to be found to stimulate conversation about the crime. But how could you bring up the subject without arousing Conroy's suspicion that his phone might be tapped?

Then in June 1966, Hogan read a newspaper account of a University of Ohio professor, also a nuclear physicist, who had committed suicide with a .25-caliber pistol. "Wasn't that the same type of gun used in the Gallagher case?" Hogan asked Keenan.

Keenan nodded. Suddenly, he got a wild idea, and rushed back to his own office. There Keenan typed up a phony newspaper headline:

KILLING IN COLUMBUS, OHIO, CONNECTED TO MURDER IN CENTRAL PARK?

Underneath, he invented a three-paragraph item on the death of the rocket research scientist in Ohio, suggesting that the revolver was linked to the death of Professor Gallagher. Keenan of course omitted the fact that the Ohio death had been suicide.

The next day, Keenan took his bogus news story to a friend who worked as a typesetter for *The Irish Echo*, one of Manhattan's numerous ethnic weeklies. The *Echo* printer linotyped the story into a dummy page, buried between such headlines as "RFK Asks $2M More for Elders" and "Pontiff Raps Poland."

Regular *Irish Echo* readers would never see the dummy story. "Perfect!" Keenan grinned as the printer held up the tearsheet for inspection. "I'll take two." Keenan mailed the dummy page anonymously to Conroy and sent the second copy to the suspect's seventeen-year-old girlfriend. Then detectives sat back with their earphones and waited for a phone call.

The call came the next day. Conroy picked up the receiver and heard his girl on the line: "Do you think Billy went to the police?" In that same conversation, she named bartender William Rachun, who became a witness against Conroy. The girlfriend, too, ultimately testified, and her testimony helped put Conroy in prison.

Hogan's own crime-solving genius lay in his ability to cut his way through legal obstacles and labyrinths of logic, putting his finger precisely on the issue at stake. Consider, for example, the assistant who came to him one day with this problem. A man had been arrested with a key to a safe-deposit box in his pocket. The assistant had located the man's bank in Brooklyn, and suspected that the evidence being sought was stashed in the safety deposit box. What the assistant needed to know was the box number—and he couldn't find it.

There were 400 safe-deposit boxes in the bank, and the law allowed a search warrant for only one box at a time, provided Hogan's office could indicate to the judge precisely what they were searching for. In his free time, Hogan played an amateur Houdini—making quarters vanish and performing handkerchief tricks for children of staff members when they visited the office. Intrigued by the "locked-box" puzzle, he thought about the brain-teaser for a few minutes, then announced, "Eureka! Get a search warrant for the lock."

"Huh?"

"The lock the key fits. Say you're searching for the correct lock. Once you find the box, get another search warrant for the box!" It worked like . . . well, like magic.

The courtroom may be, as some critics charge, a theater of illusion in which the jury hears only obfuscations of the truth. But there is one crime-solving gimmick that Hogan felt contributed to legitimate deception—the lie detector. There had always been a police polygraph operator assigned to the office. At a defendant's request, Hogan would usually give him a lie-detector test on a risk-free basis. If the machine said the fellow was lying, Hogan put no further credence in his word. But if the polygraph said the defendant was telling the truth, Hogan would, in ninety-nine cases out of a hundred, drop the case. Although he often accepted the "innocent" verdict of a lie detector, he seemed to have reservations, as evidenced by the following incident.

Homicide assistant Terry O'Reilly remembered working a murder case one day when a bill for $400 came across Hogan's desk. The bill was an outside consultant's fee for an independent polygraph operator whom O'Reilly had hired on his case. Frugal Hogan was tight about squandering taxpayers' money on what he called "Dick Tracy" gizmos. If he thought the case warranted it, he would occasionally spring for something expensive—he once flew an undercover informant to Chicago for a day just to call a gangster from a local phone booth. But there were other times when his men complained that he wouldn't even spend the money for office supplies.

On the day the $400 invoice arrived in the mail, Hogan called O'Reilly on the carpet. "What's the story on this lie-detector test? You know we have all this equipment right here. Why did you go outside for one?"

"Because I hate lie-detector tests," said O'Reilly. "They're absolutely unreliable. Their only value is psychological. Lots of times a guy will say to me, 'You don't believe me, give me a lie-detector test.' So what are you gonna do? You have to call his bluff. So I give him a lie-detector test and no matter what the results are, I tell the guy he failed. Three times out of six, the guy will say OK and tell me what I want to know."

Why, then, spend $400 on another test? O'Reilly explained. He was working on a homicide case with two eyewitnesses to the murder. Their accounts of what happened were contradictory, "one hundred and eighty degrees apart." So O'Reilly gave both witnesses polygraph tests, one by the office expert, the other by an independent operator. Neither expert knew of the existence of the other witness. The results: each expert reported that his witness was telling the truth.

"Chief," said O'Reilly, "to me, that's proof that this lie-detector business is just a bunch of shit. Both witnesses couldn't have been telling the truth!"

"When I told Hogan the story," O'Reilly recalled, "he laughed like a son of a bitch and said, 'I'll gladly pay the bill—it was worth it!' "

One of the problems that plagued Hogan, as it does any prosecutor, was that of urging witnesses to come forward.

"What we need isn't more judges, but more witnesses," a Manhattan jurist once complained of society's apathy in the face of violent crime. But people don't want to get involved in criminal cases for many respectable reasons: fear of reprisals, press notoriety, financial hardship. One of the prison reforms instituted after the October 1970 riots in the Tombs was the installation of telephones, so that today, the defendant has the right to pick up the phone and call a prosecution witness and inquire, "How's the wife and kids? Everybody healthy?" The witness often gets the message. He either refuses to appear in court, or clams up on the witness stand. The case often goes stale, or gets dismissed.

Hogan cited one example of the witness problem. A man was shot to death in a bar and grill near Madison Square Garden. Two bartenders, anxious to avoid giving their place a bad name, hoisted up the corpse, slung the arms over their shoulders, and pretended the victim was just a drunk they were bouncing off the premises. "Okay, Charlie, you've had enough for one night. Time to get home to the wife and kids." They boisterously "walked" the limp corpse around the corner and dumped it on the sidewalk, then ran back to the bar as if nothing had happened.

Hogan *did* get wind of what happened, and started questioning patrons who had been at the saloon that evening.

There were twenty-one customers lined up at the bar when the gunfire erupted. Yet it took Hogan eight months before even one of them, a foreign visitor from Austria, could be coaxed into admitting, not that a slaying had occurred, but just that a shot had been fired. Everybody else claimed they had been in the men's room and had seen nothing. (The men's room had a seating capacity of one, plus standing room for two at the urinals.)

Hogan next discovered that nearly half of the drinkers at the bar had a good reason for seeing no evil. Each had some sort of prior arrest record. The others who played deaf-and-dumb were average decent citizens, stopping off for a drink after work at the real-estate office or the accounting firm.

Getting people to testify is only part of the problem; there are other dangers for the prosecution when witnesses *do* come forward. Rarely are deliberate attempts made to frame an innocent defendant. More often, mistaken identifications are honest mistakes made by honest eyewitnesses. Hogan introduced a number of safeguards—his trial assistants would examine the witness's eyesight as well as his credibility, find out the wattage of every light bulb in the room and the last time the bulbs had been cleaned, and look for endless other possible defects of vision before taking the witness to court. Hogan estimated his office's percentage of error to be "one hundredth of one percent in all convictions."

Still, on several occasions, Hogan imprisoned men for crimes they did not commit. The sad case of Bertram Campbell was a notable one. A bookkeeper, Campbell was sentenced to ten years' imprisonment in 1938 for forgery. Even the judge chastised him with bitter irony: "You could have drawn a lighter sentence if you had implicated others in the forgery ring."

Campbell, a mistaken-identity victim of Dewey's "100 percent clean-up" crusade, endured three and a half lost years in Sing Sing before he was paroled in 1942. He would have died falsely accused if the master forger who committed the crime hadn't suffered pangs of conscience for Campbell and confessed in 1946. The newspapers were saying that the real forger, Alexander Thiel, a white-haired, florid-faced man, bore a "striking resemblance" to Campbell. Actually, the "look-alikes" were poles apart. Campbell had dark hair and a mustache. Yet five eyewitnesses, bank tellers of proven honesty, made the error.

A shamefaced Governor Dewey pardoned Campbell, who eventually received $115,000 of the $140,000 he sought in damages. He no sooner collected than he dropped dead of a heart attack. His physician said the years in prison had taken their toll.

The haphazard way in which police investigations are conducted has often served to convict the innocent. Until the U.S. Supreme Court restricted the practice in recent years, many police lineups fit the pattern of what happened to George Whitmore, Jr., on April 24, 1964. Police treatment of the dim-witted, acne-scarred Whitmore, a nineteen-year-old black youth accused of attempted rape, later figured in at least one Supreme Court decision on the Constitutional rights of defendants and set in motion an upheaval in the practice of U.S. law enforcement.

The Whitmore case began when Mrs. Elba Borrero, a practical nurse, reported to Brooklyn police that she had been attacked by a young Negro man who forced her into an alleyway and threatened to rape and kill her. Twenty-four hours later, police picked up Whitmore on a nearby street corner and asked him to accompany them to headquarters. They put him alone in a squadroom at Brooklyn's 73rd Precinct station and left the door ajar. Then, while Mrs. Borrero, a heavy-set Spanish woman, peeked through the crack in the door, the cops ordered Whitmore to say, "Lady, I'm going to rape you. Lady, I'm going to kill you."

At the sound of Whitmore's husky voice, Mrs. Borrero began to tremble. "That's the man."

It took George Whitmore, Jr., nine years—three of them in jail—and the ordeal of four trials and three hearings to reverse the devastating effects of that peephole identification. Within twenty-two hours after Mrs. Borrero made her identification, Whitmore was brainwashed into confessing not only to the attempted rape but to three murders as well—charges that might have slipped him into the electric chair had Frank Hogan not intervened.

Long before the Whitmore case became a *cause célèbre*, Hogan had been skeptical of police interrogation and identification tactics. And so he conducted his own lineups, which were almost theatrical exaggerations of fairness. The goal: to find "look-alike" policemen, resembling suspects, to join the lineups. Hogan's chief civilian investigator, Thomas Fay, Jr., ran an eleven-man "midget squad"—plainclothesmen who fell under the minimum 5-feet-7-inch height requirement of the police department. The "D.A.'s Squad" commander, Inspector Paul Vitrano, had goaded

the police department into waiving the height requirement for many of his own men. They were cops who looked like crooks, many of them foreign-born, multilingual, and masters of decoy disguise: black cops in electroshock Afros and calypso hats, white cops in Serpico-style sleazy chic, cops masquerading as Hell's Angels, Hassidic rabbis, Con Ed construction workers, pony-tailed Hare Krishnas, Good Humor men, and other assorted street people.

Both squads provided a manpower pool of diverse ethnic and physical types. Hogan dragooned these men into special duty three or four times a day during lineups in the seventh-floor mirror room. The mirror room looked like an ordinary office, with a wooden desk and straight-backed chairs—ordinary except for the one-way viewing mirror bolted to the wall. The room reflected Hogan's open-door policy toward defense lawyers: when a client was in the lineup, the suspect's lawyer was always invited to the mirror room. Choosing from a miscellaneous assortment of cops of every physical description and skin color, the lawyer himself selected five look-alike stand-ins to be seated alongside his client. If, for example, the suspect was a bearded Negro, the lawyer was allowed to select five other bearded Negroes (in the days before Hogan's rule police might have stuck the Negro in with five whites). The lawyer then picked the seat number where he wished his client to sit and stand up for the viewers.

To ensure fair identification for the "other side" (Hogan's side), the D.A.'s investigators studied the original description of the suspect that had been given to police when the victim first reported the crime. If the suspect had grown a beard in jail since the crime, Hogan obtained a court order to shave it off. If the man had originally had a beard and shaved it off, Hogan possessed a wardrobe supply of fake beards, mustaches, toupées, golf hats, porkpies, sun visors, baseball caps—a duplicate of whatever the suspect had been wearing at the time of his alleged felony. Before a lineup, Tom Fay scurried around the premises—a frenetic makeup man, giving haircuts, dabbing spirit gum on one man's cheek, touching up another's gray temple.

Eventually, the criminal lawyer was permitted backstage, behind the viewing-room mirror. Suspicious that many of the briefcase-toting Mafia lawyers were themselves mobsters in masquerade, Hogan hid his witnesses behind an improvised shower curtain: "They're protecting their people, so we're protecting ours." Witnesses weren't permitted to speak, only to write out their answers to questions, as they peered through the mirror and tried to pick an accused loanshark or gunman out of the lineup.

Hogan's lineup methods were a proven success. In 75 to 85 percent of cases, the lawyer would consent to pleading his man guilty after a "positive I.D." had been made. Defendants, Hogan reasoned, do not plead guilty because confession is good for the soul (although modern penologists claim that an admission of guilt is the first step to earnest rehabilitation—an argument that makes plea bargaining morally neutral). Rather, defendants plead guilty because their lawyers can demonstrate to them that they have no hope of winning in court.

Hogan would invite the lawyer to the lineup, lay out the People's evidence, then begin to negotiate the scope of the charge to which the defendant should plead. In other jurisdictions, the defendant's lawyer might have to arm-wrestle the D.A. for a bill of particulars on the crime charged.

Hogan preferred to deal with them more candidly. Except in organized rackets cases, the defense lawyers often revealed whatever evidence they had to prove their man innocent. This was really unheard of in other jurisdictions. But the Manhattan office reputation for integrity was so intact that a criminal lawyer in New York County knew he had a better chance of persuading Frank Hogan to dismiss a case than persuading a jury to acquit.

Had the same lineup safeguards been in force in Brooklyn on the morning of April 24, 1964, it seems doubtful that the George Whitmore controversy would have undermined police credibility to the extent that it has today. (Under *voir dire* examination in sunnier days, Hogan's trial men would ask a prospective juror if he would automatically assume a policeman's testimony to be more truthful than that of a civilian witness. Today, the same trial assistants ask jury prospects if they automatically take a cop's word to be a lie.)

What happened to George Whitmore, Jr., during the twenty-two hours he spent in that Brooklyn police station has become the subject of four books, one motion picture, and countless scholarly articles on the revolution in criminal law forged by the liberal Warren Court of the 1960s.

Two months after Whitmore's arrest, the Supreme Court, in its landmark *Escobedo* decision, issued a devastating attack on the use of the confession—the traditional backbone of police work in the United States. The *Escobedo* ruling, incorporated into the later *Miranda v. Arizona* decision, extended to guilty as well as to innocent defendants every citizen's Constitutional right to remain silent under interrogation, his right to counsel at the time of his arrest, and his right to know the precise reason he is under arrest. Predictably, the police guidelines written into the *Miranda* and *Escobedo* rulings sent shock waves through the nation's courthouses. Prosecutors charged that the nation's highest court was "coddling criminals" and "handcuffing" police. District attorneys quoted the legendary Justice Benjamin Cardozo's lament, "Why punish society for the blundering constable!"

An impassioned Brooklyn prosecutor jumped to his feet in court and shouted, "We have reached the point in our jurisprudence where the District Attorney is seen no longer as prosecutor, defender of the people. Every prosecutor today is an ogre. Identification is no good today. Confessions are no good because they are beaten. We will reach the point where any criminal who escapes from the scene of the crime can never be convicted . . ."

One of Hogan's top assistants was so passionately aroused that he violated the office rule against talking to the press and harangued reporters about "how unrealistic and naive the Court is." Hogan himself was perturbed that the Brooklyn District Attorney, Aaron Koota, went on radio to applaud the Court's decision. "I don't know what's come over Aaron," Hogan said a few days later. "Perhaps it was a leftover campaign speech. Obviously the whole purpose of police investigation is frustrated if a suspect is allowed to have a lawyer during preliminary questioning—any lawyer worth his fee will tell him to keep his mouth shut."

The District Attorney made his denunciation with full knowledge that on the day of Whitmore's arrest, an experienced assistant D.A. from Hogan's own office had taken down a sixty-one-page confession from George Whitmore to two murders he did not commit.

As for the low-I.Q. George Whitmore, the "confession" he made to Hogan's office was unwittingly the smartest thing he ever did. It saved his life.

When asked in 1972 to enumerate his greatest successes as America's "Mr. District Attorney," Frank Hogan replied simply, "I exonerated George Whitmore."

The full narrative of the Whitmore confessions has consumed thousands of pages of court transcript and miles of newsprint. Details of Whitmore's grotesquely deprived upbringing in an auto graveyard on Cape May, New Jersey, the stigmata of his running acne sores and acute nearsightedness, the twin scourges of poverty and an eighth-grade education that afflicted him—all are admirably captured in a 1969 book, *Whitmore*, by Fred Shapiro.

Working as an investigative reporter for the now-defunct New York *Herald-Tribune* in the 1960s, Shapiro devoted three years of intense legal scholarship to the Whitmore confessions, concluding in private that Frank Hogan was the "real villain."

Hogan's side of the story can now be told. It is a story of detective work upon detective work—a tragic tale that encompasses the tragedy not only of George Whitmore, Jr., but of one of society's "blundering constables."

Detective Edward Bulger, a heavy-set man with a corrugated face, was a twenty-six-year veteran of the police force. He had been a first-grade detective for seven years when, on August 28, 1963, he and several other Brooklyn homicide men were pulled off their regular assignments to go to Manhattan and search for the slayer of career girls Janice Wylie and Emily Hoffert.

The grisly details of the double murder had sent a collective shudder through the spine of a city thought to be immune to urban horror. But then the victims had also seemed immune—young, pretty, rich. Janice Wylie, twenty-three, the niece of author Philip Wylie, and her schoolteacher roommate, Emily Hoffert, were found slashed to death in their East 88th Street apartment, in the center of a "luxury district."

The murder of the two girls, living on their own in a "safe" neighborhood, frightened parents with unmarried children living alone all over the country: *They could have been our daughters!* The heat was on, then, to find the killer. Looking for the slayer during the eight months that followed the deaths, police conducted the most extensive dragnet in the city's history; they questioned more than 1,000 people.

For three months, Detective Bulger had worked on the Wylie-Hoffert case. The day after the murders, he had examined the dead girls' apartment—the bloodied bed and bathroom. He memorized the floor plan, knew the color of the bedspread, the time the electric clock had stopped, and other details that only the killer might have known. One such detail: before the girls were hacked to death with butcher knives, they had been stunned by blows from an empty Coca-Cola bottle. Also, three butcher knives had been used to inflict a senseless repetition of death wounds— thrusts so forceful that one knife blade had broken off.

Detective Bulger also knew that Janice Wylie had been menstruating;

that the killer had pulled out a sodden Tampax and molested her sexually. The girls' hands had been bound with bedding cut by a razorblade. Bulger memorized the position of the kitchen wall rack that had presumably held the knives, tried to visualize the man running back for a second knife, a third. As gory as the murders had been, Bulger also knew that the killer had meticulously tidied up the apartment after his orgy—wiping away fingerprints, mopping up pools of blood.

The finishing touch: the man had actually stepped into the bathtub for a blood-spattered shower. When he left the apartment, he could be presumed to have been immaculate.

Bulger had been assigned to the case after the crime-scene photos were taken. He came from Brooklyn, twenty-four hours behind the Manhattan team. When he checked out the apartment, he was amazed to find a clue the "Park Avenue boys" had overlooked: a Gillette Blue Blade wrapper on the bathroom floor. This wrapper became a pawn in the traditional rivalry between Manhattan and Brooklyn detectives. Manhattan dicks resented a Brooklyn boy's showing them how things ought to be done. The disdain heaped upon Bulger by the Manhattan homicide men was rumored to be the reason why, abruptly, after three months on the most important case of his life, Bulger was shipped back to Brooklyn. Taken off the case!

After that humiliating put-down, Bulger sulked around Brooklyn's 73rd Precinct stationhouse for several months. One day, he heard that up in the squadroom, a stupid, illiterate black kid was confessing to an attempted rape and a murder. Bulger asked to be briefed on the arrest.

He was told that shortly after midnight on April 23, 1964, a young patrolman had been walking his Brooklyn ghetto beat when he heard a scream from an alleyway. He beamed his flashlight on a young Negro who appeared to be molesting a heavy-set Spanish woman, Mrs. Elba Borrero. The patrolman fired a shot and the man fled. Six hours later, the patrolman saw George Whitmore, Jr., loitering in the doorway of a laundromat. Whitmore asked what the shooting earlier had been about. "Why? What do you know about it?" the cop asked.

"I heard shots and then I saw a guy running down the street," Whitmore said. Twenty-four hours later, the policeman and a detective returned to the laundromat and found Whitmore standing in the same doorway. The officers asked him to accompany them to headquarters where he would "answer a few questions."

By 10:30 that morning, the day of his arrest, Whitmore had confessed to the Borrero rape attempt. By noon, he had admitted the April 14 knife slaying of Mrs. Minnie Edmonds, a charwoman.

Being interrogated in a stationhouse was the most exciting thing that had ever happened to George Whitmore. He had frequently entertained fantasies of himself as a respected witness in an important police investigation. Now, as high-level police brass crowded into the squadroom to have a look at him, the attention made him eager to tell them anything they wanted to hear. Part of Whitmore's fantasy life, his only escape from the reality of life on a junkheap, was the dream of being loved by a white girl. He documented this fantasy with a snapshot (actually found in the town dump in Wildwood, New Jersey). The photograph was that of a pretty girl in a convertible, her blond tresses fluttering in the breeze. "To George from Louise," Whitmore had penciled across the back of the snapshot before tucking it in his wallet, where it was found at the time of his arrest.

Bulger asked to see the photograph. Almost at once, the detective's mind began racing. "I could swear this is a picture of Janice Wylie," he said, keeping his voice tightly controlled. "I'd like to talk to him about this picture." Bulger was invited into the squadroom to "ask a few questions."

Shortly after 10:00 P.M., a call for an assistant D.A. came into Hogan's office. On homicide duty that night was Peter J. Koste, who was ordered to "roll" over to Brooklyn with a stenographer. In the 73rd Precinct stationhouse, Koste was told, sat the perpetrator of one of the city's grisliest murders.

By four o'clock in the morning, George Whitmore had confessed to killing Janice Wylie and Emily Hoffert. The formal confession, dictated in question-and-answer form from Koste to Whitmore, was unusual: sixty-one pages of transcript filled with details "that only the killer would know": the broken knife, the Coke bottle, the Tampax, the razorblade. The police interrogation had begun late Friday and lasted into early Saturday. By 2:00 A.M., when Koste began taking down Whitmore's formal statement, the New York *Daily News* was already on the streets with the headline:

ADMITS KILLING 2 CAREER GIRLS

Bulger had tipped police reporters to "something big" at the stationhouse. A battery of newspaper reporters, photographers and TV camera crews converged on the precinct house. The media flock stampeded into the squad commander's office. Reporters outshouted each other with questions:

Was there any corroborating evidence other than the confession to indicate Whitmore's guilt?

"We've got the right guy, no question about it," insisted a chief of detectives. "We have a lot more than a confession."

Such as?

The chief said that a 4-by-2½-inch snapshot of Janice Wylie had been found in Whitmore's wallet.

When Hogan arrived at his office on Monday morning, his first order of business was to read over the Whitmore confession. Immediately, Hogan had a few questions of his own. He buzzed Assistant D.A. Melvin Glass on the intercom. Didn't Mel already have a suspect in the Wylie-Hoffert case? Glass said, well, he wasn't sure; he was preparing a rape trial. The defendant, a convicted burglar, had been picked up because of a fingerprint in the Greenwich Village apartment of his rape victim.

The man admitted the rape but was quick to put himself outside the Manhattan jurisdiction on August 28, 1963, the day the career girls had been murdered. The suspect said he was in Washington that day, attending the Freedom March. This Freedom March alibi struck Hogan as out of character. Would a burglar-rapist really travel to Washington as a civil-rights activist? It didn't make sense. Hadn't Glass also discovered that the defendant was once an East Side delivery boy, whose grocery errands might have taken him into 57 East 88th Street, the building where the girls had been slaughtered? Glass said yes, he'd like to see the Whitmore confession, too, "just to satisfy my curiosity."

Together, the men began reading over the confession, Hogan pointing out several dubious answers Whitmore had given to Detective Bulger's questions about the Wylie-Hoffert building:

Q: What kind of building?
A: About a four-story house.
Q: Four-story house you think it was?
A: Yes.
Q: What did you do when you spotted this four-story house? You think it was four stories?

Here the transcript was interrupted with a notation: "Detective Bulger leaves room." Twenty questions later, Bulger had returned to the squad-

room and the confession was interrupted again to go back to the height of
the building:

> Q: You mentioned that this building was about four or five
> stories. Could it have been eight to ten stories?
> A: I don't know if it's quite that high or not.
> Q: Could it have been eight stories?
> A: Yes.

Hogan and Glass exchanged worried glances. "Spoon-fed?" the D.A.
suggested.

Glass wasn't sure. "One of our men, Pete Koste, took the statement. If
it was spoon-fed, the detectives got to Whitmore before Koste got to the
stationhouse." Glass pointed out the snapshot Bulger believed to be of
Janice Wylie. Whitmore maintained he found the picture on a dump in
Wildwood, but under questioning, he admitted to Bulger that it was
taken from "the end table where the lamp is" in the Wylie apartment.

Whitmore had already been formally charged with the double homicide. But as the morning's work progressed, Hogan and Glass enumerated
as many as thirty glaring discrepancies in Whitmore's confession.

The whole thing stank, Hogan said in disgust. A sixty-one-page confession to one of the most sensational crimes in New York history had been
taken down by a Hogan assistant—and it smelled to high heaven. Hogan
would later pass that judgment along to Brooklyn D.A. Aaron Koota,
warning him, with wonderful understatement, "Uh, Aaron, we've found
certain infirmities in the Whitmore statement." But Koota had evidently
decided to press ahead with the Borrero and Edmonds prosecutions anyway. And to Hogan, the wisest course seemed not to interfere with the
work of a brother prosecutor.

Work proceeded on the case against George Whitmore. But the results
of the suspect's psychiatric tests at Bellevue Hospital stirred up more
doubt that he was the killer. Mel Glass had reason to remember something his sister had suggested at the time of the murders a year earlier.

"My sister is a psychologist and she said the killings sounded to her as
if they'd been done by someone who was compulsively clean—an anal
compulsive—because the killer had washed the knives afterward in the
bathroom, had mopped up the blood, and had gotten into the tub and
taken a shower. Koste and I were having lunch one day and I asked him
if Whitmore was a fastidious fellow. Koste said, 'He's totally filthy!' "

This was true. George Whitmore lived in unbelievable filth. His T-shirts were alive with body lice and thick with blood coagulated from the running acne sores on his back. Baths were out of the question—he slept in hallways and foraged in garbage pails.

"I kinda convinced myself that Whitmore wasn't the killer," Glass recalled. "But proving it was something else. The first thing Hogan had me do was read about fifteen hundred D.D. Fives [Detective Division No. 5: an investigation report]. I also read the Medical Examiner's reports and whatever else I could get my hands on.

"I was interviewing detectives in the case. Brooklyn detectives," Glass recollected. "They didn't know why I was speaking to them, so they may have been a little freer with me than they would have been with somebody on the other side."

Unaware that he was under suspicion, Detective Bulger dropped by Hogan's office in late August 1964 to discuss the case with Mel Glass. Disarmed by Glass's smiling face in the D.A.'s squadroom, Bulger confided *sotto voce* to the assistant D.A.: "I could tell Whitmore was lying when he said he didn't know anything about the Wylie apartment."

"How could you tell he was lying?" Glass grinned.

"Because," said Bulger solemnly, "his stomach was going in and out under his belt, and whenever a Negro lies, his stomach goes in and out."

That was all Glass needed to hear. "It doesn't take much imagination to figure out how Whitmore got the facts," he told Hogan. "He got them from Bulger."

"How could Koste have been so taken in?" Hogan demanded to know.

"Because Whitmore was brainwashed," Glass insisted. "That confession came from the police."

From that moment on, Hogan's investigation of the Wylie-Hoffert case concentrated on Detective Bulger instead of George Whitmore. Probably at no other time in the history of U.S. law enforcement has so much money, manpower and painstaking investigative work been devoted to proving a "suspect's" innocence.

Hogan dispatched an undercover man to eavesdrop on the 73rd Precinct squadroom. Cops who spy on other cops are called "shoo-flies." Hogan's shoo-fly reported back that a Brooklyn sergeant had heard Bulger say during the Whitmore interrogation, "I'll tell you how it happened. You saw the door open so you went in there and you came across the first girl . . ."

Trying to establish an alibi for George Whitmore, the D.A.'s squad fanned out into South Jersey and Pennsylvania. Among other things they were trying to track down the person who had taken the snapshot Whitmore had found on the Wildwood garbage dump—the photograph that Bulger described as "clinching" evidence because the girl was Janice Wylie, and Whitmore admitted taking the photo from an end table in her apartment. By October, Hogan's men had traced the snapshot through a photographic studio and identified the blonde in the picture as a New Jersey girl, now a Mrs. Arlene Franco. The only explanation Mrs. Franco could offer for the presence of her picture in George Whitmore's wallet was that, as he had maintained before the Bulger brainwash, he had picked it off the garbage dump.

Police next located a mother and daughter in Philadelphia who provided an alibi for George Whitmore—swearing they were with him in a Wildwood, New Jersey, hotel on the day of the Wylie-Hoffert murders, watching a telecast of the Washington Freedom March.

In New York, new leads were being followed up on what looked like the first real suspect in the Wylie-Hoffert case.

The new suspect had been fingered by an emaciated junkie named Nathan Delaney, a thirty-five-year-old addict with stringy hair and starved cheekbones. Delaney faced a possible life sentence on charges of killing a heroin pusher. Trying to build a cushion for himself on the murder rap, Delaney had a strong incentive to open up. His ace in the hole, he claimed, was knowing the *real* killer of Janice Wylie and Emily Hoffert.

"You guys have the wrong man," Delaney told detectives, who listened intently: if Delaney elected to supply information on an apparently solved case, he must really know something.

Delaney confided in quick, nervous specch that on August 28, 1963, an addict friend had come to his apartment in blood-spattered jeans and announced, "I just iced two girls." The friend was Richard Robles. The twenty-two-year-old Robles seemed a likelier killer than Whitmore. Robles lived only a few blocks away from the girls' apartment. He knew a pusher who lived in their building. Nor was Robles any stranger to police: he was out of prison on parole after serving thirty-eight months for burglary. His own confession: more than a hundred break-ins on the East Side.

This suggested the logical "opening"—a break-in, a beautiful, naked blonde, then the knives, the razor . . . The problem for Frank Hogan was that Delaney's testimony wouldn't stand up in court—a three-time loser trying to save his own skin. And so another extensive investigation would have to be carried out to substantiate Delaney's account. While the public, and Robles, believed that police were still concentrating on Whitmore as the killer, in fact, the focus had turned to the slight, hyped-up Richard Robles. Delaney agreed to work undercover for the office, in exchange for total immunity from prosecution on his unrelated homicide charge—killing a pusher. Delaney figured he was getting a terrific deal. What Hogan's office didn't tell him was that the pusher's death was a clear case of self-defense—a case too weak to go to trial.

Time was now working against Hogan. Over in Brooklyn, D.A. Aaron Koota was impatient to try Whitmore on the Borrero rape attempt and the Minnie Edmonds murder. Hogan needed time to trap Robles and disprove the Whitmore confession: what he needed was conclusive proof that there was a frame-up. Hogan found that proof in late October.

Mel Glass was sifting through the avalanche of police reports and medical findings on the case, reading the Whitmore confession over for the hundredth time and analyzing the crime-scene photos. Flipping to a photo showing the contents of one of Janice Wylie's dresser drawers, he made a curious discovery: in the jumble of lipsticks, cold creams, hair and eyelash curlers, there was a Gillette Blue Blade dispenser.

Leafing again through the pages of Whitmore's confession, Glass returned to a scene in which Whitmore told Detective Bulger that he had taken a razorblade from the medicine cabinet of the Wylie bathroom and dropped the *wrapper* on the floor. Whitmore then stated that he used the blade to cut strips of bedding—the cloth used to bind the victims' hands together.

The assistant D.A., the image of that Blue Blade dispenser clearly before him, snatched up the phone and dialed the Manhattan precinct in which the murders had occurred. He asked to see the razorblade found at the crime scene.

When the blade was delivered, Glass took one look at it and saw that the face was engraved with tiny arrows. In 1963, Gillette wrapper blades did not show these arrows. The evidence suggested that the blade had been taken from the dispenser in Janice Wylie's bureau drawer.

Checking further, Glass learned that "when Bulger was assigned to the investigation, he came across the wrapper of a Gillette Blue Blade in the Wylie apartment. He thought it was an amazing find. What he didn't realize was that a cop had been assigned to guard the death apartment overnight. In the morning, the cop had shaved in the bathroom, and *he* had dropped the wrapper.

"Detective Bulger, knowing the material that had bound the girls had been cut by a razorblade, said to himself, this must have been the one. So this makes nice reading in the confession: George Whitmore supposedly told Bulger that he took this blade from the medicine cabinet and dropped the wrapper on the floor. The same place Bulger recovered it. But Bulger didn't count on the photograph of the death room revealing that in one of the bureau drawers there was a Gillette Blue Blade dispenser. And the blade found at the scene, which Bulger never saw, was from a dispenser. A blade with the arrows! To me it was conclusive proof that Bulger had fed those words into Whitmore's mouth."

Glass brought his information to Frank Hogan, who congratulated the assistant on his discovery. The image of George Whitmore as a confessed killer had disintegrated like chalk dust. But now there was another problem to consider—the "new" suspect, Robles. Hogan's men were already installing a hidden recorder in Delaney's apartment and wiring the addict's arm with a miniature transmitter, so he could work undercover. Hogan had to avoid blowing Delaney's cover and, at the same time, convince Robles that he was off the hook as long as Whitmore was still charged with the crime. How could the D.A. dismiss the indictment against Whitmore without arousing Robles' suspicion?

Hogan decided in favor of a technicality: instead of dismissing the indictment outright, he ordered Whitmore "DOR'd"—discharged on his own recognizance—but not cleared of criminal charges. This technicality was carefully exploited in Whitmore's later murder trial in Brooklyn when the prosecutor in the Minnie Edmonds case pointed out that Whitmore could still be tried for the Wylie-Hoffert slayings. One result was to confuse the jury, which reported itself deadlocked after thirty-four hours of deliberation. The judge ordered a mistrial.

Although civil libertarians accused Hogan of deliberately delaying the dismissal to help his Brooklyn colleague win a conviction, the fact is that Hogan was merely trying to buy time. Three days later, on January 27, 1964, the Wylie-Hoffert indictment *was* dismissed, but only after Robles had been arrested, taken into custody, and charged with the crime.

Mel Glass was walking to the courthouse next morning when Hogan's limousine cruised up to the door and the Chief called out, "What happened last night?"

On the way up in the elevator, Glass told Hogan the details of Robles' arrest—details that until now have never fully been made a matter of public record.

The D.A.'s office had had Robles under surveillance since October 19, 1964, the day that Delaney fingered Robles in the crime. In the interim, investigators had amassed over 200 tapes from the hidden recorder in Delaney's apartment. Robles' voice could be heard on several of the tapes, rehearsing false answers he planned to give to a lie-detector test, reciting sordid intimate details of the murders—details not reported in the newspapers. By January 25, 1965, Hogan had listened to enough of these tapes to conclude that Robles was the killer without any doubt. But he summoned the Homicide Bureau men to his office and went over the evidence one more time. Hogan closed the meeting by praising Melvin Glass for the "outstanding job" he had done. Then, as an afterthought, Hogan told the staff that even in the event of a hung jury, the prosecution of Robles would be justified—because there existed a confession from another man. And, Hogan said, considering every angle as always, "It's just conceivable the jury might have a doubt."

Robles was to be taken into custody the next day. Delaney would be immunized from prosecution to appear as a People's witness against Robles, to testify that the killer told him how he had entered through a window and surprised Miss Wylie while she was asleep, and that when Emily Hoffert had opened the door and walked into the apartment, Robles had killed her, too.

Robles was indeed picked up the next day—in Delaney's apartment. Shortly after he was booked at the stationhouse, about 6:30 P.M., he asked to see someone from the D.A.'s office. Mel Glass reconstructs the occasion:

"I went into the detention pen and said, 'What's on your mind, Ricky?' He said, 'What can you do for me?' I said, 'It's not what I can do for you. It's what you can do for yourself. You've been living with this thing for a long time, so you might just as well get it off your chest. You've asked for a lawyer, so until you see one, nothing you say can be used against you.' He said, 'What about psychiatric help?' I said, 'Right now, it's an either/or situation. They say you did it; you say you didn't. If you give a full statement from which a court and a psychiatrist could analyze and determine whether you need psychiatric help, that would be one thing. Did you panic in the apartment?' He said, 'It wasn't panic—something went wrong.' I said, 'Do you want to tell me the whole story?' He said, 'I'd rather talk to my lawyer first.' "

So Glass left Robles alone in the detention pen, sick with heroin withdrawal and shivering under his black leather jacket. Despite a $15-a-day heroin habit, the prisoner's face looked like that of a choirboy—only the needle tracks in his arms gave him away.

Robles' defense attorney, Jack S. Hoffinger, a former Hogan assistant, arrived and spent twenty minutes alone with his client in the counsel room. Then, stepping outside, Hoffinger suggested to Glass: "What about a recommendation of life imprisonment?" The death penalty was still on the books in 1965.

"If there was a chance that they were offering to save his life, I would at least have to put it to Robles," Hoffinger explained recently. "I'd have had to say, 'Listen, Ricky, if you did this, you'd better think over whether you should confess—because there's a chance you will die.' It was a tight spot. I assumed they had some damning evidence against him. But I was also aware that they had held him incommunicado since his arrest at noon and were trying to get him to confess. Telling him the only way to save himself and avoid shaming his mother—who was dying of cancer— was to confess. At no time did I ever suggest to Mel Glass that I thought the boy was guilty. At no time did I suggest that Robles confessed to me. In fact, I wouldn't let him say much to me at all, because I was afraid the room was wired."

Hoffinger conceded that he negotiated by telephone with Homicide Bureau Chief Alexander Herman during this period outside the counsel room. Herman said, "A double homicide like this, we can't make any kind of commitment." While Hoffinger was out of the room, a detective named David Downs was assigned to guard the prisoner. Before Hoffinger had time to get back to his client, Robles broke down and confessed to Downs. Then Robles repeated his confession to a police lieutenant, a sergeant and two other detectives.

"You know," Detective Downs recollected, "I never would have repeated what Robles told me if he hadn't said it in front of four other people—because after Whitmore, who would have believed me?"

Riding up in the elevator with Hogan next morning, Glass told him: "If you'd been in the precinct stationhouse last night, you'd have seen a half-dozen detectives race to the Wylie apartment house to see whether a step from the stairway window to the kitchen window was possible—the way Robles says he got into the apartment."

Hogan paused in the corridor and shook his head, suddenly—and uncharacteristically—emotional. "You know, you know, don't you . . . how I feel about the electric chair. . . . But I don't see how, in this case, we can *not* try him, for murder one."

Fortunately for Richard Robles, the death penalty was no longer mandatory for "murder one" convictions when he was convicted of first-degree murder on December 1, 1965—a conviction unanimously affirmed by the appellate division. Robles was sentenced to life imprisonment.

The question of George Whitmore's innocence or guilt in the Borrero rape attempt has three times been put to Brooklyn jurors, and three times they have found him guilty. A Kings County jury also found him guilty in the slaying of Minnie Edmonds. Each of these convictions was reversed on appeal, because when the appellate judges threw out the tainted confessions, there was really no evidence to convict him of anything. Today, George Whitmore is free at last, currently suing the city for $5 million in false-arrest damages. Detective Bulger was allowed to resign from the police force with full pension. And those whose responsibility it is to worry about such things say that what happened to George Whitmore could never happen again.

The story of his ordeal has many more facets to it than the tale of Rashomon. If there were twenty different men in the room with Whitmore at different times during his stationhouse "confession," there are twenty conflicting versions of what happened—the truth distorted by the warped perceptions of human prejudice and self-deception. What really happened to George Whitmore during those twenty-two hours? Certainly the truth has eluded the one person who might tell us—the victim himself. At one of his trials, Whitmore had trouble remembering his own name, let alone the details of his signed "confession." And who would believe him anyway?

5
FIVE WILL GET YOU TEN

For the People, Your Honor."

With those words, the man destined to become the nation's most famous prosecutor rose in the courtroom to try his first case before a jury. The year was 1945, and *The People v. Fay and Bove* would become a Hogan milestone: the first and only trial he ever argued himself during his career as Manhattan District Attorney.

Hogan had been touted as a winner long before the trial began. By the end of his very first year, the D.A.'s office had won 97.4 percent of 2,788 felony cases, a record that washed out Dewey's high-water mark of 94.2 percent for the previous year. The press tributes poured in.

While his assistants cleared the calendar, Hogan channeled his own energies in a single direction. New York's leading newspaper muckraker, Westbrook Pegler, had spotlighted the corruption of labor in a series of direct and angry articles. By the middle of 1943, Hogan had taken the cue and begun constructing the biggest extortion-conspiracy case then on record. He and his right-hand man, Assistant D.A. Alfred J. Scotti, pitted themselves against the father of modern labor racketeering, Joseph S. Fay.

The D.A. knew that he was in for a good deal of public and political resentment when he brought one of the AFL's most shadowy powers to trial. "Anti-labor" hisses were heard as soon as the indictments were announced, and howls of "union-busting" drowned out Hogan's previous reputation for racket-busting.

Who was Joseph Fay? On paper, he was the fourth vice president of a relatively small union in Newark, New Jersey—the International Union of Operating Engineers. Actually, Joe Fay was the union's brass-knuckled boss, the shakedown czar of building trades from the Atlantic to the Mississippi.

His union jurisdiction gave him leverage to exact tribute from virtually every steamshovel and crane operator working construction sites along the Eastern seaboard. Hogan concentrated on the biggest of these construction jobs, the $4-million Delaware aqueduct water-supply project. On the strength of evidence gathered by Hogan's Rackets Bureau, Fay and his scar-faced confederate James Bove, international vice president of the Hod Carriers, Building and Common Laborers Union of America, went on trial in February 1945, charged with conspiracy to extort $703,000 from contractors on the aqueduct job.

A man of minimal illusions, Hogan knew how much he was stretching his jurisdictional authority by extending it across the river to New Jersey. Fay boasted that Jersey politicians were his "asshole buddies." The indictment was certainly an embarrassment to the Acting Governor of the Garden State, who had publicly hailed Fay as "a real force in American life." And Jersey City Mayor Frank ("I am the law") Hague once sent a band of police bagpipers down to welcome Big Joey ashore from a chartered boat ride to and from Europe. Jersey was Fay's turf—his infiltration of weaker unions went so deep, his activities were so well hidden, his mouthpiece attorneys so well paid with union funds, that it took fourteen months of pre-trial investigation and a three-year struggle up to the U.S. Supreme Court to put him away.

When the trial finally opened, the menace of Fay's underworld clout was so strong that fifty blue-ribbon jurors filed excuses not to serve in the case. Hogan, battered by anti-labor epithets, apologized for the presence of so few workingmen on the jury: "Workmen are out earning $10 a day. They don't want to be tied up for weeks at $3 a day." To leftist editorial writers, the explanation wasn't good enough. Hogan's popularity diminished as Fay's image as "labor martyr" grew.

Martyrdom was the last thing anybody expected of Big Joey Fay. Beneath his gruff exterior there was a gruff interior. His temper and drinking habits had made him the scourge of bartenders and waiters in Newark. Sometimes, full of whiskey and enraged, he used his fists on waitresses if they didn't jump when he snapped his fingers. Once, he slugged the AFL's David Dubinsky with brass knuckles; another time, he kicked in a minor labor leader's cheekbone.

Nobody ever kicked back.

While many of Fay's union members were themselves on relief in bad times, their leader squandered as much as $50,000 a night in Atlantic City gambling casinos. Union funds bought him a new Cadillac every year, and a chauffeur to go with it. The union financed an opulent mansion in Newark, and an endless supply of booze and expensive floozies.

At the trial, contractors testified to what Fay gave the membership in return: "scabs" who showed up for work on the "black-listed" aqueduct job were attacked by Fay's hired goons. When a local union hall refused to play ball with Fay, he used money from the contractors to hire thugs to smash the hall. The contractors were then summoned to hotel rooms where Big Joey asked them for big sums to prevent a recurrence of such "labor troubles."

Seated at the defense table, the fifty-four-year-old Fay and his sidekick Bove sneered as Hogan, his voice somber, began: "Labor is not on trial here." He went on to say who *was* on trial:

"These men are business partners in crime, and the business of the partnership is extortion . . . they are shakedown artists—ruthless, grasping thieves who have lined their pockets at the expense of the laboring man they represent."

Giving what was, indeed, the court performance of his life, the D.A. declared: "They had the power to ruin the contractors. It would have made no difference if they had used a gun." Dramatic pause. "I have more respect for a robber who uses a gun because at least he takes a chance! These men took no chances: they double-crossed labor."

After deliberating for fifteen hours, the jury found the pair guilty, but Fay stayed free on appeals until 1947, when he was finally sentenced to from seven and a half to fifteen years in Sing Sing.

Prison doors slammed on Big Joey Fay, but the world of labor racketeering was not shut out. That world came to him. Mayors, state senators, a former U.S. Senator, union and big-business executives, all came to his Sing Sing cell to pay homage, seek favors, get things fixed that only an empire builder like Fay could get fixed. But at least he was in jail— and gradually his power ebbed. Hogan could do no more.

The District Attorney next turned the Rackets Bureau's attention to an almost limitless source of illicit business in New York City—the Big Apple's own municipal departments, Fire, Sanitation, Hospitals, Building and Housing, Board of Education. Students of home-grown law enforcement had always suspected the city's departments were up to their necks in graft.

The opportunities for corruption were irresistible. All these departments hired inspectors to issue permits and check for regulatory-code violations. Millions of dollar's worth of permits were issued yearly. Everyone from a pushcart peddler to Aristotle Onassis needed some kind of license to do business in Manhattan. Restaurateurs, saloon owners, fashion retailers, building tradesmen, engineers, landlords—all were easy marks for official shakedown artists. For a fee, building inspectors would look the other way while investigating a broken elevator or a defective oil burner. Fire inspectors could fatten their bankbooks by approving faulty electrical installations. Sanitation patrolmen, rather than quarantining rat-infested tenements, could wink at slumlords and accept payoffs.

Unlike in a robbery or rape case, there was no complaining witness. Both parties were happy with the illegal arrangement. The slumlord felt he could avoid high-cost renovation work by forking over a $50 or $100 payoff, so he was getting a good return on his investment. The private contractor, "expediting" his architectural plans with a bribe, shrugged it off as the cost of doing business with the city.

A "sign-off" approval was required on virtually every phase of a city construction job—from architectural plans to final paint job. Permits were required for electrical work, plumbing, cement pouring, elevator installation and a thousand other jobs. An inspector might encounter a newly erected wall and question whether the electrical wiring behind the wall was in compliance with the building code: "Perhaps we ought to tear down that wall and check behind it." It was only a matter of time before the construction supervisor meekly inquired, "Can't we talk about this?"

To "talk about" violations meant overlooking them in return for payoffs that could total $10,000 for a single skyscraper.

Tradition held that there was one taboo usually upheld in the Buildings Department: an inspector never took money to overlook major violations, structural flaws, construction shortcuts that could actually collapse a building. Yet some men would do that, and when they did, it was called "leaving a monument"—presumably a pile of brick.

Infiltrating the corrupt marketplace of mutually acceptable bribe-giving and receiving was difficult. The conspiracy of silence would be broken only when a deal went sour. Hearing of a double-cross, Hogan showed little sympathy for the bribe-giver.

"It takes two to tango," he'd say, insisting on equal punishment for the bribe-giver and bribe-taker alike.

Some shakedown victims, fearing official reprisals, camouflaged the graft payments in their accounts or destroyed records altogether. Many restaurant and saloon owners kept two sets of books: one for themselves, one to show Hogan's ledger sleuths when and if subpoenas were issued.

The man who headed Hogan's counter-camouflage corps was Alfred Scotti—next to Hogan, the most feared career prosecutor in New York City. Scotti was named Chief of the Rackets Bureau in 1947 and in 1953 became Chief Assistant—next in line for the title "Mr. District Attorney." The dual responsibility gave Scotti direct control of investigations, a base of authority upon which he built an incredible record as a trial lawyer. His persuasiveness with juries was such that after taking over the Rackets Bureau, he lost only one case and suffered only a single reversal on appeal.

A peppery little man with a toothbrush mustache, Scotti epitomized the fundamentalist school of crime fighting. He believed in the "criminal mentality" and the brotherhood of crime. The enemies of human decency were "the crooks." Prosecutors were "the good guys." Life was a constant struggle between the two.

"To me, it always seems out of character when a crook commits suicide," Scotti once told the author. "Essentially, crooks are optimists. They think they can get away with it."

As had Hogan, Scotti began his career on Special Prosecutor Dewey's staff. He himself carried the rackets-busting mystique of the 1930s into the 1950s and '60s. During those latter years, Hogan, a more subtle thinker, became sensitized to the socioeconomic values of organized crime—the American entrepreneurial pursuit of personal profit and instant gratification at the expense of human equity. He became a convert, if gradually, to Chief Justice Earl Warren's theory of the criminal law as a humanitarian instrument, flexible enough to effect social change rather than simply wield punishment.

Scotti brooked no sympathy for the wrong-doer. He claimed to find modern parallels of greed and mayhem in the classic works of Cicero, St. Augustine and Cellini: "I am constantly struck by how little moral or spiritual progress has been made between those times and our own." Scotti's singlemindedness gave him the air of the Holy Avenger. He viewed the law as "a wonderful weapon." A frail, almost sparrowlike man in spectacles, he wielded that weapon with pleasure—and took delight in discovering new wrinkles in organized crime: "Hoooeee! Bootleg stereo cassettes. Tape pirates are re-recording ten-dollar Frank Sinatra cassettes at three for a dollar, duplicating cheap labels and bootlegging them back to the record stores at ten bucks apiece. *Everybody's* getting ripped off!"

Whenever mobsters of Italian origin turned up on the witness stand, Scotti felt shamed and betrayed. He was always on edge dealing with his fellow Italian-Americans. He may even have been sterner than usual when a young fellow named Rocco Barbella came before him.

Barbella was better known in the boxing world as Rocky Graziano.

Graziano, the clown prince of prizefighting, adored by late-night TV audiences in later years, met Scotti in 1946, when the prizefighter called off a scheduled middleweight bout with Reuben (Cowboy) Shank. Graziano had pleaded a sore back. But Scotti suspected that somebody was working on him with more than Sloan's Liniment: a confidential source had already tipped the D.A.'s office that there had been a bold plan to fix the fight.

Probing into the matter, Scotti learned that the slugger's life had been threatened by a "mysterious stranger" who had popped into the champ's dressing room at Stillman's Gym. This stranger, flashing smart money like neon, offered the pug-faced Graziano $100,000 if he would assume a restful position on the canvas sometime after the buzzer sounded in the Shank fight. Rocky's only reply had been, "I'll see ya later."

When the slugger was finally called down to the D.A.'s office ("Wha' happened? Did I pass a red light again?"), Scotti told him matter-of-factly, "I'm glad you didn't go through with it, Rocky." There was no specific reference to what he had in mind. Graziano played it cute:

"Hey, *paisan!* Gimme a break, will ya? When I say 'I'll see ya,' it's just my way of givin' dese wise guys da brush-off."

Paisan was the wrong word to use with Scotti. Any suggestion that he, Scotti, who read Cicero and Cellini, would play favorites with some pizza-parlor punk off the streets of Little Italy was offensive. Scotti tore into Graziano's explanation: "You mean to tell me a fellow comes in and offers you a hundred grand and you don't even know the guy's name? Isn't it true you called the fight off because these fellows were betting against you and you didn't want to double-cross them? Didn't you know they had money bet all over the country?"

Scotti pounded away, but the rope-weary Graziano refused to name the fixers ("Gee, Mac, I don't wanna get nobody in trouble.") He did admit he knew certain people in the fight mob ("How could I help knowing them? Dey come from my old neighborhood, da Lower East Side.")

Graziano survived the sparring match, but not without injury to his pocketbook. His boxing license was revoked for three years—"failure to report a bribe offer to the State Athletic Commission." And he never forgot what it had been like to meet with Scotti: "Before he got through with me," the slugger recalled, "he made me feel I'd been knocked out ten times by Tony Zale."

Scotti's professional credo may have been inspired by the language of Cellini and Cicero, but he was given to using—and mixing up—the clichés of an American baseball umpire: "We call them as we see them," he told each new grand jury. "And let the chips fall where they may."

No man to wait for crime to come to him, Scotti went out hunting for it. In the late 1940s his sharp eye lit upon the J & B Contracting Company, which he suspected was shortchanging the city's hospitals with shoddy paint jobs—approved by city inspectors. But how? The company's accounts did not fudge the usual "entertainment expenses" and other dodges with which graft is usually hidden. Scotti became convinced that the company was cheating by applying only one coat of paint and billing the hospitals for two.

He proceeded to City Hall with his information, only to be told: "We've received the same complaint. But we can't think of a way to distinguish a primary coat of paint from a finishing coat."

"Can't think of a way, hell," snorted Scotti. "Hasn't anybody around here ever heard of *field* work?"

He proceeded next day, wearing the overalls of a painter, to one of the hospitals being refurbished by J & B. Lugging bucket and brush past the information desk, Scotti found a dropclothed area and a crew to join. He passed himself off as a new man arriving late on the job and somehow managed to seem professional long enough to learn, in casual conversation, what he'd come to find out: you can spot a shoddy paint job by the "holidays." A holiday turned out to be painter's jargon for a nearly invisible missed spot. The law of averages dictates that a workman who applies a second coat of paint will seldom if ever miss the same spot twice.

To search for "holidays," Scotti came back after the work day with a magnifying glass and found enough missed spots to verify that J & B's was indeed a once-over-lightly racket.

The paint scandal broke. Company officials and city inspectors who had passed on their work were indicted. Scotti "turned" witnesses, one by one, to testify. He planned to wind up the investigation with an important but as yet unturned J & B foreman named Libratorre. Libratorre couldn't be budged from his insistence that two coats of paint were always applied. Scotti went to reinspect a paint job and took the foreman with him. Inside the hospital, Scotti whipped out his magnifying lens. "Was this spot missed?" he demanded. No answer. "Did you miss it twice?" Still no answer. "Listen. You're only victimizing your fellow workers by your silence. None of you will be able to find work if this matter isn't cleared up." Scotti resorted to further interrogation in Italian: *"Se non parla, meti i tuoi colleghe in pericolo."*

Libratorre stared in bewilderment at his accuser as Scotti brandished the classic prop of detective work, magnifying the holidays one by one.

"Well?" Scotti shouted. *"Beh, perche non mi rispondi?"*—Why don't you answer me?

Libratorre dropped to his knees then, almost sobbing: "I'm Greek!"

The Rackets Bureau casebook continually provided exceptions to the axiom that there are no new crimes under the sun. New industries, new sources of revenue, would *always* stimulate new crimes. Soon after World War II's G.I. Bill of Rights was passed, for example, Hogan discovered systematic swindling: non-student veterans were submitting fraudulent bills amounting to millions for "books and tuition."

Also after the war, nonscheduled charter flights, brought about by a surplus of propeller planes and skilled pilots, provided a catch-as-catch-can service that met the requirements of the ordinary pocketbook. But Hogan soon found himself confronted by group after group of college students stranded in New York City as their prepaid charter flights to Europe were mysteriously canceled. The Bureau prosecuted several slick operators who passed themselves off as brokers for the "nonsked" carriers, then took the students' money and ran.

To detail all the Hogan-Scotti exposés of tax irregularities and real-estate abuses in the postwar housing boom would be to write another book. In one case alone, Hogan and Scotti themselves analyzed more than 3,000 tax-reduction cases and questioned more than 600 witnesses before the grand jury. To retain so many facts and figures, they exercised the memory skills of a data bank. The investigation directly affected the city's borrowing power by revealing that fully half of the tax assessors assigned to the Manhattan Tax Commission office were improperly influenced by real-estate owners who were seeking reductions in the valuations assessed against their properties.

The postwar era led to Hogan exposés that became national scandals: the black-market sale of unwanted babies to foster parents; fake charity rackets; the hot securities market; counterfeit unionism.

Scotti served as factotum of the monarch—always there when Hogan needed him, an interlocutor who argued the cases in court. Hogan pinch-hit for Scotti just once after the Fay-Bove trial. The case centered on Frank Erickson, the so-called "King of American Bookmakers."

Frank Erickson was a man ahead of his time. He was the first American gambling entrepreneur to streamline the crude telephone-bet system, clearing his books by mail and paying customers' obligations by check— an innovation copied many years later by New York's parimutuel Off-Track Betting Corporation.

Erickson's operation was so profitable that when professional bookies from Nevada and other states were occasionally overloaded on a particular horse, they could lay off any part of their bet with Erickson. Though Erickson was notorious, he had never spent a day in jail. Those in the gambling underworld made it 30 to 1 he never would.

The fat, blubbery-lipped betting tycoon's annual turnover came to $10 million. In April 1950, he boasted to a Senate committee that he had been a bookmaker for thirty years, handling $20,000 to $40,000 in bets every day. He operated out of telephone headquarters in Bergen County, New Jersey, an anything-goes jurisdiction famous as a sanctuary for the underworld. Across the river from the long arm of Hogan's law, Erickson felt out of reach.

But Hogan watched and waited—and made countless efforts to assemble a dossier on Erickson's New York clientele. Discreet inquiries were conducted at the National Democratic Club in New York and at some of the posher dinner hangouts where Erickson would always have reserved the best table. Surveillance of his own customers revealed that many were respectable businessmen, equally guilty at any moral tribunal, but personally subscribing to the idea that gambling was sport, not crime.

Hogan hated high-stakes gambling. He felt that the inevitable payoffs contributed to police corruption, and that the racketeers also subsidized more serious crimes, such as narcotics traffic. At the same time, Hogan was aware of the case for legalized gambling, and governmental hypocrisy in trying to control it.

Hogan himself played poker. On Sunday afternoons, when his staff wound up its six-and-a-half-day work week, Hogan, Scotti and the rest of the gang would unwind with an office game of high-low. No one ever lost more than $30. Because of his own light interest in the game, and simple common sense, Hogan had no desire to harass small-fry bettors. He wanted to nail the kingfish.

Over the years, trying to stretch his jurisdictional foothold into Erickson's Jersey swamp, Hogan tried everything: wiretapping, undercover infiltration, harassment charges of "loitering." Erickson had an edge: money. He hired expensive, adept legal counsel, and he sidestepped every ruse. But the "Kingfish" made a mistake when he thumbed his nose at Hogan from the Jersey side.

His boasts of corporate success proved his undoing. Erickson became increasingly loose-lipped before a Senate committee, thinking it could not touch him either, and he let slip the fact that he kept an account at the Pennsylvania Exchange Bank. He must not have realized a crucial fact: the main office of the Pennsylvania Exchange Bank was not in Pennsylvania. The office was in Manhattan. And so was Frank Hogan.

When the bank opened next morning, Hogan's accountants were impatiently shuffling on the doorstep. Armed with grand-jury subpoenas, they pored over the Erickson account. They suffered an initial letdown.

The account looked innocent—an innocuous record of Erickson's legitimate affairs: rent payments, charity contributions. Then the D.A.'s men looked further. The subpoenas were couched in language inclusive enough to allow the team to dig into any accounts at the bank held under the names of Erickson's business cronies. One such account was discovered under the name of an "employee": Harry Richards.

There was no Harry Richards. A dummy account! Now, the file yielded its evidence: canceled checks identifying Erickson's well-heeled clients. Now, the high-rollers would have to testify to their personal dealings with the Mr. Big of bookiedom when he stood trial. There were documents that revealed Erickson's partnership in Florida gambling casinos with Joe Adonis and Meyer Lansky, the "Jewish Godfather." Other documents recorded oil-well deals with Frank Costello and George Uffner, who had been a gambling protégé of Arnold Rothstein's. Erickson's tidy corporate management system could at last be destroyed.

Hogan wanted to be the one to shut the case, and he arrived in Justice Nathan D. Perlman's courtroom on June 19, 1950, for the showdown. The weight of evidence, along with the announcement that the D.A. would try the case himself, convinced defense attorney Sol Gelb, Hogan's old prosecutorial buddy from the Dewey days, that there was no point in bucking such heavy odds.

Hogan nodded to Gelb. Gelb nodded to Hogan. Erickson stood up, perspiring heavily in the muggy courtroom. Erickson nodded to the judge. There were sixty counts of bookmaking and conspiracy against him. Fat Frank pleaded guilty to every one of them. He was sentenced to two years in prison, and fined $30,000. Judge Perlman warned him that if he ever went back into business, he'd also go back into a jail cell.

By declining to stand trial, Erickson took the rap for his clientele. To the touts, the turf accountants, and his own nervous bettors, the King of Bookmakers had proved himself a stand-up guy. But across the Hudson, Frank Hogan could look out his office windows and feel content. In this case, he'd been the long-shot winner.

Shortly after Scotti took over the Rackets Bureau in 1947, he bounced into Hogan's office one morning with another "long-shot" case, involving gambling of a different sort. A young man, a George Washington University law student who was co-captain of the school's basketball team, had come to Scotti's office with a story.

The student, David Shapiro, had been working as a counselor in an upstate boys' camp that past summer. A letter arrived one day from a stranger, Joseph Aronowitz. The letter urged Shapiro to telephone the writer as soon as he got back to New York City. Returning home in September, Shapiro called Aronowitz and agreed to a get-together where they could "discuss basketball games." The meeting took place, but all Aronowitz wanted to discuss was "the point spread," the margin of victory upon which baseball, football and basketball bets are based.

Hogan was aghast. He recognized, of course, that sports betting had long been a way of life to millions of respectable Americans—there's hardly a business office or a factory crew in the land that hasn't set up its own basketball or football pool at some time or other. Compared with horse racing, in which gambling has a takeout of 15 percent, the bookie's 5 percent commission on sports betting seems small. And the chances of picking a winner are much better. As any Las Vegas analyst will tell you today, the combined proceeds of church bingo, horse racing and casino gambling can't approach the sports action on a single weekend of televised baseball, football and basketball. Unlike horseplayers, heavy sports bettors do their homework. Their willingness to "bet the mortgage" is traditionally based on an edge—insider's information culled from record books, weather forecasts and player injury reports from trainers and team physicians.

Hogan knew that gamblers often infiltrated college locker rooms to get chummy with the players. But the possibility of enticing them into dishonest point-shaving—a fumbled rebound or a muffed jump-shot in the final seconds of play—seemed utterly unthinkable.

David Shapiro agreed to work undercover for the Rackets Bureau. His mission: make himself an easy mark for Aronowitz and other gamblers who would be under observation by the D.A.'s men. Scotti himself posed, over the telephone, as the athlete's uncle, instructing him on what to do next as a widening ring of bookies and hustlers surrounded the basketball star between games in New York, Washington and Miami.

Eventually, Shapiro arranged to "accept" a $1,000 point-shaving offer. The game was scheduled for Madison Square Garden. The money would guarantee his team's defeat by Manhattan College. The point spread was ten. If George Washington University lost by more than ten points, the man who put his money on the team would win. Instructions to Shapiro were: "Play your best game for three quarters. In the fourth quarter, watch the scoreboard. If it's close, dump a few rebounds and keep your shots away from the rim."

In a tense pre-game meeting near the Garden, the gamblers agreed to turn over the money to Shapiro's "uncle," this time a Manhattan detective. Other detectives closed in as the money changed hands. The fixers surrendered. They ultimately pleaded guilty and were sentenced to prison terms. Scotti thereafter kept a keen eye on the point spreads of virtually every collegiate and professional game from season to season, carefully scrutinizing upset victories.

In 1951, the office detected another pattern of under-the-table "coffee money" paid to college stars who had dumped games by giving less than their best efforts. The master fixer was Salvatore Sollazzo, a neighbor of mobster Frank Costello's in a luxurious Central Park West apartment building. Sollazzo received eight to sixteen years for corrupting fifteen basketball stars.

Among the indicted athletes was superstar Sherman White of Long Island University. Scotti had spearheaded the investigation, but his point-blank style of interrogation bounced off White, who refused to talk. Hogan's manner was one of ingratiating warmth. Left alone with White, Hogan the sports fanatic reminisced about his own athletic career at dear old Columbia.

Hogan trotted out all the Knute Rockne platitudes. He spoke of the "purity of sport." He explained how White could help himself as well as his teammates by spilling the whole story. The D.A. communicated such kindness that White's beanstalk physique began to tremble and his eyelids moistened. Hogan too began to bawl. The accused and his accuser had a good cry together. Then the basketball center made a clean breast of it and implicated the others.

Hogan had all the guilty players arrested and jailed. Then he made a remarkable appearance on television to warn other college players who might consider throwing games for gamblers:

"I fervently wish that any person who is so tempted could have seen these young persons when they admitted their guilt; tears, remorse, self-reproach, the scalding thoughts of the perpetual heartache their disgrace had caused mother, father and loved ones . . ." Suddenly, before a nationwide TV audience, Mr. District Attorney, worshipper of college sports, dissolved in tears again and had to swallow hard through the rest of his speech.

Sentences were suspended for most of the players, but White and another received six-month to one-year penitentiary terms.

The New York basketball scandal caused out-of-state college teams to raise their hands in horror. Players of the Bradley University team in Peoria, Illinois, for instance, righteously spurned an invitation to play in a National Invitational Tournament at Madison Square Garden. Coach Adolph Rupp of the University of Kentucky sanctimoniously observed that New York gamblers "couldn't touch my boys with a ten-foot pole."

Well. Three months later, Hogan revealed that a fixer named Eli Klukofsky, apprehended outside a nightclub in Miami, had left a trail of person-to-person phone calls to Peoria and Toledo, Ohio, during the 1950–51 season. Hogan's investigators checked the toll slip dates and discovered that each call corresponded to a game day on the basketball schedule of Bradley University and Toledo University. Hogan's men booked flights to the Midwest, bought tickets for the games, and studied each contest for dubious outcomes or sudden shifts in the pre-game betting odds. Development of these leads led to the exposure of score rigging by Bradley and Toledo players, and ultimately to Nicholas Englisis, a one-time University of Kentucky football player who had returned to the Kentucky campus in 1948 to sound out the possibilities of rigging basketball games. He induced two of Coach Rupp's varsity athletes, Ralph Beard and Alex Groza, both All-Americans and former members of the U.S. Olympic Team, to shave points.

The trio's original bankroll of $350 yielded more than $8,000 in winnings by the time the Invitational came to Madison Square Garden that season. The prospects for a real killing were excellent.

Englisis talked the Bradley five into rigging a scheduled game with Bowling Green for a price of $500 each. Everything went like clockwork until the closing seconds of play, when a Bradley substitute, unaware of the plot, sank a jumpshot and ruined the point spread. The Englisis trio was wiped out by the fiasco, and there were no payoffs.

In the face of accumulated evidence, men from the D.A.'s office traveled to Lexington for the start of a lengthy extradition battle; it involved University of Kentucky trustees and the Governor of the state. There were cries of "Yankee invasion," but Hogan succeeded in bringing several Kentucky players before a New York County Grand Jury—along with Coach Rupp, who now allowed that point-shaving was less reprehensible than outright dumping.

Despite Hogan's revelations, there were very few signs of moral awakening in the sports world. (A city official of Wilkes-Barre, Pennsylvania, wrote to Hogan asking how soon Sherman White would be out of jail, as he wanted to hire him for a professional team.) As the big business of scouting college athletes accelerated, the fixers were two steps behind the scouts.

By 1960, Scotti had amassed volumes of wiretap transcripts and "KG" (short for "known gambler") files on suspected fixers. The prime fixers, of course, were the colleges themselves. In many cases, a college awarded "scholarships" not to earnest students but to muscle-brained "phys. ed." majors who had trouble spelling even the word "basketball." Their scholarships amounted to under-the-counter paychecks.

Following Scotti's leads, assistant D.A. Peter Andreoli, a senior staff member who later became chief of the Supreme Court Bureau, spent two years investigating college basketball—and then lifted the lid on five years of corruption in the sport. (It could have been worse; the statute of limitations had already run out on crimes committed before 1955.)

The second major basketball-fix scandal broke into banner headlines over the winter of 1960–61, and it quickly sparked other investigations. At the height of the inquiry, Andreoli had detectives working in fifty cities in twenty-five states. More than 200 college ball players from all over the country booked flights to New York—and these weren't field trips. Plainclothesmen picked up the athletes at airports, and threaded their way back down through Manhattan traffic in unmarked cars. One by one, the players were spirited into Hogan's office for questioning. These players were never prosecuted, but their "innocence" was left open to question.

"The insidious part of it was the atmosphere of bribe-taking created by the college athletic departments," Andreoli recalled in later years, explaining his decision to "go after the fixers" and use the players merely as witnesses against them. "The atmosphere began when the kid was recruited out of high school. Twenty different scouts would fly the player and his family from one school to another, each college trying to outdo the other with lavish dinner parties and salary offers for no-show after-school jobs.

"Most of these kids didn't even belong in college. I asked one 'honor student' what his major was. He says, 'Numbers.' I said, 'Whaddya mean, numbers?' He says, 'Well, you know—plus and minus.' I said, 'You mean mathematics?' He says, 'Yeah, that's the word. I couldn't think of it.' "

By the time the inquiry had' ended, thirty-eight players at twenty-two colleges had been implicated in shaving points over five seasons. "Think of it," said the jowly Andreoli. "There are only a hundred major colleges listed on the point spread. Nearly one-fourth of the teams were shaving points. And that's just one investigation from the little island of Manhattan. I've been disillusioned with basketball ever since."

Each morning during the basketball probe, Andreoli remembered, Frank Hogan would drop by the Rackets Bureau with a worried look. Each morning, he would ask the same question: "Is it coming close to Columbia yet?" The day Andreoli had to nod, "Yes," Hogan suffered total disillusionment. Not only had his adored alma mater been betrayed, but the man suspected as the master fixer was a former Columbia All-American, a Hogan hero.

Six-foot five-inch Jacob "Jack" Molinas had somehow escaped detection in the basketball fixes of the 1950s. Andreoli learned that Molinas had been fixing scores at Columbia only since graduating and becoming a star rookie with the Fort Wayne (now Detroit) Pistons in 1954. Soon thereafter, Andreoli learned that Molinas was "betting on himself," a useful phrase for dumping pro contests. NBA officials called Molinas on the carpet. Although there was never any evidence to prove it, league insiders said that Molinas confessed. The player denied it. He was suspended for life anyway.

Molinas was bounced off one court, but landed in another. No dummy, he enrolled at Brooklyn Law night school, breezed past his bar exams, and in 1957, hung out his shingle in Manhattan. "The sharpest-looking, fastest-talking patent-leather con-man lawyer in the United States," as Andreoli called him, was soon earning $25,000 a year as a whiplash lawyer, specializing in personal-injury cases.

Molinas was a walking encyclopedia of basketball statistics. He knew the key players on every team. He was still working the angles, jockeying to win.

Midway through the basketball inquiry, in January 1962, Dennis William Reed, a Bowling Green player, was flown to New York for questioning. Reed was accompanied to Newark airport by a New York City detective. From the airport, the detective phoned Andreoli: "You'll never guess who showed up to meet us when the plane landed. Jack Molinas! He says he's representing Reed."

"Put Mr. Molinas on the phone," Andreoli ordered. When Molinas picked up the receiver, the prosecutor let him have it: "You're the target of this investigation! I direct you to have this witness in court tomorrow morning."

That night, Molinas took Reed to a midtown hotel room and pressured the player into signing a two-page affidavit. In it Reed states: ". . . I never accepted any money, or any promise of any money, from Mr. Molinas, directly or indirectly, or from anyone, not to do my best in any athletic contest in which I participated."

What Molinas didn't know was that Reed had been "wired" by the Rackets Bureau. "Like Watergate, it was the coverup that gave us the corroborative evidence to make the case." Andreoli chuckled in recollection. "As a matter of law, we had no case and Molinas would have gone scot-free if he hadn't tried to cover his tracks."

On March 17, 1962, Hogan announced a five-count indictment against Molinas, charging him with conspiracy to bribe twenty-two players from twelve colleges to shave points in twenty-five games. The jury returned a guilty verdict on all five counts. Bounced off to Sing Sing, for a ten-to-fifteen year prison term, Molinas was already dribbling into position for another clutch play—an early release. He cooperated with authorities in an abortive probe of harness-race fixing and scored a parole after serving only four years.

The basketball scandal went down in Hogan's book of memories as the "most heart-wrenching case of my professional career." For millions of sports fans, it was a sour revelation. To the U.S. Congress, it was a national disgrace, leading to the passage of laws that now make basketball fixing a federal crime.

For Jack Molinas, it was only the beginning. He moved to Los Angeles after his parole in 1968 and began financing his gambling ventures with investments in the fur industry, 16 mm pornographic movies, and the Indian shrimp market. In 1974, his business partner, Bernard Gusoff, was beaten to death. The murder was never solved. The police said they went to question Molinas at his $60,000 home, but were chased away by three barking dogs. The detectives had wanted to question Molinas about the $500,000 he collected from an insurance policy he held on the life of his deceased partner. The policemen never knocked twice.

In the early-morning hours of August 3, 1975, Molinas heard noises in the back yard. Leaving a luscious "playmate" warm in bed, Molinas strolled outside. There, among the eucalyptus and lemon trees of Hollywood Hills, he listened to the cicadas. The girl got dressed and came outside to join him. Then, from the bushes, a shot. The girl screamed. The basketball fixer fell dead, a sniper's bullet lodged in his gifted, busy brain.

"He just loved to be a hustler," a friend said after the funeral.

"Yeah, we find a few dead pornographers now and then," remarked a federal investigator. "It's not a question of whether Jack had any mob connections. The only question is which mob and which connection."

6
THE UNPOLITICIAN

If there was one person in 1948 who understood better than Frank Hogan the ways of evildoing at the municipal back door, that person was New York City Mayor William O'Dwyer. Hogan had the criminal investigator's comprehension of the problem: suspicious evidence. O'Dwyer had something more: an insider's view.

Common gossip had long singled out James J. Moran as a symbol of O'Dwyer's corrupt regime. When the Mayor appointed his friend Deputy Fire Commissioner, Moran proceeded to organize a shakedown racket that victimized almost every city contractor installing oil burners and storage tanks. This systematic extortion netted Moran an estimated $500,000 a year.

The growing clamor for an end to the scandals of O'Dwyer's first-term administration left O'Dwyer himself dangling on a political string. Hogan's exposés were killing him. In the course of one investigation—a phony "Fireman's Ball"—the president of the Uniformed Fireman's Association, John P. Crane, was granted immunity from prosecution so that he could testify before the grand jury. Crane did testify. He swore that he had given Mayor O'Dwyer $10,000 in cash on the steps of Gracie Mansion as "evidence of support" from the UFA. Crane further testified that, over a period of three years, he had transmitted a total of $55,000 as a token of "good will" to the Mayor's friend, Deputy Commissioner Moran.

The only vital question that remained to be asked in Democratic circles was who O'Dwyer's successor might be. The Mayor himself suggested a candidate by inviting Frank Hogan over to City Hall one after-noon for a heart-to-heart chat.

The ritual pleasantries over with, O'Dwyer got down to apparent busi-ness. "Come here, Frank," he said, ushering Hogan by the elbow to the big leather swivel chair behind the Mayor's desk. "Now," O'Dwyer said with a ham actor's flourish, "sit down and test the Mayor's chair out for size."

Hogan sank into the leather upholstery. O'Dwyer spun him around: a kid getting his first joyride in a barber's chair.

Hogan swiveled and laughed—he had no inkling that he was in for what he later called "the biggest double-cross in New York political his-tory."

O'Dwyer announced in September 1948 that he was "definitely" out of the running for reelection, vowing that he would "take no part" in the selection of a successor. Hogan's name had come up in Tammany Hall, and with three of the five city Democratic bosses supporting him, the nomination seemed within his grasp. If Hogan accepted it, he was a shoo-in to win the election. He could plunk himself down in the Mayor's chair for more than a joyride.

At first, the only serious opposition to Hogan's candidacy came from Representative Franklin D. Roosevelt, Jr., son of the former President. F.D.R., Jr., bore a serious grudge against the District Attorney. In 1944, Hogan had been a delegate to the National Democratic Convention that nominated Franklin D. Roosevelt for a third term. When Roosevelt's name came up on the ballot, Hogan walked off the floor and surrendered his vote to an alternate. This display of devotion to his old boss, Dewey—the Republican standardbearer who was found to oppose F.D.R. in the general election—struck young Roosevelt as outright betrayal.

Other delegates regarded it with more kindness—a "misguided sense of Irish loyalty," as one expressed it. Only a few skeptics saw the act as a self-serving political maneuver: there was talk that if Dewey got into the White House, Hogan would be named to replace FBI Director J. Edgar Hoover.

Hogan's short "walk" for Dewey left him branded an "anti-New Dealer" by Roosevelt. Five years later, in 1949, F.D.R., Jr. sided with the two county leaders, Bronx boss Edward J. Flynn and Borough President John Cashmore of Brooklyn, who refused to support Hogan's mayoral candidacy.

At a July 12 meeting of the county Democratic leaders, Hogan's spon-sor, interim Tammany chief Hugo Rogers, pledged to support Hogan if

O'Dwyer was still out of the running. But as late as 11:00 A.M. the same day, O'Dwyer was still playing peek-a-boo with the bosses, demanding that they "get wise to themselves" and pick a "successor" immediately.

O'Dwyer's strategy was obvious. He considered Hogan's candidacy nothing but a wedge, carefully driven between the bosses to create internal friction while O'Dwyer himself offered party unity. The bosses must get together to support him at once, or face a chaotic primary battle over the nomination.

The plan boomeranged—Hogan received the nomination anyway. Rogers of Manhattan, James A. Roe of Queens and Staten Island boss Jeremiah A. Roe all voted for him. Bosses Flynn and Cashmore refused to cast a ballot. When Rogers returned to his office, he found an urgent message: "Call O'Dwyer at Gracie Mansion." Nearly a quarter of a century later, Rogers recounted the scene for the author:

"O'Dwyer was boiling mad," Rogers recalled. "He was almost inarticulate with rage—lambasting Tammany and carrying on about me as if I was some kind of poison snake.

"I said, 'Fella, this is your own doing. You've been telling me you're not going to run again. I played it on the level with you. Now, if you want to start playing games, you've got the wrong man. You start banging me on the head and I'm gonna get a baseball bat!' "

The next day, Rogers learned that Judge John Mullen, who had arranged Hogan's nomination, had spent half the night arguing with O'Dwyer at Gracie Mansion. O'Dwyer tried to convince Mullen that Hogan should resign. Meanwhile, the Tammany designation had already been announced in the morning papers. O'Dwyer accused the leaders of a "squeeze play" against him. In the midst all of this confusion, Rogers' home telephone rang with another urgent call.

"This is Frank Hogan." Hogan had just talked to his old mentor, Judge Mullen. Perhaps it would be better if the District Attorney sidestepped the mayoralty offer? "I don't want to start up a ruckus in the organization," Hogan said. "It would just lead to some nasty primary fights."

Rogers was stunned. The Tammany sachem hadn't expected an eleventh-hour letdown. He pleaded with Hogan to stay in the race. Call the Mayor's bluff. "That guy won't bite!" Rogers huffed. "He's just volatile. Honestly, Frank, I don't know what the hell's in that jerk's mind. He's completely unpredictable. I've heard him make a speech that would charm the ears off a jackass, then turn around and cut a guy's heart out, just for the hell of it. If you hold your ground another eight hours, I'll guarantee it—he'll back away from you. I'm the county leader, dammit. I want to show everybody I can have this thing if I want it!"

Hogan seemed serene. He'd made a private decision—the lies and double-dealing and fractured egos that went into the making of a Mayor were not for him.

"I'm sorry to be acting like a reluctant debutante," he told Hugo. "But I suppose I love my job too much to give it up for this kind of thing."

"You don't have to give it up," Rogers insisted. "Just give it eight more hours. If you stay in the race, you'll have the nomination. You get the nomination and you'll run away with the election!"

Hugo Rogers went on to paint a triumphant picture of Frank Hogan as Mayor, rooting out the corruption of city departments, sweeping O'Dwyer's flunkies out of City Hall, restoring the Criminal Courthouse to a temple of justice. His pleading was in vain. Hogan said his dropout decision was final.

"I was double-crossed," he kept repeating, his voice trailing off. Rogers finally understood. He was wasting his breath on someone who refused to act like a politician. "Frank," he said before hanging up, "you would have made a damn good Mayor."

Ten years later, in the spring of 1958, Frank Hogan was expected by many to become the next United States Senator from New York.

The Democratic State Convention that year was in Buffalo. The District Attorney attended, along with 1,100 Democratic delegates and Governor Averell Harriman, the party's standardbearer for the convention.

Everybody assumed Harriman's reelection to the governor's mansion was a matter of course. The convention would simply sit back and await the word on the rest of the ticket. The delegates, their wives and families, looked forward to visiting Niagara Falls and enjoying a few days of catered food. Instead, they suffered three days and nights of back-room bickering and wild chaos on the convention floor—a spectacle of bossism that undermined the Harriman platform by Election Day.

The shadow of influence fell upon Hogan instantly: Carmine DeSapio, then Democratic boss of New York County, was waiting for him in the hotel lobby. Closeted in an upstairs conference room with the District Attorney, DeSapio asked, "Are you still my man for Senator?" Hogan nodded. The two men had discussed the endorsement a month earlier. Hogan had wanted DeSapio to make a public announcement, but DeSapio had so far kept his support a secret.

The meeting over, Hogan slipped from the room and headed for a staircase, hoping to escape news reporters lying in wait by the elevator. The reporters spotted him and gave chase. Hogan broke into a sprint and raced down six flights of stairs, the newsmen after him. They chased him all the way to his room, where he told them finally: "Sorry, gentlemen, I have nothing to say," and firmly closed the door.

That was virtually the last glimpse of Hogan during the convention. The next morning, when the gavel pounded, rumors buzzed through the crowded corridors: DeSapio had hand-picked Hogan for the Senate nomination. Why had he picked Hogan? Out of personal friendship? Because of pressure from the rest of the Democratic hierarchy? Or did DeSapio simply want to get an overly efficient prosecutor out of office?

Long before the era of media manipulators, DeSapio recognized the importance of selling a political image to the electorate. At fifty-six, Hogan *looked* like a Senator. His prim figure, wreathed by pipe smoke, exuded unassailable probity. His style of dress—vests, gold watchchains, collar stays—reinforced the impression. If the leprechaun face was more wrinkled now, the hair thinner and grayer, the afterglow of his smile still asserted stamina and friendship. He could be articulate about government, but not in the egghead style of his chief rival, Thomas K. Finletter, the dry attorney who had once served as Secretary of the Air Force. Hogan was younger and less reserved than his other rival, the sixty-eight-year-old engineer Thomas Murray, former head of the Atomic Energy Commission and the apparent favorite of Governor Harriman.

While Hogan and the other two candidates occupied center stage, another dapper man waited in the wings: Robert F. Wagner. Few delegates doubted that the shrewd, oxlike Mayor of New York City would make the strongest Senatorial candidate. But the year before, Wagner had pledged: "I will not run for higher office if reelected Mayor."

Sure enough: "I'm here as Mayor of New York City," Wagner announced upon his arrival in Buffalo the day before the convention opened. "The job of Mayor is a lot more important than being the junior Senator from New York."

In his hotel suite, Wagner was met by Charles Buckley, county leader in the Bronx. Buckley came straight out with it. "Are you interested in the Senate nomination?"

Wagner said, "No, I've told you that, Charley. I just came up so my wife and kids could visit Niagara Falls."

"Well," said Buckley. "If you *are* interested, then I'm for you. I'd frankly prefer to have you as Mayor. There's no patronage in the Senate. But if you're not interested, I told Carmine I'd get busy up here and line up the votes for Hogan. Carmine is still saying he's not for anybody."

DeSapio's tiptoeing in the tulips irritated Wagner, who knew he was the obvious choice for Senator. If the convention drafted him out of desperation, no one could blame the Mayor for breaking his "I won't run" pledge. That was the position Harriman and DeSapio took when they met with Wagner in a hotel room the next evening: they all but twisted his arm to get in the Senate race.

"You fellows didn't think of this just a little while ago," Wagner purred. "Why me all of a sudden?"

"We need you," said Harriman.

DeSapio said, "I haven't any candidate. I'm for you if you want it, Bob."

Wagner turned on the Tammany boss with a mixture of incredulity and rage: "Now stop kidding everyone, Carmine. You may be conning the Governor here, but you're not conning me. You're for Frank Hogan. Jesus! Admit it!"

DeSapio refused to admit it. By two in the morning, the exhausted Harriman asked Wagner to "think it over" until the next morning.

"Look, I'm sure the answer will still be no—but in deference to you, Averell, I'll think it over."

Next day, Harriman made the tactical mistake of accepting the renomination for Governor publicly at the convention—before straightening out the rest of the ticket. Boss DeSapio seized the opportunity to ram the Hogan nomination down his throat.

"We have him over a barrel," the grand sachem shrewdly announced to the other bosses. "What's he gonna do now—*deny* that he's going to take the nomination?"

The third day of the back-room convention produced a showdown. Harriman shouted at DeSapio in front of all the other leaders: "I want you to be for Finletter. You're my Secretary of State. I want you to be for *him!*" Harriman's personality could cool to sub-zero at times. His words chilled the other leaders. Not DeSapio. With an arrogance that would have stunned Bismarck, DeSapio stiffened his shoulders and shook his head. "I'm sorry, Governor. I'm for Hogan."

Word of Harriman's humiliation leaked onto the convention floor, creating havoc. Former Governor Herbert Lehman telegraphed from

Switzerland: "Shocked and deeply distressed . . ." The convention lapsed into bedlam.

Hogan won. Murray and Finletter lost. Their opponents branded the back-room deals as bossism, and Hogan "the candidate of the bosses." Many felt this a disservice to Hogan: he had been hopelessly stranded in the crossfire between the reformers and DeSapio.

"Hogan was completely innocent," Wagner reminisced about the 1958 debacle in later years. "There were probably twenty-five angry meetings in those three days and Frank Hogan was never invited to attend even one of them."

Hogan's alliance with DeSapio will always remain controversial, perhaps shadowing the bright light of Hogan's integrity. He knew Tammany's tie-in with gangsters Frank Costello and Frank Luchese had been investigated by the State Crime Commission. Two years after DeSapio became head of Tammany, the Kefauver Senate Committee asserted: "Costello's influence continues . . . strong in the councils of the Democratic Party of New York County."

In the aftermath of the "bossed" convention, Hogan proved a lackluster fighter against the GOP's Senatorial nominee, snowy-haired Kenneth Keating. Wagner tried to rev up Hogan: "Look, Frank. You're not charging a jury. You're running for Senator. Get angry, for Christ's sake!"

The Hogan-for-Senate campaign limped toward Election Day, and collapsed when James Farley, New York's elder Democratic statesman, ad-libbed that "Hogan's knowledge of foreign policy extends from Yankee Stadium to the Battery."

John Bonomi, a Hogan campaign worker, recalled the 1958 contest as "the best example I know of Frank Hogan as an amateur politician. I'll never forget his first appearance before the Young Democrats, then headed by William Fitz Ryan, a former assistant district attorney. There were still vestiges of McCarthyism in those days. But Hogan gets up after dinner and says he thinks Red China should be admitted to the United Nations as soon as she has proved her peaceful intentions. Next day, the newspapers splash the first part of the statement rather than the last. Headlines: 'Hogan Favors Reds in UN.' Now, he should have said what a thoughtful professional would have: Red China should *not* be admitted to the UN until she proves her peaceful intentions. Just by the turn of a phrase, Frank was off on the wrong foot."

With DeSapio an albatross around his neck, and Nelson Rockefeller, making his debut in state politics, whipping the "bossism" issue, the rest of the Hogan campaign lumbered toward defeat. Election night itself? Years later, Hogan remembered the sparkle of chandeliers in the Hotel Biltmore Ballroom. The yellow-jacketed saxophone players, whooping it up with "Hail, Hail, the Gang's All Here." And the mood of the party workers: unrelieved gloom.

Up in his hotel room, Hogan had nibbled Swiss cheese and pickle slices, watching Rockefeller pile up a plurality of more than half a million votes. Carmine DeSapio, hair and shades gleaming blackly, every inch an operator, walked in to report Keating's margin. Over at the Hotel Roosevelt, Senator-elect Keating was already chuckling on the phone to Richard Nixon: "Well, Dick, it was wonderful of you to call."

When the time came, DeSapio escorted Frank and Mary Hogan onto the "winner's platform," strewn with Oriental rugs. An unpretentious blackboard on the platform behind them told the story: the Rockefeller landslide was the most dramatic overturn in the state since Theodore Roosevelt's over the Democrats in 1898. Harriman's entire ticket was beaten, except for state comptroller Arthur Levitt. The Democratic Party that had dominated the state since the days of Franklin Roosevelt and Herbert Lehman would be plunged into the abyss of reform, replaced by the sixteen-year regency of the Rockefeller family.

Good sport Hogan conceded defeat gracefully: "The jury decided. Never quarrel with the jury."

7
THE PROTEGES

The New York State Supreme Court is a curious misnomer: the court is in no way "supreme." Actually, it is the court of original jurisdiction in New York State, answerable to the Appellate Division. For years, it was called the Court of General Sessions, a title that more accurately described the various courtrooms devoted to bail motions, felony trials, homicide cases, youthful offenses and sundry legal applications.* The Manhattan courtrooms were designated "Part V," "Part VII," "Part X," and so on, until Hogan realized one day why many of the poor and ignorant defendants got lost in the corridors—they couldn't read Roman numerals. Hogan asked the court administrator to put up signs in Arabic numerals. Traffic speeded up considerably.

Manning these courtrooms were members of the largest bureau in the D.A.'s office, the "Supreme Court," formerly the General Sessions Bureau. A promising young advocate was eligible for the frenetic work of the Supreme Court after apprenticing two or three years in the Complaint Bureau and in Criminal Court, where preliminary hearings and misdemeanor cases were tried. Promotion to the Supreme Court Bureau was a big step in Hogan's army.

The advocate became the most visible representative of the office. His legal battles were reported and analyzed in the media. When the young lawyer voiced that resonant phrase, "In the interest of the People, Your

---

* This venerable tribunal, descended from colonial times, is the oldest court of criminal jurisdiction in North America. Appeals from felony convictions are taken first to the Appellate Division, First Department, then to the state's highest court, the Court of Appeals.

Honor," what he often had in mind was the interest of just one man—
Frank Smithwick Hogan.

Hogan realized that the trial men of the bureau were not always the
paragons of fairness he lauded in after-dinner speeches and glossy year-
end reports. The legal fraternity's exalted Canon of Ethics looked good on
paper. But a personal, more flexible code of combat was also necessary to
overcome the obstacles of an adversary system in which the scales of justice often seemed tipped in favor of the defendant.

Hogan's best trial men were the real go-getters of the office, driven to
long hours of preparation by the Chief's emphasis on convictions. They
had to be anti-intellectual, aggressive infighters. If a defense lawyer produced conclusive evidence of his client's innocence during a trial, there
were some prosecutors in the land who would have fought to the bitter
end. Hogan, however, with a great deal of pride, would order a motion to
dismiss the case. Under all other circumstances, acquittals were inexcus-
able. After any acquittal, Hogan demanded an inquest. Poll the jury after
the verdict. Find out what went wrong. Was it lack of preparation? Did
you have insufficient evidence to go to trial in the first place?

Veterans in the bureau went through the same theatrics that defense
lawyers have used for decades. Supreme Court men smashed furniture in
court to dramatize the force of an assault blow. They trained themselves
to read upside down so they could decipher an opponent's notes in court.
Hogan's men would have a hardbitten prostitute dress in a demure
jumper and wear her hair in Shirley Temple sausage curls if they thought
that would improve her image as a witness for the prosecution. A scruffy,
unsanitary, gap-toothed ex-convict might appear as a People's witness in a
new suit and tie, clean-shaven, with cosmetic dentistry if he needed it.
All to impress jurors.

At the actual *voir dire* selection of a jury, senior prosecutors instructed
junior men to exclude certain types as jurors automatically. Sociologists,
part-time workers, psychologists, artists, musicians, writers and free-
thinkers in general were undesirable. Better to empanel the kind of people who marched in Veterans' Day parades—Elks and Rotarians,
plumbers, electricians, housewives, secretaries, retirees on Medicare and
government pensions. The prosecution's case always rested on respect for
authority. The object was to make the jury box a sounding board for conventional values, not a seminar on the social dynamics of crime.

Mild-mannered, academic types never endured in the bureau. "I had to
leave," a former Hoganite recently recalled, "because I began to feel that

every time I prosecuted a defendant, I was really prosecuting myself . . . that I was somehow to blame for the society that produced this defendant."

Those who succeeded were complex, tenacious men, some destined for higher achievement in the political maelstrom: Burton Bennett Roberts, who became the Bronx County District Attorney; New York Congressman William Fitz Ryan; Samuel Pierce, who went from Hogan's office to Washington as counsel to the U.S. Treasury Department; District Attorney Carl Vergari, of Westchester County; and Maurice Nadjari, who left Hogan to become Chief Assistant District Attorney of Suffolk County.

G.K. Chesterton once remarked, "The horrible thing about all legal officials, even the best . . . is not that they are wicked (some of them are good), not that they are stupid (some of them are quite intelligent), it is simply that they have got used to it."

Unfortunately, the self-image of many Hogan assistants fit the stereotype of the flinty-eyed prosecutor who derived thin-lipped satisfaction from his power to inflict human misery. This defect was vivified in a speech Maurice Nadjari made to a group of law students after he left Hogan's office. Hogan later referred to it as "Maury's orgasm speech."

"Your job requires your all-enveloping attention," Nadjari began his pep talk to the prospective young prosecutors in the audience. "You've got to love it more than yourself, your wife, your children and your future. . . .

"Man's greatest experience is the act of lovemaking. I sometimes wonder if the moment when the jury foreman rises to utter those sweet words of verdict—'We the jury find the defendant guilty as charged'—is not as satisfactory an experience."

A lifeguard in his teens, Nadjari remained a physical-fitness specimen into his forties. Dark and handsome, he kept in fighting trim by doing push-ups on his office floor.

His determination was first evident to Hogan in 1965, when the 563-carat Star of India sapphire and $350,000 worth of other precious gems were stolen from a display case in Manhattan's Museum of Natural History.

Three bronzed beachboys from Florida had borrowed their script for the caper from the motion picture *Topkapi*, which they saw twenty times, studying every scene and taking notes. Accordingly, they broke through the museum's skylight and lowered themselves by nylon cords to the fourth-floor jewel chamber. The heist went like clockwork. The boys shinnied back up the rope with their precious loot and fled into the night.

The trio—Allan Kuhn, Roger Clark and Jack (Murph the Surf) Murphy—were muscular, gold-fuzzed sun-worshipers who earned their livings in Miami Beach by laying out air mattresses for hotel guests (big tips) and rubbing suntan lotion on middle-aged ladies with waffled thighs (bigger tips). They pulled the gem heist to maintain a high-on-the-hog Florida lifestyle that included lots of B-girl sex, snazzy convertibles, a sailing schooner and a speedboat.

They were so noisily immodest about their museum adventure afterward that a friend got fed up with their bragging and turned the beachboys in to police. Detectives arrested the trio within forty-eight hours of the jewel theft.

The gem thieves were out on bail when Nadjari came across Herman Gordon, a New York fence. Gordon claimed to be a rare-coin dealer, but his real passion was dabbling in stolen gemstones on the New York–Paris–London axis. Nadjari threatened him with a grand-jury subpoena unless Gordon agreed to help expedite recovery of the museum jewels, now in the hands of the Miami underworld. Gordon agreed. Nadjari gave the beachboys a chance to think things over, too. He upped their bail so high that they had to go back to a sunless jail cell in the Manhattan Tombs.

Kuhn, the brainy one of the bunch, immediately sent out word that he would cooperate in the recovery mission—in exchange for leniency. Accordingly, he was spirited out of the detention pen. Three indoorsy-looking New York City detectives handcuffed him aboard a Miami-bound jetliner in the company of Nadjari.

Yet almost from the moment their plane touched down in Miami, Nadjari and the detectives ran into trouble, most of it from Kuhn. When he wasn't dozing in his motel room or watching Captain Kangaroo on TV, Kuhn was hemming and hawing on the telephone with his underworld contacts.

Nobody wanted to keep the jewels, Kuhn assured Nadjari. The Star of India, the largest star sapphire in the world, had proved a bitch to fence. The 116-carat Midnight Star sapphire and 110-carat DeLong Ruby weren't moving very well, either. The underworld's problem in wanting to turn over the gemstones was the fear of capture—not by the FBI but by news photographers. The Miami press had gotten wind of Nadjari's mission and staked out the beachfront motel where he was holed up with

Kuhn and the detectives. There were already pictures in the paper of Nadjari in scuba mask and flippers, diving under the beachboys' sailing yacht on a phony tip that the jewels might be found there. The prosecutor splashed back to shore emptyhanded and stepped up his personal negotiations with the underworld.

The situation became so tense that one of the detectives suffered an anxiety attack of diarrhea and locked himself in the bathroom for two days. A second detective whined that he was about to have a heart attack and wanted to check himself into a Miami hospital. There were death threats against all of them, and the press pursued them like foxhounds. Meanwhile, Herman Gordon, having also flown down from New York, was on the phone with *his* underworld contacts, trying to set up a rendezvous for the return of the jewels.

Eventually, Gordon and the detectives were instructed to drive to an all-night pizza parlor. They choked down coffee and anchovies. They waited. Nothing happened. They returned to their car. There, on the floor, was a key to locker number 682 at Miami's Greyhound station.

With Gordon behind the wheel, they sped to the bus depot. One of the detectives went inside. He opened the twenty-five-cent locker. Inside, he found two water-logged chamois bags. He pulled the drawstrings and out rolled the missing gems, minus only the DeLong ruby.

In no time at all, Kuhn was back on a New York-bound jetliner in handcuffs. The missing ruby was later ransomed for $25,000. Herman Gordon became a gangland victim: his eagerness to help in the transaction was rewarded by a bullet in the head. The beachboys won their place in the sun, ending up in a Florida penitentiary. The successful recovery earned Nadjari a shower of press coverage, threatening to dampen Burton Roberts' reputation as the celebrity lion of the Supreme Court Bureau.

Roberts and Nadjari reigned as twin princelings of the bureau, with an ongoing rivalry for Hogan's attention.

They even ran to him with tattle-tales about each other. Nadjari squealed that on the day the jewels were returned, Roberts sidled into his office, picked up one of the gems and shrugged, "I don't see what everybody's getting so excited about." He then dropped the gem on the floor and walked out.

"He's lying!" Roberts bawled. Hogan didn't know whom to believe (an occupational hazard when dealing with lawyers). Of the two protégés, Hogan personally favored the forty-eight-year-old Burt Roberts.

For sixteen years in the D.A.'s office, Roberts was a renegade—a red-haired, rambunctious prosecutor with a flaming temper and an ego that made Muhammad Ali sound like Mahatma Gandhi. Staff members found Hogan's affinity for Roberts hard to understand.

"Burt's tenacity was what Hogan liked," recalled a former colleague, John Bonomi. "Somehow, I always had the feeling that many of Burt's qualities, his flamboyance and love of fun, were qualities that Hogan secretly admired because he did not have them himself. Perhaps the reverse was true of Burt Roberts. He sought the Boss's approval because he envied Hogan's courtliness and quiet dignity."

Hogan himself had once said, "I like Burt because he likes to win and so do I." Hogan was referring to Roberts' prowess on the softball diamond, not his courtroom triumphs. But one couldn't help inferring that the same was true for the courtroom. During his years in the Supreme Court Bureau, Roberts negotiated over 1,000 felony pleas and prosecuted more than 200 jury trials, with amazing success.

Aside from four reversals on appeal and a couple of hung juries, Roberts could boast, "I don't think I had more than five acquittals." He would never be precise about his losses because Hogan was wary of prosecutors who kept batting averages.

"We only present the evidence," Hogan was fond of saying. "The jury acquits or convicts."

Roberts worked just as hard as Nadjari to get a conviction. But on sentencing, Nadjari, by his own admission, went for the jugular, while Roberts aimed for the central nervous system. Roberts' objective was to confront the defendant with his criminality and make him face up to his own guilt. That, he figured, was punishment enough. Roberts usually recommended the lightest sentence provided by law. A suspended sentence, if possible.

Roberts had gained the upper hand in Hogan's affection from the outset, as star second baseman for Hogan's Hooligans, the office softball team. Apart from the office, his wife, and Columbia University, the team was Hogan's great passion. Legal careers were rumored to advance or decline on the strength of a pitching arm or a good eye at the plate. When a bureau chief complained on one occasion of an inept assistant whom he thought ought to be fired, Hogan said, "I know he's lazy and incompetent, but what are we going to do for a third baseman?" Hogan himself held down third base until he retired himself in the 1950s to third-base coach.

The Pete Rose of office softball, Roberts was a real hotshot—screaming at the ump, diving headlong into the bag, running roughshod over the catcher if it meant a score at home plate. His razzle-dazzle, lotsa-chatter-in-the-infield gamesmanship built the team into a juggernaut.

Teams assembled from big Wall Street firms accused Hogan of offering athletic scholarships. His team consistently outclassed the opposition so badly that at the annual upstate D.A.'s conventions, the Hooligans played the best men the other sixty-one counties could lump together. Hogan usually picked up the bronze trophy.

Roberts' courtroom tactics matched his softball style. Judges shook their heads over the fact that someone with such a brilliant and precise legal mind could transgress the minimal standards of dignity and court decorum by acting *mishugana* so often.

Roberts was a one-man vaudeville act when he tried a case. He banged his fists on tables, made faces at the jury, and grilled defense witnesses as if they were ants on a skillet. Provoked by this finger-snapping behavior, silver-tongued defense attorney Nicholas Atlas once stormed up to the bench and intoned with grandiloquent wrath: "Your Honor, I will not be intimidated by the golden cockerel of the District Attorney's office!"

Roberts reacted by playing the hayseed legal bumpkin, sidling up to the jury box with a subdued, "Your Honor, so the record will not remain blank to this insult—" a dramatic hesitation—"I wish to state that I'd rather be a young rooster than *an old cock!*"

This exchange occurred during a case which involved Manny Lester. Lester was accused of attempting to extort $535,000 from shady millionaire Serge Rubinstein, who had been slain before the trial. Detectives ran out of ink before they could complete an enemies list of people who might have had some motive to see Rubinstein dead. He was "the most hated man in New York," police said. "The Prime Minister of Hell," Atlas called him.

"A dead scoundrel," Roberts acknowledged, "but saint or sinner, angel or devil, there shall be equal justice for all who become victims of crime in New York City." As usually happened after one of Roberts' summations, the jury voted to convict.

Roberts often skated on thin ice with his insults. They proved too provocative to one defendant, a 240-pounder, who jumped up and socked the prosecutor. Roberts lay flat on his back for the count and stayed there for three minutes before court attendants revived him by dashing cold water in his face.

One Roberts tantrum even landed him in hot water with Hogan.

It happened during the trial of a securities dealer accused of kidnapping a former U.S. Attorney and holding him at pistol point for four hours. Roberts' insolence toward Judge Charles Marks, who had granted a defense adjournment in the case, provoked the jurist into apoplectic rage. The judge threatened Roberts with a contempt citation—the first such action in a New York court for an assistant district attorney. Hogan was mortified. He ordered a senior trial man to sit at Roberts' side in court and "monitor" Burt in action.

The only assistant with enough moxie to talk back to the Boss, Roberts slammed the trial folders down on Hogan's desk and demanded to be taken off the case.

"You goddam prima donna!" Hogan trembled with anger. "You come back here and pick up those folders and try this case!"

Roberts answered in a sing-song little brat's voice: "Not unless you get rid of the monitor."

Hogan finally gave in. All right. No monitor. But with one condition: Roberts had to swallow his ego—just as Hogan had swallowed his temper—and apologize to Judge Marks.

Next day, with Hogan seated at the back of the courtroom, Roberts put on a sheepish face and told the judge, "I have had time to reflect. I most respectfully ask Your Honor to accept my apology. I attribute my intemperate conduct to overzealousness . . . ."

Judge Marks was unimpressed. He noted that Roberts' behavior had already brought "discredit" to Hogan's office in the case of *People v. Steinhardt*. In that case, the Court of Appeals had reversed the conviction Roberts obtained in a $140,000 robbery case. The court's ruling berated the assistant for "the incredible incident wherein the two lawyers and the court refought the battle of Anzio in the Second World War"—a typical mouth-foaming Burton Roberts production. The defense counsel, trying to establish the good character of one of his witnesses, had noted that the man was a wounded veteran of the Anzio campaign. Anzio! Anybody who told Anzio war stories in court was stealing Roberts' material—he himself was a veteran of that battle. The prosecutor leaped to his feet and cross-examined the witness in detail about the campaign, discrediting his recollection of mountain ranges, battalion strength, firepower. "This military symposium went on for twenty pages of the record," the court noted in disbelief, with Roberts "listing all the military honors he himself held."

Hogan was not amused by the court's ruling. But he defended his *en-*

fant terrible: "There are some defense lawyers—happily, not many—who feel they can say practically anything and the assistant D.A. has to take it, because the Appellate Division will single out *his* responses to lawyer-baiting. Burt is an outstanding trial lawyer. Even those with whom he has crossed swords would not deny that he is exceptional. Many jurors have written to me after his cases expressing admiration for his zeal and professional competence."

Hogan, open in his admiration of Roberts' triumphs both in court and on the softball diamond, was also impressed by Roberts' office reputation as a ladies' man. Seldom did Roberts' romantic reach exceed his grasp. Attending a movie alone one night, he developed a crush on screen star Grace Kelly. Probably thousands of moonstruck men across the nation entertained the same fantasies about her that Burt Roberts enjoyed as he watched *To Catch a Thief.* But while others might have stayed content to worship her screen image from afar, Roberts went from the movie house to a pay phone, obtained the actress' unlisted number from the police, and telephoned her.

When Miss Kelly picked up the phone, Roberts somehow persuaded her to come down to the District Attorney's office the following day for a guided tour of the place.

Hogan was astonished to look up next morning and see Burton Roberts standing in his doorway with a big cigar in his mouth, one hand holding an Afghan on a leash, the other cupping the elbow of Grace Kelly. That vision was memorable, even though celebrities did appear frequently at the office.

Hogan enjoyed his VIP guests and was always happy to pause and entertain them by remembering bits of business that had amused him over the years. There was the day Leopold Stokowski came in to testify that his car had been burglarized and Worgan delivered the standard opening line: "What is your occupation, Mr. Stokowski?" Or the time Alan Funt stormed in to complain that a business partner had embezzled him out of a cool million—and Hogan just sat there with a dopey smile because he thought he was on *Candid Camera.* Or the day Sophia Loren sashayed in after a jewel thief had robbed her of $20,000 in glitter. It took two hours for the sex goddess to answer ten questions. Each time her lush lips parted, another junior assistant popped into the room "by mistake," interrupting the Q and A.

Over the years, the office mug file had garnered short takes of Norman Mailer (wife-stabbing), Debbie Reynolds (weapons possession), Swifty

Lazar (bludgeoning Otto Preminger with a wine goblet at "21") and a star-studded cast of drunk drivers, dope heads and famous (but never prosecuted) closet queens. Even Humphrey Bogart had brushed with Hogan after a "woman scrape" at El Morocco one night.

Hogan's favorite complainant was Tallulah Bankhead. In 1950, while starring on Broadway in *Private Lives*, her checking account mysteriously dried up. She appeared at Hogan's door one day to announce in her elegant drawl: "Dahling! I'm being embez-zled!" Fishing into her purse for a flask, Miss Bankhead comforted herself with bourbon as she poured out her tale of woe. Her maid had been adding extra digits to the weekly paychecks, changing $50 to $250 after Tallulah signed them. The maid was convicted—but not before her defense lawyer threatened to expose Miss Bankhead's kinky sex habits and alleged drug addiction if the case went to trial. Tallulah flew into a temper tantrum in Hogan's office.

The great Southern belle had learned the harshest four-letter word for love, and she used it to set to rest any impression that a Bankhead of Alabama could be intimidated, Hogan recalled: "I was wonder-stricken that a woman could bring out so many amazing nuances of that word and still retain her insouciant charm."

Grace Kelly confessed that she had found the morning most diverting, but when Roberts asked for a date as she was leaving, she gave him the polite brush: Prince Ranier of Monaco had just come into her life.

"To tell you the truth, I was disappointed," Roberts shrugged when Hogan asked him later how he'd made out. "She isn't *nearly* as pretty as she looked in that movie."

The light that Burton Roberts brought to Hogan's office ended in 1965. The New York Bar Association had lodged complaints that year about the way certain political cases were being handled in the office of Bronx County District Attorney Isador Dollinger. His office, in the weatherbeaten Bronx County Courthouse overlooking Yankee Stadium, was still a place for patronage. The office creaked with deadwood; do-nothingness pervaded.

With an election coming up in November, the Democratic bosses were running scared. Dollinger needed change if he was to survive. A way had to be found to Hoganize the Bronx office (thus allowing the bosses to run against their own records; in New York City, this is known as "reform").

Hogan was called upon to recommend someone for the post of Chief Assistant D.A. in the Bronx, and he didn't have the heart to refuse Burt

Roberts the opportunity. Hogan and his old Columbia Law classmate Justice Mitchell Schweitzer arranged with Dollinger for Roberts to take over. Within a year, Dollinger was reduced to a forgotten man—Chief Assistant Burt Roberts had become the real power of the Bronx D.A. office.

Like Hogan in 1942, Roberts swept out the political hacks and professionalized the office. He eliminated moonlighting and recruited idealistic, full-time prosecutors out of the best law schools. He revitalized salary scales. And he made news.

With information provided by Hogan, Roberts began investigating the biggest case of his career: charges of grand larceny and perjury against a Democratic candidate for state senator, Eugene Rodriguez, in an alleged attempt to fix a narcotics case for $100,000. Roberts' prosecution of Rodriguez made explosive headlines at the end of the trial. With the jury excused and out of earshot, Roberts accused Rodriguez of having threatened, if found guilty, to shoot "that son of a bitch Roberts" and then himself in the courtroom. The media lapped it up. Roberts' name started cropping up in the society pages as the most eligible bachelor in the Bronx and the man destined to become the next "Mr. District Attorney."

Rodriguez, a leading member of the Bronx Democratic organization, was found guilty. Dollinger was pressured to resign under the inducement of a State Supreme Court judgeship. Roberts automatically succeeded him as Acting D.A., and by Election Day 1966, Burton Roberts had become—like Frank Hogan in 1942—a District Attorney with four-party backing. The torch had been passed. But neither man had heard the last of Maurice Nadjari.

8
GREAT IMPOSTERS

The office of Hogan's Complaint Bureau chief looked like a pawnshop. Tables and chairs were piled with junk—dusty furs, tarnished jewelry, dubious appliances. An inventory of the office was a con man's catalogue: radios that looked terrific, but tuned in only static; shiny wigs labeled "100% human hair" that shed like yak's fur (which they were). The file cabinets were crammed with certificates to the variety of human vanity: fake doctorates, diplomas, marriage licenses, beauty-contest awards. And there were chest drawers of "miracles"—pills that would grow hair on bald pates, vitamin compounds that would cure brain tumors, creams to give erections to the impotent, salves to make flat chests bloom.

The Complaint Bureau was proof that for every human want, there is a way to exploit that desire. Nearly 15,000 cases of consumer fraud and related rackets poured into the D.A.'s office every year.

The complainants came in depressed droves to the seventh-floor bureau. Ushered by police officers into suitable dreary cubicles, the victims would choke out their gyp stories. The lawyers assigned to listen to the unending woes were the greenest of Hogan assistants. The Boss deemed this job the best way to break in young prosecutors. Experience in the Complaint Bureau became a cram course in the human comedy.

Housewives ranted, "They said it was Chanel No. 5. When I opened the bottle, it was plain water!"

Pretty young girls sobbed out stories of being "discovered" by talent scouts who took their "audition fees" and ran. Amateur art lovers brandished shellacked canvases, maintaining, "I thought it was a real Vermeer. Two hundred dollars! It had better be *somebody*!"

The decibel count in the Complaint Bureau was the highest in Hoganland. Behind foggy glass partitions, accusations and countercharges reverberated between natural enemies: the discount salesman and his bargain-hungry customers; landlords and tenants; medical quacks and hypochondriacs. Those who did not want revenge ("I want to see that shyster in *jail*") wanted refunds ("At least make him give me back the five hundred").

People appealed to the D.A.'s office as if to an omnipotent bill collector. The office was not a collection agency, Hogan would explain. But a measure of good government is the courtesy with which government responds to the complaints of its aggrieved citizenry. He conceived of the Complaint Bureau as a waystation for the "average citizen who too often gets bounced around from one city agency to another."

Justifiably indignant complainants were joined, of course, by cranks and mental cases. To screen them out, the office developed files on chronic complainers—"the scolding woman, for instance, who had complained about her last three doctors, her last three lawyers, and her last three Social Security checks." These deluded people were always appealing for help in imaginary crimes. A common complaint was the telepathic "theft" of million-dollar ideas and famous song lyrics: "Oscar Hammerstein has a mind lock on me. He read my thoughts and robbed me of 'Oh, What a Beautiful Morning!' "

Former Complaint Bureau assistant Irving Lang recalled a "scientific solution" he applied to solve the problems of one overweight brunette. She complained that a clairvoyant industrialist had stolen her original idea for diet soda.

"He still has my mind in an electronic vise," the woman explained.

"Do you have an umbrella with a metal tip?" Lang inquired earnestly. The woman said yes.

"Well, always carry it with you. The metal tip will ground his electrical brain impulses into the sidewalk. You'll be rid of him forever." The woman gushed in gratitude: "I won't even bother you with the other idea he stole from me," she said as she began to leave.

"What idea was that?"

"Coca-Cola."

In cases of real grievance, the Complaint Bureau gave Hogan an opportunity to rectify injustices that other District Attorneys might automatically have shunted off to other agencies. One case, in 1961, even involved Hogan in international diplomacy.

The case began with the bureau's receipt of hundreds of complaints from Iron Curtain immigrants in New York. The complaints were all directed against one man: Leonard Tankel.

Tankel was himself an immigrant New Yorker who ran a chain of shops in New York where other Russian émigrés could buy made-in-U.S.A. babushkas, blouses, fabrics and food-parcel items to ship to relatives in the U.S.S.R.

Comrade Tankel, a licensed Soviet postal agent, was authorized to accept prepaid customs duties on the packages. But instead of paying the U.S.S.R., Tankel was siphoning the money into his own pocket. Because the duty monies did not get through, the packages were being returned to the U.S. Thousands of parcels piled up in the New York Post Office for want of double postage and uncollected customs fees.

On the strength of evidence gathered through the complaints, Hogan's office prosecuted Tankel on charges of grand larceny. Then U.S. postal authorities stepped in and capped the conviction with additional charges of mail fraud. Tankel went out of business.

This solved one problem, but created another. The packages were still gathering dust at the Post Office. Hogan was bothered by the idea of "a little old lady in Leningrad" waiting for her gifts to arrive from loved ones in America. He resolved to get the merchandise delivered.

Over several days, Hogan drove around town to pay calls on foreign-package corporations that had ties to the Soviet Union. Then, after a visit to the Soviet UN Mission, he coaxed several Russian trade officials into mini-summit talks with the D.A.'s office.

Together, they sat down and worked out a way to take over the responsibilities incurred by Tankel's bankrupt operation. Thus, during a brief thaw in the Cold War, the Iron Curtain was lifted for Frank Hogan and that little old lady in Leningrad—the packages were delivered.

Occasionally, a small complaint mushroomed into a national scandal. One such case began in 1957 when Herbert M. Stempel, a graduate student at New York University, walked in with the standard opener that he'd been double-crossed.

"I took a dive on television," Stempel said, and explained that he was a former champion of the nation's most popular TV quiz show, 21. He had won $49,500 with answers to questions posed to him in a studio isolation booth. On December 5, 1956, millions of Americans had watched him sweat out tough questions while pitted against a contestant in the opposite booth.

The man in the other booth: Columbia University English professor Charles Van Doren. Van Doren, thirty-two, had captured more or less instant celebrity status by already winning $129,000 on 21. The December 5 program was to be the showdown between Van Doren and Stempel.

Stempel proved that, in the long run, he was smarter. Hogan's office heard this behind-the-scenes story from him. On December 4, an NBC producer had informed Stempel: "You've reached a new plateau and we have to find a new champion and so we are going to drop you." For the good of the show, the producer explained, Van Doren would be a better champion. He had class. He had an attractive wife. And his father was Pulitzer Prize-winning poet Mark Van Doren. Stempel was a klutzy-looking egghead with brilliantine-slick hair.

Upset by NBC's cavalier treatment, Stempel decided to get even. All the TV quiz shows, he now revealed, had been rehearsed from start to finish.

"Did you see me perspiring in that isolation booth?" he asked the Hogan assistant with whom he talked. "That's because the producer deliberately kept the air conditioning off. He wanted to create a realistic effect." In accordance with the wishes of the producer, Albert Freedman, Stempel said he went on the December 5 show and "lost" by failing to recall the name of the 1955 Academy Award-winning movie *Marty*—a film he had seen three times—and by missing a question on American history. "I knew both answers," he said.

Stempel's complaint was sent up to Hogan, who immediately summoned Van Doren before a Manhattan grand jury. Hogan listened to the professor's denials for several days. To hear Van Doren tell it, TV quiz shows were as clean and honorable as final exams at a theological seminary. Hogan doubted that, but it took him nine months to short-circuit the world of electronic sham.

The D.A. ordered Joseph Stone, then chief of the Complaint Bureau, to take charge of the investigation. A consumer-frauds expert, Stone had spent years prosecuting trademark counterfeiting of names like Bulova and Benrus on cheap imitation wristwatches. He exposed phony trademarks—"Ford," "Delco-Remy"—on bootleg auto parts distributed across the country. And in the late 1950s, Stone prosecuted disc jockey Alan Freed and other DJs in the payola scandal, proving that they received "royalties" each time they spun certain records. It was also Joe Stone who uncovered one of the biggest pharmaceutical scandals of all time, the famous "Regimen" racket, by disproving several "doctor-tested experiments" with the phony diet pills.

On one occasion, Joe Stone provided Hogan an introduction to Marc Chagall. The renowned French artist was working at Lincoln Center, supervising the installation of his famous murals, when Stone uncovered two forgeries of Chagall's signature on canvases painted in his style. Stone took the paintings up to the artist, who clambered down from a scaffold. Chagall took one outraged look at the fakes and grabbed them. Chagall wanted to smash the phony "Chagalls" against the scaffold. But Stone clung to them for dear life, pleading with Chagall alternately in English and French: "The evidence, *monsieur*, the evidence!"

Stone's suspicions about the TV quiz shows had already been aroused by a series of TV columns in the New York *Post* and *Journal-American*. A *Journal* reporter, Martin Steadman, had urged Stempel to go to the D.A.'s office. But Stone reacted cautiously to the contestant's charges; the allegations raised the possibility of larceny and commercial bribery. Stempel himself might be an extortionist. A thorough investigation was required.

"I urge you to tell the truth," Stone told Van Doren and his fellow contestants. "If we find that it's all been a hoax, but no crimes of larceny or bribery have been committed, then I assure you that none of your names will get out."

Instead of taking this advice, Van Doren stuck to his alibi: all the quiz shows were legitimate. "All right," said Stone, calling the professor's bluff, "let's see how you do on some of the questions and answers."

Sitting Van Doren down in a dreary cubicle of the Complaint Bureau, Stone proceeded to grill him with some of the same questions emcee Jack Barry had earlier put to the contestant in the studio isolation both. Van Doren sweated out the answers in earnest this time.

Joe Stone, now a retired Criminal Court judge, recalls that the professor didn't do too well. "He missed some of the answers he had previously given correctly on television. Then we dug up some of the questions he had *missed* on TV. You'd have thought he'd have looked up the answers by this time. But he didn't know those answers either."

Gathering evidence on *21*, *Tic Tac Dough*, *Dotto*, and other TV giveaways—all of them high in audience ratings—Stone's office interrogated more than 300 quiz-show contestants. A few told the truth.

Bandleader Xavier Cugat and another man, the manager of child star Patty Duke, admitted the contestants had been spoon-fed questions on *The $64,000 Challenge*, winning a combined total of $40,000. Some contestants insisted they were never coached. Dr. Joyce Brothers, for instance, a $64,000 winner on *The $64,000 Question*, said she relied on a "photographic memory" to answer queries on her specialty: prizefighting.

Digging deeper, Stone learned that the producers of *The $64,000 Question* and *Challenge*, both sponsored by Revlon Cosmetics, had interviewed some contestants at length before going on the air. The producers did not feed them answers directly, but as Stone recalled, "They knew what the contestants knew and what they didn't know. The promoters kept their eyes on the Trendex popularity ratings for each contestant. If they wanted to keep a certain contestant on the air, they led into his strength. If they wanted to get rid him, they led into his weakness. . . . We found out, for example, that Dr. Brothers' specialty was originally supposed to be home economics. But the promoters preferred paradoxical interests for each contestant: a Navy captain who was an expert on cooking, a cop who knew Shakespeare, and so on.

"So they make Dr. Brothers, a female psychologist, an expert on prizefighting. Her father is a big fight buff, see. A friend of Nat Fleischer, the editor of *Ring* magazine. They pick Fleischer as the fellow who will make up the prizefight questions for the show. Then they give Joyce a prizefighting encyclopedia and claim she's able to memorize every ring statistic since the days of John L. Sullivan. Okay. I ask her if she's ever talked to the producers about prizefighting before she went on the air. The great memory expert says, '*I can't remember.*' "

Stone also called in Charles Revson, the cosmetics tycoon, but absolved him of any complicity in the rigged programs: "Revson was really the only guy who came out ahead. Many of the contestants invested their winnings unwisely and lost everything. But the publicity helped make Revlon one of the biggest glamour stocks on the market."

Hogan and Stone eventually put together a grand-jury presentment on the ways the programs operated, indicating that although there was no evidence of larceny or commercial bribery, the FCC should put a stop to the shows. Unlike an indictment, a presentment does not allege criminality. It merely suggests that something is rotten somewhere and that the D.A. can't pin it down with hard evidence.

Judge Mitchell Schweitzer, whether acting on a strict interpretation of law or responding to pressure from big TV sponsors, suppressed Hogan's presentment as illegal. He ruled that a grand jury "is not empowered to submit a report critical of a private person engaged in a strictly private enterprise, as distinguished from a person occupying public office."

Hogan wrote a lengthy memorandum pointing out that since colonial times there had been historic presentments against private entrepreneurs. Critical reports had emanated from Hogan's office on construction-industry shenanigans, substandard nursing homes, snake-pit psychiatric hospitals, ptomaine slaughterhouses. Schweitzer was upheld by the Appellate Division, however, and the presentment was permanently sealed in a municipal vault. To this day, the contents have never been released.

The names of Van Doren and the other contestants might still be secret if the presentment material hadn't become public knowledge through the revelations of a Senate investigation committee headed by Senator Estes Kefauver. As the nation would soon learn, a great many contestants lied before the grand jury.

Hogan advised them to change their stories voluntarily or face the consequences. Among those with a strong incentive to "correct" his testimony was Charles Van Doren. Hogan confronted him with seven sealed envelopes. They were self-addressed, registered letters which one of the 21 contestants, James Snodgrass, had mailed to himself after being fed questions and answers before appearing on an April 22 show. Among the questions the letters contained was one asking Snodgrass to name the seven dwarfs in *Snow White*.

Hogan warned that if the fraud investigation went to trial, he would play the kineoscopes of the NBC program to the jury, then open the letters one by one. Snodgrass promised Hogan that one of the envelopes contained not only the answers to the seven-dwarfs question, but a "script" on how the answers should be delivered: "Sleepy, Sneezy, Dopey, Happy (pause) . . . the Grouchy one . . . Grumpy (pause) . . . Doc (pause) . . . Bashful!"

Hogan shuffled the envelopes and whistled a tune from *Snow White* while Van Doren thought it over. It didn't take the professor long to find the right answer. "I did something very foolish," Van Doren said, as he began spilling out the whole story. "I acted like a child."

In today's post-Watergate world, accustomed as we are to being hoodwinked, the national furor over the quiz-show scandals of the 1950s seems out of proportion. But the *Readers' Digest* mentality of the Eisenhower years became so exercised that the President ordered a Congressional inquiry, based on Hogan's information. A House subcommittee subpoenaed Hogan's grand-jury minutes, took the sealed envelopes out of his hands, and called Van Doren to Washington to make a public confession.

The real-life melodrama unfolded in a tense Capitol Hill setting, the college professor, once America's intellectual hero, admitting it was all a fake:

"I have deceived my friends, and I had millions of them," he said. "I would give almost anything I have to reverse the course of my life in the last three years. . . . I've learned a lot about good and evil. . . . They are not what they appear to be. . . . The fact that I, too, was very much deceived cannot keep me from being the principal victim of that deception, because I was its principal symbol."

This dramatic confession taught Frank Hogan something, too—he learned just how viscerally many Americans react to notions of crime and punishment. In the eyes of the nation, Van Doren became an object of more scorn and hate mail than all of Hogan's sex maniacs, corrupt politicians and coldblooded killers combined.

"It's amazing to me," Hogan said, "that such a great percentage of the letters are vindictive, almost sadistic." The Chief wasn't about to satisfy national venom with a prison term for Van Doren, even though the legislators were screaming for his scalp.

"Changing testimony doesn't automatically perjure a person," Hogan informed the grand jury, "especially if he shows signs of contrition."

Van Doren had, by now, lost his Columbia teaching post. NBC had cancelled his lucrative contract as a commentator on the *Dave Garroway Show*. Hogan decided the professor had suffered enough.

But what could he do about Van Doren's statement to the committee, in which the professor admitted he had lied to the grand jury? Producer Freedman—at Hogan's urging—had agreed to come forward and tell the truth. Hogan really had no choice: he had to turn the entire matter over to the grand jury and let the jurors decide.

They decided: on October 17, 1960, Van Doren and nineteen other quiz-show contestants were indicted on charges of second-degree perjury, punishable by prison terms up to two years. Van Doren pleaded guilty on January 17, 1962. Justice Edward Breslin let him off with a suspended sentence, noting: "I see in your eyes the remorse and shame you must feel . . ."

What the judge never saw in the defendant's eyes: an offer to return the

$129,000 he had won in the quiz-fix. "I'm going home and forget this whole thing," Van Doren said. "In fact, I'd like to drop out of sight altogether."

He was as good as his word. When last seen by his attorney, Carl Rubino, the former professor was living somewhere in Chicago, writing children's history books under a pseudonym.

It would be several years before the D.A.'s office would have to tarnish the reputation of yet another Golden Boy.

The James Marcus case, soon to swell to enormous proportions, began with an almost imperceptible leak in 1967. Assistant District Attorney Frank Rogers (who would head the Complaints Bureau after 1969) was, in 1967, still doing routine work in the Frauds Bureau. Rogers had an unusual background. Before taking his law degree, he had been an Air Force criminal investigator in Germany. He remained eagle-eyed while on Hogan's staff, and when a letter from a Philadelphia lawyer came through the Complaints Bureau, Rogers gave it closer scrutiny than one might have thought the subject—a missing $6,000—would have merited.

According to the Philadelphia attorney, a client in Switzerland had given an American acquaintance $6,000 to invest in a stock called Xtra. Xtra manufactured piggyback railroad containers, and was said to be a booming company. The Swiss businessman never received a receipt or the stock certificates. His calls and letters to the American went unanswered.

It seemed a possible case of stock fraud, except for one element: the American in question was New York City Water Commissioner James Marcus.

A photocopy of the $6,000 check showed that it had been deposited in a bank, co-signed by Lily Lodge Marcus, Marcus' wife. She was also the daughter of one of America's most famous political families. Her father, John David Lodge, had been the Governor of Connecticut, and an uncle was Ambassador to Spain.

Rogers checked on Marcus' background and found that his marriage to Lily Lodge had been a crucial factor of change in his life. Marcus was a middle-class, bright, but anonymous Schenectady boy. By marrying Lily, whom he had met at a theatrical colony in Maine, he had hoisted himself umpteen rungs up the social ladder into the highest echelons of Republican politics. Everyone liked Marcus, who was darkly handsome, upwardly mobile and charming. His wife's friends became his; one new friend was John V. Lindsay, then still a Congressman. Marcus served as a volunteer for Lindsay's 1965 mayoral campaign. Lindsay won—and so did Marcus. He became the Water Commissioner. One would have thought his cup runneth over . . . but the $6,000 check implied that he had wanted more.

Rogers quietly subpoenaed Marcus' bank records. A checking account showed that the $6,000 deposit had been diverted to groceries, telephone bills and other mundane household expenses. No stock transfer.

After getting Hogan's go-ahead, Rogers called Marcus. "I'd like you to come and see me, Commissioner," he said.

"Marcus came down and I started off by reading him his Miranda rights," Rogers recalled, reconstructing the interrogation. "There was no obligation to give him his Miranda warning at the time, but I find it's a great equalizer. Here's a supercommissioner in Lindsay's office and I'm a lowly assistant D.A. in Hogan's office so I start off by saying, 'You have a right to counsel. You have a right to remain silent. You have a right to know that anything you say may be used against you.' Now I had taken him out of that commissionership and brought him down to the level of a target.

"Marcus's whole position after I hit him with the check question was: 'Do I have to tell you?'

" 'No, Commissioner, you don't have to tell us anything.' "

"Well, you're going to get suspicious if I don't tell you?'

" 'Yes. That's true. I would get suspicious. What was this money for?'

" 'Xtra.'

" 'Well, how much Xtra stock do you own?'

" 'Do I have to tell you?'

" 'No. You don't have to tell me.'

" 'Well, I have over $100,000 in Xtra stock.' "

Marcus told Rogers that back in April 1966 the stock had been touted to him as one that would boom. But it had not taken off—it had gone from 100 a share down to 37. He had bought too early. In November 1966 he had bought another 2,000 shares to even off, at 54, and it went over 100. So Marcus had ended up in pretty good shape.

"The question in my mind," recalled Rogers "was where he got the cash to meet that margin call. I said, 'I don't mean to be personal, Commissioner, but this is part of an investigation. Do you make that kind of money? I know that your wife is Governor Lodge's daughter and Ambassador Lodge's niece, but do you really have that kind of money?'

" 'No. I really don't.'
" 'Where did you get the money?'
" 'I factored my margin account to a friend from school.'
" 'Who is that?'
" 'Do I have to tell you?'
" 'No, you don't.'
" 'You'll probably find out?'
" 'Yes, I will.'
" 'Okay, I'll tell you. He's at Koenig & Co.' "

Rogers knew that Koenig would factor a client up to a certain point, but "Marcus needed fifty to sixty thousand dollars in cash to save his first investment. If he had had to sell out at 37 he would have been wiped out."

After five hours of "Do I have to tell you?" interrogation, Rogers went to see Frank Hogan: "Chief, I don't know what I have, but I have something by the tail. This man is guilty of something. I don't know what it is, but I never met a guiltier man in all my life. If I was a supercommissioner in Mr. Lindsay's administration and facing an assistant D.A. and innocent, I would have told *me* a long time ago to shut up and mind my own business."

Hogan told Rogers to go to it. Hogan remembered something that Rogers (known around the office as "the man with total recall") had forgotten: there was already a little shadow over Marcus' name.

A year earlier, Marcus had been mentioned as an investment partner of rogue labor lawyer Herbert Itkin, then under investigation for defrauding the owner of a motel in Tucson, Arizona. Rogers was preparing indictments in the $1.5-million mortgage swindle when the FBI told him that Itkin was a paid informant, perhaps the best informant the FBI ever had: "He's never lied to us. His information has always been right."

An arrangement was worked out with Hogan whereby the mortgage complaint would be shelved on condition that Itkin produce state information of use to the D.A.'s office. For the next six or seven months, Itkin walked around with a miniature tape recorder strapped to his belly, but it was all a farce. He provided no information for the D.A.'s office. Itkin was too busy working angles with the FBI. His "double agent" status was a laugh over there, too. He gave information all right—but only on cases in which he'd been caught. Were there other shady deals? Nobody knew.

Having inveigled his way into Marcus' life back in 1965, Itkin had conspired endlessly to make political connections with City Hall.

"Attorney for the People"—Frank Hogan takes over from Tom Dewey at swearing-in ceremony, December 29, 1941. Judge George L. Donnellan administers the oath. (N.Y. Daily News)

The District Attorney and Mrs. Hogan at home (1942). (N.Y. Daily News)

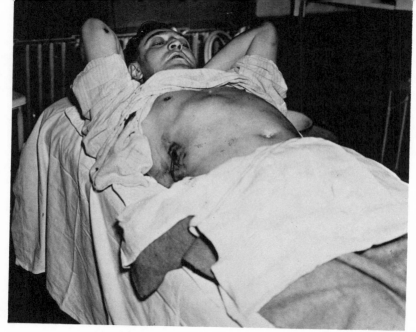

Numbers racketeer Dutch Schultz still conscious in Newark emergency ward after being gunned down by unknown assailants (1935). (Wide World Photos)

Jimmy Hines, still riding high in Democratic politics, on trial for protecting the Dutch Schultz gambling empire (1938). (Wide World Photos)

Lucky Luciano is crowned "Public Enemy No. 1" in 1940. (Wide World Photos)

New York Mayor William O'Dwyer has a close shave in 1949 when Hogan's wire-tap evidence stops just short of stowing Hizzoner behind bars. (New York Post photograph by Calvacca. © 1949, New York Post Corporation.)

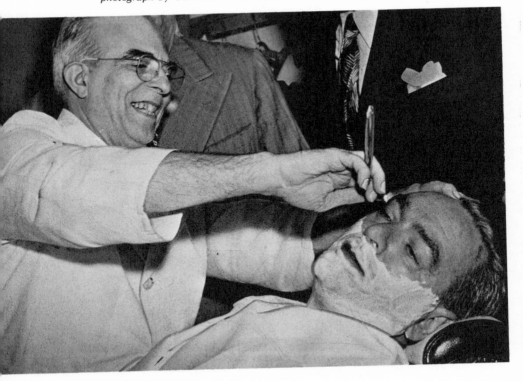

"A Hepburn gone haywire"—G-string dancer Madeline Webb, a murderess, narrowly escapes the electric chair (1942).

"The King of Bookmakers"—Frank Erickson is a long shot loser (1951). (New York Post *photograph by Stein.* © 1951, New York Post Corporation.)

Slot machine czar Frank Costello gets a free ride (1961). (New York Post photograph by Stein. © 1961, New York Post Corporation.)

Rocky Graziano is middleweight champion in 1947, but loses his boxing license for neglecting to report a fight fix. (New York Post photograph by Stein. © 1947, New York Post Corporation.)

All-American basketball star Jack Molinas, a pastmaster at rigging the point-spread (1954). (New York Post photograph by Calvacca. © 1954, New York Post Corporation.)

Why are these men laughing? Emcee Jack Barry and star contestant Charles Van Doren hype NBC-TV's quiz show, "Twenty-One." (1957). (New York Post photograph by Stein. © 1957, New York Post Corporation.)

(Left to right) Detective Edward Bulger, the "blundering constable," with prisoner George Whitmore, Jr., the wrong man (1964). (New York Post photograph by James. © 1964, New York Post Corporation.)

Political whisperings of Tammany boss Carmine De Sapio (middle), once the most powerful Democrat in New York State, do not concern Mayor Robert F. Wagner or Harry Truman during the Hogan-for-Senate race of 1958.

"Dah-ling!"—Tallulah Bankhead is being ripped off by her maid when the actress appeals to Hogan for help (1951). (Wide World Photos)

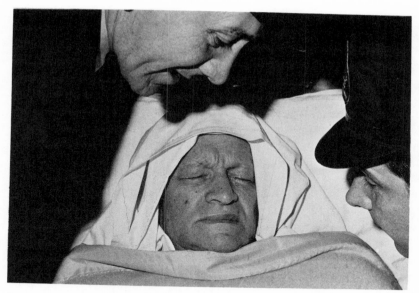

State liquor chairman Martin Epstein, looking like a Pharoah's mummy, is hauled before the grand jury on an ambulance stretcher. Epstein, who has just had his leg amputated, remains tight-lipped about liquor license bribes (1964). (N.Y. Daily News photo)

Hogan's biggest mistake—prosecuting Lenny Bruce for poor taste. (1964). (New York Post photograph by Jacobellis. © 1964, New York Post Corporation.)

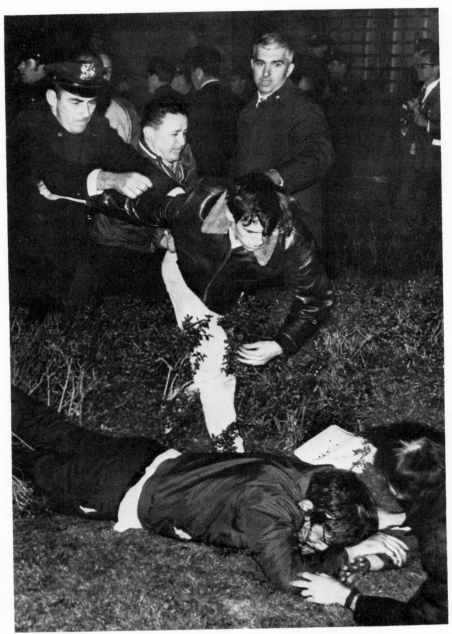

Nightmare at Hogan's alma mater: Columbia University during the SDS rebellion of 1968. (Wide World Photos)

Black Panthers flank the Criminal Courts Building as Hogan charges twenty-one of their members with an alleged bomb plot (1969). (New York Post photograph by Liotta. © 1969, New York Post Corporation.)

Bearded detective Frank Serpico blows the lid on police corruption in the Big Apple. Serpico, testifying at televised hearings of the 1971 Knapp Commission, is accompanied by his lawyer, former U.S. Attorney General Ramsey Clark. (New York Post photograph by Stein. © 1971, The New York Post Corporation.)

David Levine caricature of Frank Hogan appeared in the December 6, 1971 issue of New York magazine. (Courtesy of the artist)

"Marcus was a beautiful front," the pudgy-faced Itkin later reminisced. "He gave it real dignity. Instead of introducing Herbie Itkin, a Jewish lawyer from New York, we could introduce James Marcus, the son-in-law of Governor Lodge."

As Marcus described it, a Svengali-Trilby relationship soon developed between the two men. Little mesmerizing was needed to get Marcus interested in what Itkin had to offer. When the Xtra margin call went out in April 1966, Itkin arranged to undertake the needed loan through a racketeering friend named Antonio (Tony Ducks) Corallo. The Water Commissioner and the Mafioso arranged to meet in an East Side restaurant, while Marcus' chauffeur waited in the limousine outside.

Corallo agreed to a four-for-one loan of $10,000. For every dollar he put up, he would get back four dollars' worth of stock—plus this agreement: all emergency cleaning contracts on the Jerome Park Reservoir, which provided most of the city's drinking water, would go to a contractor friend named Henry Fried.

Hogan's office and the FBI could never agree at what point the reservoir bribe became known to Itkin's FBI contact, Special Agent William Vericker. Vericker said he learned of the Marcus affair after it was all over—in August 1967. Hogan maintained that the FBI didn't know a thing about it until Assistant D. A. Rogers dredged up the truth in grand-jury proceedings between October and December. At any rate, Hogan heard nothing from the FBI. If the Bureau had prior information, as it claimed, then it had reneged on its agreement to provide state information of use to Hogan's office. Hogan had delayed the earlier Itkin indictment for one year so the informer could be of service to the FBI. Now, the Bureau came back through the U.S. Attorney's office and wanted Hogan to give Itkin, in effect, a suspended sentence. The Chief refused to do it.

On April 14, 1967, Hogan indicted Itkin on charges of grand larceny in the Arizona motel swindle. The self-styled informer had still never squawked about any financial shenanigans between Marcus and Tony Ducks. But Frank Rogers had reconstructed the wheeling-dealing through grand jury action:

"We started to lay the subpoenas on in earnest: brokerage firms, savings accounts, checking accounts. We got brokers to testify, bankers to testify. Marcus resisted throughout."

Hogan, deciding it was time to alert Lindsay to the investigation, called City Hall: "Mr. Mayor, did you know we have questioned one of your commissioners several times and we're not satisfied with his answers?"

"No," said Lindsay. "Which one?"

"Marcus."

"Marcus? But there's nothing wrong with him! What are you suggesting?"

"I'm suggesting that if one of *my* assistants were called to the District Attorney's office and didn't come back and tell me directly, I'd fire him!"

Lindsay took the cue fast. On December 12, Marcus drew up his resignation at the Mayor's request. Lindsay had been told nothing by the FBI.

Three days later, Rogers walked into a Manhattan grand-jury room and hit Marcus with the name Corallo: "Do you know Tony Ducks?" Marcus denied it. He left the courthouse that day and ran to Itkin: "They're asking about Corallo."

"Well," said Itkin, "you better give up and come on over to the Feds. They'll give you a better deal than Hogan." Water Commissioner Marcus went to the office of then U.S. Attorney Robert Morgenthau and shrewdly recounted what he called the whole "nightmare" from start to finish. At one point in the four-for-one deal, Marcus told Morgenthau, the mob pressures became so intense that Marcus had contemplated jumping out a window.

Marcus and Corallo were now scheduled to reappear before the Manhattan grand jury on December 18. Rogers was waiting outside the grand-jury room at 1:34 P.M. when the phone rang. It was Hogan. The Chief had just received a call from his wife, who was listening to the radio that day.

"Frank," said Hogan. "You got that grand jury going?"

"Yes, sir," Rogers replied.

"You expect Marcus?"

"Yes, sir."

"Corallo?"

"Yes, sir."

"Well, I think you can apologize to the grand jury and explain that the two of them won't be there after all. They've just been indicted."

"You're kidding," said Rogers. "There must be a mistake. It can't be *our* Marcus . . . it must be another one."

Hogan said: "Is this other Marcus the Commissioner of Water Supply?"

Rogers said, "Holy Christ!"

That same morning, Marcus and his co-defendants had been taken before a federal grand jury. Then they were politely escorted to lunch while indictments were drawn up against them. The office of U.S. Attorney Morgenthau released the story to the press while Hogan's men waited "like idiots" at the door of their own grand-jury room. Three months of vigorous investigation had gone down the drain. The FBI had robbed them of one of the juiciest political scandals in the city's history.

Hogan was furious with Morgenthau, who by this time was being referred to as "the germ" around the D.A.'s office. Hogan telephoned the U.S. Attorney and all but yelled at him: "That case was absolutely stolen from us!"

Hogan's fading relationship with the quiet, bespectacled Morgenthau, grandson of the Secretary of the Treasury, came to an abrupt end. Morgenthau went on the offensive, calling Hogan's accusation of "stealing" a "destructive thing . . . It will hurt informants and ruin stool pigeons."

By this time, Itkin was squealing on Carmine DeSapio, whose name had come out at the Marcus-Itkin bribery trial. Itkin began sending back reports that Hogan had covered up for his old political supporter by refusing to indict him on state charges. A former federal prosecutor added that Hogan's office "had a complete case against DeSapio and did nothing with it. They kept saying we don't have a case. We went ahead and indicted him."

Such statements traveled back to Hogan, making him feel like the man who twists a bottlecap, doesn't realize he's loosened it, and hands it over to a child, who, with one touch, unscrews it. Morgenthau's work had already been done for him. The only scraps of evidence he had against DeSapio were a couple of money wrappers from a kickback deal involving city permits on an overhead transmission line. The wrappers had been turned over by Hogan because he couldn't use them without Itkin's testimony. The state law on conspiracy requires corroborative evidence other than that of a co-conspirator. The Feds had no such requirement. So they went ahead and indicted the ex-Tammany boss.

Even so, they couldn't have made a case against DeSapio without Hogan's help. On two occasions, the D.A. invited his onetime sponsor up to the office for an explanation of his dealings with Marcus and Itkin. The second time, DeSapio sat and talked to a Hogan bureau chief for nearly two hours, not realizing that Hogan had bugged the desk. The tapes that resulted helped the Feds convict DeSapio, once the most powerful Democrat in the state, on kickback-conspiracy charges involving Consolidated Edison, the giant public utility.

To this day, senior staff men maintain that the "bitter feud" that ensued between Hogan and Morgenthau was largely a difference of philosophy. Hogan's strongest venom was still reserved for FBI Director J. Edgar Hoover.

The Marcus-Itkin case brought to a head nearly thirty years of festering ill will between Hogan and Hoover. There had always been friction—healthy competition between law-enforcement agencies trying to screw each other out of cases that make headlines. The 1966 gold case was one in point.

Mel Glass was in charge of the Complaint Bureau at that time, and he received word of a sensational larceny case. "Fifty tons of black-market gold were supposed to be unloaded by the Mexican government to support the 1968 Olympic Games," Glass recalled. "I told Mr. Hogan about it, and he said, 'It's got to be a con job. Why don't you go over and tell Bob Morgenthau about it?'

"Morgenthau said the same thing: 'It's got to be a con job.'

"I said, 'I *know* it's a con job. Now what are we gonna *do* about it?'

"So Morgenthau calls the Justice Department and they speak to the Secretary of the Treasury. This is all happening in the middle of the gold crisis, remember, and after working with Morgenthau's office a few weeks, it looks like the con man behind the scheme is a federal informer.

"I asked the U.S. Attorney to find out, *discreetly*, whether the informer was involved. And to show you how the Feds work, they called the informer into the courthouse and *asked* him whether he was involved. And that blew the case."

Hogan's expert on stolen securities was bearded Assistant District Attorney Murray Gross, a man who spent most of his time negotiating with informants over flabbergasting purchases of stolen stock—more than $100 million worth annually.

"I was very aware of the feud between our office and the FBI," Gross remembers. "There were dozens of incidents where they double-crossed us. I remember when I testified before the McClellan Committee on stolen securities, one of the Congressmen asked if I had received cooperation from the federal agencies. I said we got very good cooperation. He asked, 'Including the FBI?' I said, 'No . . . excluding the FBI.' I told them the Bureau was a one-way street, that they don't cooperate. There was a Washington press conference later and most of the questions were about the FBI. I called Hogan and told him that I had gotten a very good reception. 'McClellan was nice and sends regards to you. There's only one thing there may be a little problem with.'

"Hogan said, 'What did you tell them?' I said, 'I told them the truth.' He said, '*What did you tell them?*' So I repeated what I'd told them and he laughed and said, 'Don't worry about it. The truth is the best swindle.' "

The Hoover feud posed questions that worried many of Hogan's latter-day critics. Wasn't it, after all, a little like Dracula turning on the Wolf Man? Hadn't both men suffered the same hardening of the ideologies when it came to prosecuting anti-war radicals and Black Panthers? Hadn't both men become "living legends," or, as some would have it, living anathemas?

The two men were, of course, intrinsically different types. Hoover was always a cantankerous administrator with a narrow circle of male buddies. Hogan led a more normal and certainly more gracious life. The two men had met: back in the Truman days, the FBI Director paid Hogan's office one brief visit. Afterward, the two "Chiefs" sat down to a restaurant dinner and then took in a prizefight at Madison Square Garden. But Hoover was "strictly a cop," Hogan observed later, not anyone with whom he would ever choose to spend another evening.

The personal animosity started in 1966, after Hogan began investigating a ring of blackmailers who preyed on homosexuals. The victims, all prominent closet queens, included a member of Congress who had been shaken down for $40,000, two deans of Eastern universities, several professors, businessmen, a movie star, a television talk-show personality and one of the nation's leading musicians. Hogan accused the blackmailers' ringleader, Sherman Kaminsky, of extorting over a million dollars from prominent homosexuals over a ten-year period.

The operation was carefully planned: Kaminsky recruited ex-convicts to impersonate vice-squad detectives. He even provided his confederates with bona fide police shields, made-to-order arrest warrants, and phony "extradition papers." He would dispatch a young male hustler, or "chicken," to cruise airports and hotel lobbies until he picked up an affluent-looking homosexual. The chicken would then seduce his victim and lure him into a hotel room.

As soon as the two males settled into bed, flashbulbs would explode. "Detectives" burst upon the scene. The victim was told that to avoid exposure at home or at the office, he would have to buy the nude photos of himself. If he refused, the "detectives" asked for payoffs to avoid "arrest." If he refused again, he was simply overpowered and then robbed of his wallet and jewelry.

As the investigation spilled over into other states, the list of the ring's known victims grew, and so did Hoover's interest in the case. Hoover finally seized federal jurisdiction to enter into Hogan's investigation. Urgent priority messages streaked to Bureau offices across the land: track down the blackmailers at all costs, and smash the extortion scheme. A kind of Operation Overkill was begun: gay bars were raided by the FBI in wholesale numbers; mass roundups were conducted on waterfronts and in back-alley hangouts.

"Hoover really freaked out," recalled the Hogan assistant who handled the case, Richard Wynn. "It was incredible. The Bureau was poaching on us every day. We'd set up an arrest and at the last minute, they'd rush in and nab the guy for themselves."

Hoover called Hogan to make certain that none of the victims' names would be released to the press. Hogan assured the Director that exposure of homosexuals had never been office policy and never would be. The New York press always cooperated by deleting the names of victims who testified against their blackmailers before a grand jury.

A number of the victims did agree to come forward. A California surgeon who had been shaken down made three cross-country trips at his own expense to cooperate with the grand-jury inquiry. A British producer paid his own way from England to testify. A distinguished nuclear scientist who had paid $5,000 to ransom a roll of film, agreed to take the stand. Along with the other victims, the physicist had been duped into believing the extortionists were authentic New York policemen.

The tension between Hoover and Hogan tightened to the breakpoint when Manhattan detectives raided the apartment of Kaminsky's chief accomplice, Elwood (Buddy) Hammock. Hammock produced one of his chickens, a gay deceiver who claimed to have a glossy snapshot of J. Edgar Hoover in his possession. The hustler said he had taken the snapshot of Hoover, on vacation somewhere, petting a Dalmatian dog. The hustler warned that, if arrested, he would confess to an "escapade" with the FBI director himself.

Hogan never saw the purported photograph, according to detectives who helped stage the raid. But since the FBI had elbowed its way into the investigation, Hogan decided to apprise the Director of what a key defendant intended to declare in court. By all accounts, Hoover did not react kindly to the information.

He may have thought Hogan had his own doubts about Hoover's life-long attachment to Clyde Tolson, the Director's constant male companion. Although Tolson always stayed a respectful step behind the Boss in their famous walks together, their odd-couple relationship had titillated Washington's gay grapevine for years.

The gossip had spread to Capitol Hill in 1964, when Hoover's friend Walter Jenkins was arrested. Jenkins, a Presidential assistant to Lyndon Johnson, had been picked up on a morals charge in a basement men's room of the YMCA.

The episode sent Jenkins to the hospital with a nervous breakdown. Ostracized by the Johnson Administration because of the fear that the incident might jeopardize L.B.J.'s reelection chances, Jenkins had only one important bedside visitor: J. Edgar Hoover delivered a "get-well" bouquet of flowers.

Hogan had heard all the rumors about Hoover, but hadn't paid much attention. Wasn't this the same J. Edgar who, during the McCarthy days, had "purged" the State Department of 420 "commie queers"?

Times had changed, of course. Unlike blackmail victims of the past, many of the men trapped in Kaminsky's web had no intention of burrowing into the woodwork. If they came out anywhere, it was in the D.A.'s office. Encouraged by the progress he had made in lining up grand-jury witnesses, Hogan signed a subpoena ordering one of the best-known victims to come to New York and testify.

The subpoena was served on fifty-two-year-old Rear Admiral (ret.) William C. G. Church, one of the highest-ranking officers in the Pentagon—a naval air commander during the Japanese sneak attack on Pearl Harbor. On the night before the Manhattan grand jury convened to hear his testimony, December 19, 1965, the admiral drove to a motel in Rockwell, Maryland. He inserted the muzzle of a loaded revolver in his mouth and squeezed the trigger.

The admiral's suicide tormented Hogan more than any death sentence handed down in the days of Lepke and Dutch Schultz. The fact that his signature on a subpoena had apparently driven a man to blow his brains out seemed, to Hogan, a tragedy of infinite proportions.

The episode marked Hogan, in some quarters, as a "fag-baiter," a considerable disservice to him. As District Attorney, he had always taken liberty with the archaic New York law that made "consentual sodomy" a crime. Almost all police arrests were quietly dismissed with a warning. Hogan's refusal to prosecute homosexuals as outlaws virtually nullified the law itself. The "sodomy" law was buried along with such other dead statutes as adultery and vagrancy.

Hogan never seemed to fully understand J. Edgar Hoover's personal involvement in the blackmail case. Since his role was never explained, a lot of New York law-enforcement types remained convinced that the Director's "secret file" on the sex lives of Presidents and Congressmen left out the darkest secret of them all.

"To this day," said a Hogan detective familiar with the case, "you say 'Dalmatian dog' to the FBI and twenty-five G-men run for the nearest foxhole."

* * *

Over a span of twenty-nine years, Leonard Newman, chief of the D.A.'s Frauds Bureau, had seen them all: counterfeiters, art forgers, handkerchief switch artists, check kiters, auto-repair gypsters—scavengers of every sort. Yet until the night of Thursday, January 27, 1972, the frauds expert had never encountered a set of circumstances like those behind the "autobiography" of billionaire hermit Howard Hughes, written by Clifford Irving, the obscure writer from Ibiza.

Hogan's investigations had often trapped personalities whose criminal mischief added a certain gaiety to coffee breaks and cocktail-party chit-chat. But there had never been anything to compare with the way people carried on over Clifford Irving's misadventures: the sexy Baroness Nina van Pallandt in Mexico, the blond scuba diver Ann Baxter in St. Croix, and, of course, the author's own wife, a Swiss beauty named Edith.

The eccentric nature of Howard Hughes stimulated the widening audience of the interested, and curiosity was heightened by the disembodied voice of Hughes himself labeling the book a hoax over a telephone news conference.

Hughes could shed no light on the mystery of a Swiss bank deposit of $650,000 that McGraw-Hill and *Life* magazine believed they had paid Hughes for his autobiography, written by Irving. When the reclusive industrialist denied receiving the money, the publishers went to federal authorities and initiated an investigation in Switzerland.

Irving said he couldn't understand why Swiss police were hunting for a woman identified as "Helga Hughes" who had opened a Zurich bank account in the name of "H. R. Hughes" and then vanished to become the object of an international search. Irving was "leaning" toward a theory that the "Howard Hughes" he interviewed for the book might have been an impostor.

In a way, it amused Lenny Newman that the newspapers talked of an "intriguing puzzle" surrounding "Project Octavio," code name for the secret book project that had been assigned to Irving for a $100,000 writer's fee plus $15,000 in expenses.

Unless the book deal was legitimate, someone, as Newman saw it, had committed a felony: either the "Howard Hughes" impostor, or the female who had signed the forged bank checks, or the real Howard Hughes for misrepresenting that he never got the money, or Clifford Irving for perpetrating a hoax. In any event, it seemed no more than a caper of sorts, certain of easy unraveling in the end.

The D.A.'s office was virtually deserted on the night Clifford Irving arrived with his attorney, Martin S. Ackerman.

Irving was tired, still jet-lagged after a seven-hour flight from Madrid the previous day, and catching cold in New York's wintry air pollution. He had laryngitis from talking so much about the Hughes book with reporters, not only at Kennedy Airport but back home in Ibiza, where he had been under siege by the European *papparazzi*. Ackerman said his client was nevertheless anxious to give the Manhattan D.A. a "full explanation" of the book mystery.

This was not the first time Irving had visited the D.A.'s office. He had twice been consulted by Hogan as an "expert" on art forgeries. In Ibiza, Irving enjoyed going around with a pet monkey on his shoulder, talking about his good friend Elmyr de Hory, an Hungarian art forger about whom Irving had written a book called *Fake:* "All the world loves to see the experts and the Establishment made a fool of . . . and everyone likes to feel that those who set themselves up as experts are really as gullible as anyone else."

Hogan knew of the book. He also knew that Clifford Irving frequently shuttled between *les beaux mondes* of modern art in Europe and New York. On one occasion, Irving had even been invited to the Frauds Bureau to authenticate an art forgery.

This time, Newman busied himself at his desk as Irving and Ackerman were shown into the office. Newman made it a point not to get up to shake hands with the suspect. Experience had taught him not to make that gesture. He read Irving his Miranda warning: "You have the right to remain silent and refuse to answer questions. Do you understand?"

Yes, the writer croaked (his laryngitis), he was waiving his right to remain silent. Even as he spoke, Irving was irritated by Newman's refusal to get up and shake hands with him. "I felt terribly guilty when he refused to shake hands," Irving remembered afterward.

"Worse, he kept avoiding my eyes." Irving has the kind of piercing eyes that rivet a listener, rooting him with the author's sincerity. That Newman wouldn't look him in the eye bothered Irving enormously.

Newman sat, chain-smoking, patiently listening as Clifford Irving launched into what Newman later called the "longest bullshit story" ever told in the Manhattan D.A.'s office. No one interrupted as the writer spoke for two hours, explaining how Hughes had "requested" Irving's wife to deposit the Swiss bank checks. The suspect searched the faces around him for some visual reaction. There was none.

Lenny Newman finally spoke: "Where did you meet Howard Hughes?"

Irving plopped a coughdrop on his tongue and gave his interrogator a Chap-stick smile. "Palm Springs."

"Where in Palm Springs?"

"At a roadstop outside town. I got a call at two A.M. to meet him. He drove up in an old Chevy and got out of the car."

"What did he say when he got out of the car?"

"He was talking to his passenger in the back seat."

"What was he saying?"

" 'It's all right, Spiro. This is a friend of mine.' "

Newman and his assistants exchanged glances. "Don't tell us—Spiro T. *Agnew?*"

"Yes. The Vice President." Irving seemed in earnest. Newman blinked in disbelief. But Irving stuck to what he was saying with such maddening persistence that after another hour of questioning Newman began to mistrust his own instincts.

The story of a predawn rendezvous on a California desert with the Vice President of the United States and a man who hadn't shown his face in public for twenty years was so farfetched that no rational man would dream of offering it as an alibi. Unless? Could the story be true? Or parts of the story true?

Newman had another factor to consider that night: a mysterious phone call he had received shortly after Ackerman contacted the office.

The telephone caller had identified himself as a U.S. Postal Inspector on special assignment from Washington, D.C. The caller said that he and a partner were "waiting outside the building" to serve a subpoena on Clifford Irving whenever the D.A.'s office was finished with him. This had struck Lenny Newman as a peculiar way to initiate a federal investigation. He suggested that the two men come in out of the cold and use the upstairs waiting room. But the caller declined the invitation and hung up.

Thinking back on that telephone call, Newman wondered why the Justice Department in Washington was interested in a New York larceny case. There were plenty of postal inspectors in New York. Why should two special "mail-fraud" investigators be sent all the way from the nation's capital? It didn't make sense. Newman decided to call the U.S. Attorney's office—just to confirm that the two inspectors were who they said they were. He was told that, indeed, a "coast-to-coast" task force of postal inspectors had entered the case, and there was the possibility of the FBI's stepping in, too. "Why?" Newman wanted to know.

"Because we've heard there's Carlo Gambino money behind Irving." Newman hung up, no more prepared to accept this explanation than he was ready to believe Clifford Irving. The image of Irving as a front man for the Mafia seemed totally out of character with his life style and artistic pretensions—just as his willingness to talk was not characteristic of the mob. Newman allowed an unpleasant thought to surface, then sink again into his subconscious: *Nixon doesn't want this meeting with Hughes and Agnew to come out.*

Lenny Newman was determined to get some sort of admission out of Irving before the Feds got hold of him. Lenny's talent for coaxing confessions out of unwilling suspects was greatly admired by Frank Hogan. When people asked Lenny how he did it, the Frauds chief would simply shrug, "I don't try to con anybody. I just present the alternatives as truthfully and honestly as I can."

While their book project teetered on the brink of disaster, the prospective publishers of *The Autobiography of Howard Hughes* had no unarguable proof to corroborate the author's claims of access to the eccentric billionaire. There were no tape recordings or testimony from disinterested witnesses—a tribute to how well Irving had covered his tracks. The "honest alternative" approach to a confession was the only one possible. Lenny Newman leaned across the desk and made direct eye contact with Clifford Irving for the first time.

"The time to own up to all of this is now," he said flatly. "Now, while you're still part of the nation's folklore. Let's face it. You've pulled off the literary hoax of the century. People will enjoy and admire you—so far. If you wait, you're gonna have a federal grand jury breathing down your neck. You're going to lose your charm, your allure. You'll be just a common criminal . . . a bum for letting your wife go down the drain. It's better to confess now. Now, while you still have the money. Now, while McGraw-Hill can be made whole again. Now, while we can give your wife immunity."

Newman continued with this low-key, almost *hamische* persuasion. Today, a rueful Clifford Irving remembers it as "the kindly Jewish uncle approach," adding, "He would slip in a few Yiddish words here and there. Suggest we were just two Hebes in this thing together. Suggest I understand and I'm on your side . . . that's the game he was playing with me."

Irving wasn't buying any of it. "I'm innocent," he maintained.

"Think about it," suggested Newman, writing out a subpoena for him to return the next day. Irving took the subpoena and left the building with his lawyer. Outside, the postal inspectors were waiting. "Clifford Irving?" one of them inquired as the writer climbed in a taxi. The process server lunged forward to present Irving with a federal subpoena. Irving tried to slam the taxi door on the man's arm, but it was too late. The subpoena, served, lay in a puddle of melted snow on the floor of the cab as it sped into the night.

Wild rumors reached Hogan the next day via his junior assistants. Obviously, there was pressure from Washington for the U.S. Attorney's office to get involved. One of the prosecuting attorneys, Frauds Bureau assistant Charles Clayman, had been assigned to read the top-secret galley proofs of the Howard Hughes book, now locked in an office safe.

Hogan understood from Clayman's reading of the book that it mentioned a loan made in 1960 by Howard Hughes: $205,000 to Donald Nixon, the then-Vice President's brother, in a vain attempt to salvage Donald's sagging chain of California drive-in restaurants. The fast-food franchise advertised three-decker sandwiches called "Nixonburgers." Donald Nixon had never repaid the loan. Afterward, Howard Hughes gained federal favors worth millions through tax shelters such as the Howard Hughes Medical Institute and certain airline cost exemptions. No clear connection was ever established between the loan and actual "services rendered."

However, Noah Dietrich, formerly executive vice president of the Hughes Tool Company, had an unfinished manuscript of his own which told how he had visited Richard Nixon before the payoff was made. In the manuscript (which Dietrich had loaned to Clifford Irving), the

Hughes executive warned the Vice President that the loan would become known sooner or later and cause a scandal. "Mr. Dietrich, I have to put my relatives ahead of my career," Nixon was said to have responded.

Hogan had since learned that the "Nixonburger" exposé was leaked to muckraker columnist Drew Pearson during the 1960 campaign. Irving merely added certain embellishments to the already twice-told tale. One exaggerated excerpt from the spurious "autobiography" quoted Hughes as saying he had paid $400,000 to Nixon in the 1950s, expecting him to help Hughes with his problems over Trans World Airlines. Irving maintained (if anyone could still believe him) that there was another excerpt in the original manuscript, deleted by McGraw-Hill lawyers, in which Hughes was quoted as saying, "There are other monies totaling $195,000 which I gave to Nixon for other favors through a third party whose name I can't tell you."

If Hogan had known about the coincidence of Irving's make-believe dialogue and an actual Howard Hughes "loan" of $100,000 to Nixon's 1972 campaign, the D.A. might have understood the consternation in Attorney General John Mitchell's office that month. In retrospect, Hogan would learn how seriously Mitchell's men regarded the "autobiography," even speculating that Irving got his information from documents in the safe of Hank Greenspun, flamboyant publisher of the Las Vegas *Sun.* The Senate Watergate Committee would elicit closed-door testimony that Waterbugger G. Gordon Liddy was instructed on February 4, 1972, to study the possibility of breaking into the publisher's safe and escaping by private plane to Mexico. Senate investigators believed the White House was afraid at the time—fearful that the Hughes memos might contain evidence of the "dirty deal" $100,000 in cash kept in the safe of Presidential buddy C. G. (Bebe) Rebozo in Key Biscayne, Florida.

As the Watergate scandal widened over the next two years, the younger men in the Frauds Bureau began referring to the postal inspectors in the Irving case as "the plumbers," convinced that they, too, had been Gordon Liddy operatives on an intelligence-gathering mission the night they confronted Clifford Irving and his lawyer on the icy sidewalk.

Meanwhile, negotiating behind the scenes with the U.S. Attorney's office, Hogan struck a plea bargain with Clifford Irving. Although the local charges carried a maximum prison penalty of seven years, an agreement for Irving to serve only two and a half years was worked out—in exchange for details of the hoax. Irving and his researcher, Richard Susskind, named as a co-conspirator in a federal indictment, told how they had pla-

giarized previous books and magazine articles about the millionaire industrialist, believing that Hughes was "too senile" to renounce the "autobiography." At one point, the hoaxers had even managed to smuggle a
1,500-word interview transcript out of the Library of Congress.

The assorted forgeries in the case—a doctored passport, dramatic letters
in Hughes handwriting, and the Swiss bank checks—had led Hogan to
suspect that Irving's art-forger friend Elmyr de Hory was also involved.

Irving, the son of a cartoonist, insisted he had acted alone, practicing
Hughes' handwriting for days, even weeks, on end. As a sample, he used
a facsimile Howard Hughes note printed in the December 21, 1970, edi-
tion of *Newsweek*.

"Would you be willing to give us a sample of Hughes' handwriting to
prove it?' Newman challenged Irving on the day he confessed, March 7,
1972.

"Sure," Irving shrugged and picked up a fountain pen. Newman slid
over a sheet of foolscap paper, then dictated a letter. Irving wrote out the
words in longhand almost as fast as they were spoken:

Dear Mr. McGraw,

This letter will inform you that the book in your possession was
not written by Clifford Irving.

Most sincerely yours,
Howard R. Hughes

Lenny picked up the letter and shook his head. "Fantastic."
He framed the letter as a permanent office souvenir.

9
ROTTEN APPLES

The apocalypse of Hogan's career began with a front-page headline in the New York *Times* of April 25, 1970:

GRAFT PAID TO POLICE HERE
SAID TO RUN INTO MILLIONS

The *Times* exposé sent a seismic tremor through City Hall and the surrounding granite of municipal buildings and courthouses on Manhattan's Foley Square. The reverberations left cracks in the New York City Police Department that have never fully healed.

For the first time in the Department's history, a police officer had come forward voluntarily to testify about widespread corruption in the ranks. He did so after a four-year ordeal in which high police brass and political officials had dismissed his allegations as the ravings of a psycho. Finally, in desperation, this officer had gone to the newspaper with his story. The honest cop was Patrolman Frank Serpico, the bearded, pot-smoking, hippie-cop whose defiance of institutionalized police graft made him a Hollywood movie hero—and an overnight millionaire. Serpico, ridiculed and feared by the crooked plainclothesmen he rubbed shoulders with every day, singlehandedly toppled New York's police command. The liberal administration of then-Mayor John V. Linday was scandalized, and quickly lurched into an offensive.

The city's police precincts were purged. Department commanders were banished to distant outposts, inspectors were stripped of their rank. The Police Commissioner resigned. And a Commission to Investigate Alleged Police Corruption was formed in May 1970, by order of the Mayor.

The Serpico case had a broad theatrical outline. The protagonist was an undercover narc who loved opera, girls and sheep dogs, practiced karate, and obliged his enemies in the department by getting himself shot in the head during a heroin raid. Serpico's story, told in the best-selling book by Peter Maas and in the movie *Serpico*, enriched the policeman a hundredfold over the loot he would have raked in had he gone "on the pad." A marked man after his bombshell, Serpico took his newfound riches and went off to find life anew in a Swiss mountain retreat.

It is difficult to understand the Serpico case without an overview of police graft in New York since the early 1890s. Corporate price-fixing, lethal consumer frauds, political graft, child labor, the industrial exploitation of sweatshop workers—none of this "white-collar" crime offended the American conscience over the years as did the occasional sweetening of a policeman's palm by gamblers and prostitutes. Whether real or imagined, the idea that every man in blue is on the take has always obsessed newspaper editors (and sold papers). Politicians have also known that the only sure way to banish the opposition scoundrels from public office is to form a civic committee and go after greedy cops. The exercise of this tactical principle took place in 1894 with the so-called Lexow Committee. The committee's year-long hearings produced a report that policemen were not underpaid creatures with large families and mortgages to sustain, but a complacent, oppressive caste of public bloodsuckers who had bankbooks purpled with deposit stamps. The political consequence of the Lexow report was that a reform mayor, William L. Strong, ousted the Tammany tinhorns from City Hall. Teddy Roosevelt was appointed Police Commissioner.

A few years later, after Tammany had recaptured City Hall, the Mazet Committee was formed to investigate police payoffs with gambling graft. Once more a reform mayor was elected. In 1909, John D. Rockefeller, Jr., was recruited as foreman of a grand-jury investigation of police corruption. In the fall, the reformers took five or six major offices.

The biennial police exposés that followed into the 1920s and '30s—the Committee of One Hundred, the Curran Committee of the New York Board of Aldermen, the Committee of Nine, and so on—all charged that corruption still poisoned the Police Department. After each rousing investigation, a few scapegoats would resign, their resignations making headlines. But criminal prosecutions were virtually zero. The Department insisted that it was too preoccupied with chasing murderers and rapists to pay attention to newspaper stories. The reformers seldom stayed in office longer than a single term, anyway. The odor of corruption soon wafted away.

"The people can't stand all this police corruption," declared one Tammany sachem of the period, "but they can't stand reform, either."

In 1932, the "little tin box" disclosures of Samuel Seabury's committee revealed that the Police Department served pretty much as a collection agency for the New York County Democratic Organization (Tammany Hall), a sort of enforcement arm for political shakedowns of speakeasies and bootleggers. The political dynamite of the Seabury Committee disclosures paved the way for Tom Dewey's cleanup crusade. But there was hardly a ripple of concern in the Police Department.

Having heard about the avarice of "New York's Finest" in every election campaign since the turn of the century, New Yorkers were hardly taken by surprise in 1950 when the Harry Gross scandal broke in Brooklyn. Gross, a gambling monopolist with several plainclothes squads on his million-dollar-a-year protection payroll, took the witness stand and identified twenty-one police officers as his bookmaking buddies. He balked at further testimony and was held in contempt. The defendants had to be set free. Case dismissed. Jaundiced observers knew they'd heard that song before.

The Democratic bosses were still in the saddle. And police payoffs escalated to keep pace with the cost-of-living spiral.

Hogan was having dinner with Jacob Grumet one night after the latter had left the D.A.'s office to become City Fire Commissioner. When the discussion turned to parity pay scales in the Police Department and Fire Department, Grumet said, "Frank, the firemen's union leader came to me today and said he wanted it written into the next contract: firefighters deserve higher pay than cops because firemen lack the same opportunity for 'bonuses' that the cops get. He wanted to make police graft a formal subject for contract negotiations!"

An amusing anecdote, but Hogan suspected the Commissioner of exaggerating for laughs. Hogan still clung to the "rotten apple" theory of police graft. It would be as unfair to assume that every cop was corrupt, he thought, as it was naive to believe that none of them were. One or two rotten apples didn't spoil the barrel. Moral reform by committee was, as Hogan saw it, a diversionary maneuver away from the fundamental questions of police crime. Sensational inquests into the sins of the Department overlooked the ambivalent community standards that produce the bundle of contradictions we call a crooked cop.

The policeman is daily subjected to "pig-cop" verbal abuse and physical indignities—indignities which provoke his desire to respond in kind against the despised "system." The irony: a system that encourages expense accounts, business lunches and corporate Christmas presents to politicians, slaps the hand that accepts a free hamburger from some greasy-spoon owner. An ordinary man, the cop is expected to resist the extraordinary temptations that arise in his daily contact with gamblers, pimps and dope hustlers. He justifies his share of the "pad" as a form of punishment against these "bedbugs." If turnstile justice can't punish them, the cop will. More important, the dishonest cop feels pretty safe in the narrow subculture of the stationhouse, a clique that thrives on secrecy, stereotyped enthusiasms, exaggerated masculinity and a regimental pecking order. He belongs to a secret cult in which the only commandment is "Thou shalt not inform on a brother officer."

Hogan believed the instigators of all those anti-cop crusades were sour hypocrites, enriching their own political fortunes through the exposure of a few wretched grafters and broken-down whores. Witch-hunting investigating committees had traditionally trampled over the Constitution, suspended due process, permitted hearsay evidence, and ruined decent reputations by character assassination.

Going after greedy cops was a Band-Aid remedy applied to the gangrene of entrenched corruption, Hogan felt. Given the dimensions of human frailty, you had to remove the temptation before you could remove the problem. That was the Legislature's job. Hogan submitted fifty-seven recommendations to Mayor Lindsay for dealing realistically with police graft: Hold a public referendum. Eliminate the victimless crimes of gambling and prostitution. Eliminate arrest quotas. Lift the police officer's responsibility to regulate liquor licenses and construction permits. Here was where most of the money changed hands. Also, penalize the bribe giver and the bribe taker with *equal* punishment.

Hogan waited in vain for a response from the Mayor. All that Lindsay did was appoint the District Attorney to still another anti-corruption panel, an interdepartmental committee to investigate the *Times'* exposé. The Rankin Committee, named after the city's Corporation Counsel J. Lee Rankin, included, of all people, Howard Leary, who was then Police Commissioner. Hogan wouldn't have anything to do with the panel, especially when he learned that Lindsay wanted to "go public" and televise the hearings.

"I'm a quasi-judicial officer," Hogan protested. "I can't associate myself with public hearings. I cannot develop an interest in the guilt of somebody based on hearsay. Forget it. I'm walking out."

"I assure you, Frank, there won't be any public hearings," Lindsay vowed, and begged him to stay on.

"We can't be investigating ourselves!" Hogan banged his fist on the conference table. He urged Lindsay to appoint an independent committee of non-officeholders. The conflict-of-interest question aside, Hogan wouldn't sit on any committee that included Police Commissioner Howard Leary. There had been a tense, shifting relationship between the two men ever since Lindsay had brought Leary up from Philadelphia, where Leary had built his reputation as a "liberal" police commissioner.

Lindsay had hired Leary as a yes-man to replace outgoing Police Commissioner Vincent Broderick. Broderick had opposed Lindsay's plan to implement one of the mayor's campaign promises—a Civilian Review Board to examine complaints of police brutality. A voter referendum—aided by a million-dollar public-relations blitz from the Patrolmen's Benevolent Association—eventually rejected the proposal. After the defeat, Lindsay was stuck with Howard Leary, perhaps the most peculiar public man in the city's history.

The Commissioner, a balding, turnip-faced fellow, was as exhilarating as vinegar. He had made the grade of detective years before—on the Philadelphia "fag posse." For years, Leary squinted through peepholes into public men's rooms, nabbing homosexuals as they attempted their moist pleasures behind the stalls. He divided his time between peeping and night school. A law degree finally sprang him from the toilet assignment to rise through the ranks and become Philadelphia's top cop. When Lindsay tapped him in 1966 to become the New York Police Commissioner, Leary settled into a furnished room—and his own odd life style. He would spend four or five hours a night in the back room of a tavern across the street from his Lower Manhattan digs. At the bar, he would sit alone, watch television, and silently inhale the yeasty effervescence of beer.

Leary hated New York City, and would rather have been in Philadelphia. As a matter of fact, he *was* in Philadelphia most of the time. He commuted back to Philadelphia every weekend to be with his wife, who was a high school principal there. Monday morning was a real downer for the Commissioner. So he got into the habit of ducking back to Headquarters late Tuesday. Friday, of course, was a chance to get away early and beat the traffic to Philadelphia. In between trips, he found other ways to goof off. There are almost as many expense-paid law-enforcement conventions around the world as there are taxpayer dollars to pay for them. Leary found these invitations to far-flung travel irresistible.

The jet-setting Police Commissioner was finally grounded as a result of some dramatic events at Police Headquarters: A terrorist explosion with the pent-up force of fifteen sticks of dynamite blew out the rear wall of the Headquarters, some 125 feet from the Commissioner's office.

"Is he in there?" a frantic police rescuer called out as the dust settled. "Are you kidding?" came a deputy's reply. "He's *never* in there." An embarrassed Howard Leary had to be summoned all the way back from a London freebee conference to inspect the crumble of brick and mortar dust that had been his professional domain.

New York City confused the Commissioner. Two years after taking office, he still hadn't learned where the various police precincts were located. He confused New York and Philadelphia street names. His few press conferences were fiascos. "Uh, duh . . . um . . ." the Commissioner painfully searched his memory for crime statistics. He garbled his syntax and hopscotched from one unrelated topic to another. And he was completely adrift in the sea of internal N.Y.P.D. politics. The top echelons were still captained by the so-called Irish Mafia, the law-and-order conservatives. Leary limply allowed himself to be held under their sway.

First, the Old Guard persuaded him to shift plainclothesmen from the Public Morals (vice) Squad to the Narcotics Unit. This move bothered Hogan: "If there's larceny in the Department," the D.A. protested, "it's in the Public Morals Squad. Why are you introducing it into the Narcotics Squad, which has a good reputation?" It was Department legend that the one taboo rigidly regarded by thieving cops was never touching narcotics graft "because your kids might get hooked some day." But Hogan had protested in vain.

The D.A. also complained that it was foolish for Leary to flood the D.A.'s office with penny-ante gambling arrests and hooker roundups every time Lindsay pressured him into another of the always unsuccessful Times Square cleanup crusades.

In April 1968, Hogan had surveyed one hundred of Leary's gambling arrests, which had resulted in seventy-five convictions. "Not one of the arrestees went to jail, even though some of them had long yellow sheets," said Hogan. "The total amount in fines was $5,000; in effect, a $60 gambling license. And it cost us $250,000 in manpower! Let's face it. The wave of the future is to legalize gambling. We have bingo, we have off-track betting, and we're probably going to have casinos." Leary seemed to be stuffing cotton in his ears. Maybe he just didn't understand.

At any rate, Hogan told Lindsay he wasn't about to serve now on any housecleaning committee with Howard Leary: "We'd just be irritating each other to no purpose."

Lindsay knuckled under and agreed to name an independent, five-member commission to replace the Rankin Committee. The Mayor asked Hogan to recommend a chairman. The D.A. suggested his former Appeals Chief, Whitman Knapp; a private citizen, at that time practicing law on Wall Street.

For several weeks, Leary complained to Lindsay that the Knapp Commission "would be McCarthyism all over again." But now, Lindsay was handcuffed to the commission and could do nothing. So Leary simply got up from his desk and disappeared. Sailed off to Europe. There was no letter of resignation. No press release. He just wasn't there any more. When he hadn't shown up for three days, Lindsay released a letter saying that Howard Leary had resigned. The letter extolled Leary's virtues and declared he would go down in history as one of the great police commissioners. Adieu, Howard Leary. When last seen, he was a floorwalker in a midtown department store: Chief of Security.

Although Lindsay had promised not to televise the Knapp hearings, going public now seemed the only way to help the Knapp Commission survive. The commission's legality was being challenged in court by the PBA, whose president, John Kiernan, had gone on record to say that he found nothing wrong with free meals and hotel rooms for policemen.

For nine days in October 1971, the home viewing audience was presented with another rousing spectacle of venal cops, each bleating in turn that Department pressures had gradually converted him from an idealistic rookie into a "meat-eater," grubbing for bribes and payoffs. Four "rotten apples" had been persuaded to work undercover for the commission under the compulsion of having been caught *in flagrante delicto* by Knapp's investigators.

The rottenest apple in the barrel was Patrolman William Phillips. Phillips' life style on the pad included flashy clothes, a private airplane and gambling trips to Las Vegas at $5,000 a clip. His smug glossary of graft included such quaint expressions as "grass-eaters" for meeker cops who, unlike meat-eaters, accepted only $10 and $20 Christmas "presents" from contractors, tow-truck operators and the like. The meat-eaters' monthly pad added up to as much as $3,500 in mid-Manhattan, $1,500 in Harlem. Even desk-job supervisors were entitled to a share and a half. Three other police grafters made their appearance and backed up Phillips' account of widespread corruption.

If only a tiny fraction of their charges were true, however, the scandal was sensational enough for the Police Department—and Frank Hogan —to consider abandoning the rotten-apple doctrine. Even a high-ranking police executive, First Deputy Commissioner William H. T. Smith, declared: "They [the public] are sick of bobbing for rotten apples in the police barrel. They want an entirely new barrel that will never again become contaminated."

If Serpico had proved to be a "live hand grenade" to the Department's Old Guard, Phillips was a walking time bomb to the criminal-justice Establishment. The hearings detonated when Phillips told how, apart from graft, some cops practiced unorthodox maneuvers to guarantee the outcome of court cases. The most common tactic was that of "dropsy" practice in drug busts.

To skirt their way around the 1961 *Mapp v. Ohio* Supreme Court decision forbidding unreasonable searches and seizures, undercover narcs gave identical testimony in case after case. Their heroin seizures were "reasonable," they said, because they never frisked a suspect or smashed down his apartment door.

Instead—their language was always the same—"the defendant dropped the contraband on the ground whereupon I arrested him." Hogan's press critics immediately accused him of winking at the "dropsy" fiction in order to get convictions—presuming a clairvoyance on the part of the D.A. as to which "dropsy" cases were perjured and which were bona-fide. In general, Hogan felt, news editors were sophisticated enough to understand the complicated legal obstacles of admissible evidence and cross-examinable witnesses: the difference between a straightforward criminal accusation and the ability to prove it under the rules of evidence. The tabloid mentality, however, cares not so much about what is really happening as what people *think* is happening. Obviously, it was more fun for reporters to write about Phillips taking brothel payoffs from kinky sex madam Xaviera Hollander, "The Happy Hooker," than to bore their readers with dissertations on the complexities of prosecution.

None of Hogan's critics attributed Hogan's moral bind to the *Mapp* decision itself, which, like the later *Miranda* ruling, went beyond the narrow facts of the case and drafted an unrealistic code of criminal procedure for big-city police. In the day-to-day coverage of the Knapp hearings, no attention was paid to police motives for perjuring themselves in hundreds of dropsy cases in which no money changed hands at all.

Could it have been that the *Mapp* decision, from a practical point of view, made drug busts illegal? Didn't the decent narcotics cop feel he had to tell a little white dropsy lie in order to make his arrest stick in court? The easiest answer was to ascribe the sins of the Department to the devil and attack Hogan for seeing things in "black and white."

The Knapp Commission scenario provided the official pretext for some political opportunists to enlarge the dropsy matter into a blanket indictment of Hogan's office. The District Attorney, charged defense lawyer Martin Garbus, had "consciously acquiesced" to criminal misbehavior by the police. Garbus had a strong motive to go on the offensive: he had bruited it around the courthouse that he was seeking the nomination for D.A. if Hogan could be pressured to resign.

Muckraking journalist Nat Hentoff, a board member of the New York Civil Liberties Union, went on public television to state the libertarian case against Frank Hogan:

"The guy's a phenomenon. The press set up a stereotype: here is this fearless, incorruptible man whose zeal is for justice and fairness to all . . . without looking into whether in fact the stereotype reflected complicated reality."

The complicated reality of police corruption, as Hentoff saw it, was that "any kind of input had to come first from the Knapp Commission. I don't see that there's been any investigating zeal ever by the D.A.'s office in terms of what goes on in police corruption. Hogan may be one of the worst district attorneys in the history of that office."

Hogan need not have apologized for his lack of "investigative zeal" in prosecuting demonstrable corruption cases. Since 1942, his office had prosecuted more rogue cops than all the other district attorneys, federal prosecutors and investigating committees *combined*. Hogan could have boasted of seventy-four police prosecutions in just the previous three years—involving sergeants, lieutenants and an assistant chief inspector.

His record compared favorably with the twenty-two indictments obtained by the Knapp Commission in a year's time. And the commission, with a budget of $500,000, a staff of forty, and the resources of virtually every federal and state crime-fighting agency at its command, had concentrated *solely* on police misconduct. Also—commission investigators failed to turn up evidence on any corrupt cop above the rank of sergeant.

Nat Hentoff was heated—but not necessarily well informed. His regular *Village Voice* column communicated the topical wisdom of a heavily psychoanalyzed New York intelligentsia. Hentoff's was a generation that had retreated from the bomb shelter paranoia of the 1950s into the allurements of jazz and zen. It was a jive-talking, grad-school generation that had found a vent for its pent-up sexuality in the toilet humor of suicidal sick comic Lenny Bruce. Hogan's prosecution of Bruce on obscenity charges in 1964 had pulverized the New York literati in general, and Hentoff in particular—the bearded writer had been a close friend of Bruce's. Obviously, the man who prosecuted Lenny could not be a friend—and the old grievance was still borne against Hogan.

The Lenny Bruce prosecution had been an utter disgrace. Hogan had put Bruce on trial for boorishness and bad taste; for offensiveness rather than offense. The trial brought shame not only to the Chief, but also to his young protégés in the office, many of whom were Bruce fans. A few of them tried to explain away the prosecution, accurately noting that the times had changed just a little bit faster than Hogan's consciousness.

Bruce had hardly been found guilty before Hogan regretted ever bringing him to trial. This feeling was demonstrated by the D.A.'s later decisions to allow erotic theater and hard-core porno films to flourish on Broadway. Whenever the old stick-in-the-mud epithets flew, Hogan would groan, "They've Lenny Bruced me again! Christ Almighty, that case was six years ago. Today we have stuff on Broadway that would make Lenny Bruce blush. Why don't they talk about *that!*"

Hentoff's singling out the D.A. as a target for the Knapp Commission seemed to suggest that Hogan was once again being "Bruced."

The Knapp Commission was an embarrassment: it *did* reflect poorly on Hogan. But Hentoff's theory that Hogan's "input" had to come from Knapp was off-base. Whitman Knapp had remained an affectionate Hogan loyalist and close friend since their early days together on the Dewey crusade. And Hogan admired the commission chairman. Knapp conveyed the refreshing, intelligent manner of an Archibald Cox kind of legal personality—a quiet-voiced, bookish man thrust into the sudden glare of television lights and unexpected controversy.

After Hogan recommended Knapp for the job, the new chairman arrived at the D.A.'s office one afternoon with a bold request. Would Hogan turn over to the commission his files on current corruption investigations in progress? This was not an ordinary favor. To grant it would go beyond what an ordinary man with natural survival instincts would do in the same situation. With little hesitation, however, Hogan agreed to turn over his leads to Knapp's investigators. So much for "input." There was actually *output*.

The feedback came during the public phase of the televised hearings, with suggestions that Hogan's judgment was misplaced. He had devoted less time to police graft than to conventional crime.

All the D.A.'s offices depended on policemen to conduct investigations, Knapp accurately noted. Indeed, prosecutors seemed to look upon themselves as allies of the Police Department. "New Yorkers," Knapp asserted, "just don't trust policemen to investigate each other." As validation of this distrust, Knapp produced a depressing statistic: of the 218 cops arrested since 1965, the first year such figures were recorded, ninety-one had been convicted and only twenty had received a jail term longer than one year. Phillips testified at one point that the dishonest policeman knows that even if he is nabbed red-handed, he will probably receive no more than a court reprimand; at most, a short jail term. Not much of a deterrent.

When Serpico and his friend Sergeant David Durk made their appearance on TV, they testified about how they had taken firsthand accounts of corruption to a number of higher-ups in the Police Department and at City Hall. The pattern of response had been the same—from division inspectors to the Police Commissioner, to the city's Department of Investigation, to the Mayor's office, the reaction was: don't make waves. The commission trotted out a dreary procession of Department officials, each intent on justifying his role in the cover-up. When it was all over, Serpico had gotten the same advice at the top of government as he had begun with at the bottom.

Captain Phillip Foran, head of the Department of Investigation's police squad, had put it bluntly back in August 1966, when Serpico had handed him an envelope containing $300 as payoff money from a gambler called Jewish Max. Foran gave Serpico a choice: he could either go before a grand jury with his information, after which he might wind up in the East River, or he could forget about it.

How this official ambivalence reflected on the city's District Attorneys wasn't clear to Hogan. There had been only one official action taken on Serpico's charges—this by Bronx D.A. Burton Roberts. Back in October 1967, Serpico had gone to his superior officer, Deputy Inspector Phillip Sheridan, to talk about rumors of corruption in the Seventh Division. To ensure secrecy, Roberts met Serpico in a motel room and listened to his allegations. When Serpico was finished, Roberts exclaimed triumphantly,

"Well, there's going to be a grand jury on these shitheels and you will appear as a witness against them."

Burton Roberts hadn't counted on Serpico's chickening out. The cop had good reason to be afraid, after Foran's veiled threats about winding up in the East River. Still, Roberts argued, wouldn't Serpico be hero enough to wear a wire and gather evidence on the pad in the Seventh Division? Contrary to the image provided for him in the book and movie that bear his name, Serpico got cold feet and refused.

"Look," Roberts said, "you don't have any evidence. All you're giving us is a hook. There's corruption in the division. Now put your money where your mouth is and help us catch the bastards." Serpico muttered something about the whole thing's being a farce. He wanted to start with the real culprits, the bosses in the Department, not the "schmuck cops." Roberts patiently explained investigative technique—how you have to start with small fry and turn them against the big fish.

Serpico, still wanting nothing to do with shoo-fly work, reluctantly agreed to appear before a grand jury, but balked as a witness. He claimed that Burton Roberts deliberately steered questions away from corruption by superior officers and concentrated on the flunkies. Serpico provided enough information to convict four officers on corruption charges, but it was hardly the scandal that Roberts had envisaged. It was, however, Roberts who had written letters to Commissioner Leary and Mayor Lindsay, commending Serpico for his "high moral courage" in exposing "a pattern of corruption in the Bronx." The D.A. waited patiently for an answer from Leary. When none came, Roberts persisted in dialing Headquarters until he got through to the Commissioner. Had Leary considered giving Serpico the gold detective's shield Roberts had recommended? "He's a psycho," Leary snapped.

In front of the Knapp Commission's cameras, Roberts charged that Serpico himself had thwarted the entire investigation in the Bronx. "This man didn't want to wear a wire," Roberts growled, "this man didn't want to go before a grand jury."

Leaving the hearing chamber, Roberts spoke to Hogan with less restraint. "It's crazy who they make heroes out of these days," Roberts moaned, rolling a dead cigar in his fingers. "I *created* Frank Serpico! A Frankenstein monster I created!"

It was not Frank Serpico but William Phillips who provided the entertainment value for a fascinated television audience as he reeled off stories of pads and payoffs that added up to millions. Serpico himself suggested that there were thousands of honest cops out there in videoland who must have bristled at Phillips' declarations. At times, Knapp manipulated witness Phillips like a ventriloquist's dummy:

> Q: If a gambling case arrives at court, is it too late to do business?
> A: No. It's never too late to do business.
> Q: Do you know of instances where, in fact, when a captain changed commands, that the new captain was straight but the bagman kept picking up?
> A: Yes. That happens in many instances where the superior officer is on the straight and narrow and the bagman continues his activities.
> Q: What percentage of the plainclothes men assigned to the Sixth Division do you feel participated in the pad?
> A: Everyone, to my knowledge.
> Q: Everyone?
> A: Everyone.

The sweeping vagueness of such exchanges was a constitutional lawyer's nightmare. Eventually, the hearings became too much for the civil-liberties crowd to stomach. A faction within the New York chapter of the ACLU went to bat for their old antagonists, the police. The longhaired NYCLU attorneys went to court on behalf of several cop commanders who had been transferred or demoted as a result of Phillips' hearsay allegations.

As the cameras zoomed in for a close-up of Phillips' nondescript face, one viewer itched with a peculiar sense of *déjà vu*. Hadn't he seen Phillips someplace before? The man asking himself that question was Detective John Justy. In the winter of 1968, Justy had been assigned to investigate the Christmas Eve murders of a pimp and his girlfriend at an East Side brothel. No suspects were found and the case was still open now, three years later.

There were a few clues: while fleeing the brothel, the killer had shot a john in the stomach and left him for dead. The patron, Charles Gonzalez, recovered from his wounds and helped police artists make a composite sketch of his assailant. This was the face that Justy remembered. The sketch bore a remarkable likeness to William Phillips.

On a hunch, Justy rounded up four prostitutes who had had dealings with the brothel from time to time. One by one, they identified Phillips as having some connection with the crime. One of the girls said she had heard Phillips threaten the pimp, James Goldberg, alias Jimmy Smith, on the night before the murders. Phillips was brought in for questioning.

Phillips quickly admitted that he had known Jimmy Smith, but hadn't seen him since 1965 or 1968—his memory wasn't clear. "Well, perhaps this will help to refresh your recollection," said Justy, producing Phillips' memo book. For December 24, 1968, the date of the double homicide, Phillips' entry was "Case Against Smith."

By mid-December, eight people had tied Phillips to the murders. Gonzalez picked Phillips out of a lineup and identified the officer as the man who had shot him. The murders had been committed on the eleventh floor of an apartment building on East 57th Street. The killer, as he left the lobby, had turned to the doorman and announced, "You've got two dead and one aided case on the eleventh." (In police parlance, an "aided case" is any injured person who must be rushed to the hospital by ambulance or patrol car.)

"That's cop talk," Justy told the D.A.'s office.

But the case against Phillips wasn't airtight. There was no circumstantial evidence. The .38-caliber shells removed from the victims' bodies were from a police revolver, but not the pistol registered to Phillips. Obviously he wouldn't have used that gun, Justy reasoned. Phillips also passed a lie-detector test. But what did that prove? The crooked cop admitted he had perjured himself in at least twenty-four different court cases. And, putting aside the lack of circumstantial evidence, how many times is there an eyewitness to murder?

Homicide Bureau Chief John Keenan was handling the case, and from a political point of view the timing couldn't have been worse. For the D.A.'s office to ignore the mountain of evidence it had against Phillips would have been tantamount to a cover-up. Conversely, no matter what the grand jury decided, the Phillips case was bound to be interpreted as a frame-up; an attempt to torpedo the Knapp Commission.

When Assistant D.A. John Keenan went to Hogan to announce that Phillips was under investigation for murder, the Chief blurted out, "Oh my God! Not another Becker-Rosenthal Affair!" *

* The historical reference was to the most famous legal lynching in New York history. It began with the 1912 murder of a Times Square gambling house owner, Harold Rosenthal, who had reported police corruption to the newspapers. He was gunned down next day on his way to the office of then District Attorney Charles Whitman. To placate public outrage over police corruption, the murder was charged to a known grafter on the Police Department's strong-arm anti-gambling squad—handsome, two-fisted Lieutenant Charles Becker. The frame-up has often been attributed to a young reporter on the New York World, Her-

When Phillips ran to the chairman of the Knapp Commission and reported, "Hogan's after my ass for murder," Whitman Knapp was dumbstruck. Knapp went in turn to Michael Armstrong, the commission's chief counsel, and told him, "I'm absolutely convinced that's a bum rap. Maybe Phillips is a killer. But that particular killing was not his style. Extortionists who kill do so to maintain their credibility. A peace officer maintains credibility by his power to arrest. There's no point to a crime that hurts his credibility. The idea that Phillips would shoot a guy and leave him crawling away is ridiculous. He'd be the first to tell you that if he decided to do a job on somebody, he'd do it right.

"Everybody in Hogan's office knows that. But subconsciously they don't want to come to that conclusion. The idea that our star witness is their defendant is just too damned attractive."

Hoping for more information, Armstrong got hold of Nicholas Scoppetta, a former Hogan assistant serving as a Knapp Commission attorney.

"Hogan's office is going to try Phillips for murder," said Armstrong. "Any possibility of a frame-up?"

"Who's handling the case for Hogan?" Scoppetta asked.

"John Keenan."

"Dammit, then it's legitimate," said Scoppetta. "Phillips is either guilty or they've got a helluva case against him."

The month-long trial of Phillips began in July 1972, with vivid testimony by Charles Gonzalez, the brothel customer. He described how Phillips, angered by the pimp's refusal to make a $1,000 payoff, held a revolver six inches from Smith's head and fired. A pink mist suffused the air. When Gonzalez spun his head, he saw blood clots clinging to the wall. Phillips then fired two shots into the face of the screaming prostitute, Sharon Stango. The shocked Gonzalez was sitting on a couch between the two victims. Phillips turned to him and "fired a shot into my belly," Gonzalez swore. "I'll never forget his face as long as I live."

A hoary axiom of defense advocacy holds that "When you have no case, try the evidence. When you have no evidence, try the District Attorney." Predictably, defense lawyer F. Lee Bailey began picking away at Hogan's "phony case" against the Knapp Commission's star witness.

Knapp's relationship with Hogan was as taut as catgut during this

bert Bayard Swope. He goaded D.A. Whitman into prosecuting Becker, then arranging for his electrocution at Sing Sing after Swope's advocacy journalism had enabled Whitman to become Governor. Becker was the first of three policemen in U.S. history who received the death penalty.

period. "If there was one thing Hogan was almost neurotic about," Knapp recalled, "it was the suggestion that he ever prosecuted a case to protect his own image. He was so impressed with his own integrity that he couldn't take into account his own human weakness."

Knapp had seen this Hogan superego bristle in another scandal that began making headlines about this time—the case of State Supreme Court Justice Mitchell Schweitzer. Hogan and Schweitzer had a long-standing friendship that went back to their days as classmates at Columbia Law. Schweitzer had since become the hardest-working jurist on the Supreme Court bench. His reputation was that of a judge who could "get rid of cases" without giving the courthouse away.

To keep his head above legal waters, Hogan had to show an average of twenty to twenty-five dispositions a day in Supreme Court. None of the other jurists moved cases with the "celerity" of Judge Schweitzer, Hogan noted appreciatively, adding: "If it weren't for Mitch, the Tombs would have exploded long ago."

Schweitzer ran the courtroom like an auctioneer, or a short-order cook at a busy counter. Three proceedings would go on at once—Schweitzer taking testimony on one side of the bench while disposing of motions on the other. Meanwhile, attorneys popped out of back-room plea-bargaining sessions to haggle over possible sentences. To keep this process off the record, the judge would snatch his legal pad and scribble in large Magic Marker numbers whatever prison term he intended to impose if the defendant pleaded guilty.

"Of course I can't . . . ahem . . . make any promises," the judge winked as case after case was disposed of with a noticeable lack of propriety.

This yeoman service of Schweitzer's kept the D.A.'s calendar alive. It was Schweitzer who signed virtually every *ex parte* order for bugs and wiretaps sent down from Hogan's office. It was Schweitzer who arranged with Hogan and Dollinger for Burton Roberts to take over as Bronx D.A. And it was Schweitzer who abruptly stepped down from the bench in December 1971, rather than face charges of judicial misconduct brought by the Court of the Judiciary.

Nearly 7,000 pages of court testimony detailed the charges—which ranged from obstruction of justice to improper relations with the late Nathan Voloshen, a convicted influence peddler. At the time the charges were announced, Hogan reviewed the evidence and found nothing to warrant an indictment. The grand jury found nothing to call a crime, either. The D.A. had since let the two-year statute of limitations on such offenses run out.

Knapp read every accusation in the judiciary panel's draft of charges and agreed with Hogan that there wasn't a single indication of a crime. "But the improprieties made your hair curl," Knapp said. "It was outrageous for Frank to let himself get into the position of investigating Schweitzer. Ridiculous. He could have gotten Louis Lefkowitz [the state's Attorney General] to take it over. And it never even occurred to him to duck it. His self-image was too beautiful. I pleaded with him, 'Frank, it's humanly impossible to want to prosecute judges and police on whom you rely from day to day.' His response was a human one, too: the tendency to forget the things you can't do anything about."

Meanwhile, Phillips on trial projected the same image as Phillips on television—a slimy man trying to wriggle his way off a hook. His half-joking admissions to reporters in the courthouse corridors ("I'd never off [kill] a guy for a measly grand") offended legitimate police officers like Sergeant Durk. On assignment to the Brooklyn D.A.'s squad one day, Durk had encountered a narcotics detective who seemed to feel the same way: Detective Robert Leuci.

"I'm sick and tired of having the Police Department singled out as the bad guy of the criminal-justice system," said the thirty-two-year-old Leuci. "There's a lot more wrong with the system than the Police Department." Durk asked Leuci if he'd like to do undercover work for the Knapp Commission. Leuci said okay, he'd wear a wire and see if he could ferret out heroin bribes through the Narcotics Division.

"Babyface" was Leuci's nickname in the division. Yet beneath the muscular Mod Squad appearance, the long hair and snazzy tailoring, Leuci had a true zeal for drug busts; it was said to be personal: a close relative was hooked on "skag."

Leuci went to work with a tiny radio transmitter hidden in his belt. His tan two-door Pontiac was equipped with enough supersensitive, long-range eavesdropping gear to monitor someone sucking a coughdrop. In a remarkably short time, he managed to blow the whistle on a freewheeling assortment of corrupt law-and-order types—judges, prosecutors, defense lawyers, courtroom hangers-on. At last, Knapp had the kind of information he needed to confound the skeptics and knock the Court of the Judiciary right off their swivel chairs.

The problem was how to handle Leuci's arsenal. Many of the cases were political dynamite. Indictments would be obtained, but it might take years for the cases to be ground through the slow-motion machinery of appellate review. A permanent investigative body would have to follow up. The logical choice would have been Hogan's office. But the detective branch of the office, the "D.A.'s Squad" over which Hogan had no administrative control, carried with it a tremendous risk of leakage about the undercover operation. Leuci himself insisted he could continue to work only with the federal people. Knapp decided to turn Leuci over to U.S. Attorney Whitney North Seymour.

Now—Hogan would have to be told that he could not interrogate Detective Leuci or use him as a witness. The lack of confidence would be implicit. There was no way around the insult. Seymour and Knapp converged on Hogan's inner office to deliver the bad news. Seymour still remembers it as "the most uncomfortable meeting of my entire life."

Hogan trembled when he heard the announcement. He banged down his pipe, scattering lit tobacco across the desk blotter. His blood pressure had clearly rocketed. Tears, insults, and curses came pouring out. Why were they doing this to him? Seymour's office wasn't under attack. Hogan's office was. Why not give *him* the chance to vindicate himself?

Knapp looked stricken. Seymour put on his most ingenuous, persuasive manner, trying to placate Hogan. The federal prosecutor heaped praise upon Whitman Knapp, summoning up an image of the commission chairman as a courageous human being of great common sense. Seymour implored Hogan to see Knapp's side:

"Consider, Frank. You're Whitman Knapp. You're really under the gun—everybody's out to show you're a faker. You strike paydirt with Leuci. Then you go in and have public hearings with one hand tied behind your back and you don't use the best material you've got because you realize you're working undercover. That's a courageous decision."

Doggedly, Seymour assured Hogan that the matter did not reflect on his professional staff but on his *police* staff. Hogan cooled off finally, and said he trusted Seymour. He recognized that the two of them weren't trying to show him up. He held his breath a moment, then exhaled. "Go ahead. You'll have my full support."

But the meeting didn't end at that point. Seymour said he *needed* Hogan's full support because some of Leuci's allegations came very close to Hogan's office. . . . Silence. The D.A. said not a word. Seymour talked some more. Would Hogan permit an undercover agent to pose as a defendant on the representation that his case could be fixed, "just to see if the case would be fixed?" Hogan wouldn't be told the type of case or the name of the defendant. He would just have to trust Seymour and await the outcome, an outcome that could prove the greatest embarrassment of his career.

There was no hesitation in Hogan's voice this time. He almost seemed to welcome this challenge to the absolute integrity of his staff. "You go right ahead." Hogan thrust out his chin. "You go right ahead."

Hogan's office had been free of scandal for nearly thirty years. A few former assistants had gotten into trouble *after* they left the office to go into private practice. Drugs. Ponzi schemes. Shady dealings in the commodities market. "If they hadn't left me, it never would have happened," Hogan had often complained like the proverbial Jewish mother.

"I don't want to sound like a Johnny-One-Note about this," he lectured his new recruits, "but appearances really do count. You must not give the appearance that there's anything venal about this office." On one occasion, Assistant D.A. Martin Danzinger had left Hogan to take a bureau chief's post in the office of then District Attorney Thomas Mackell in Queens County. Hogan took Danzinger aside at his farewell party: "Listen, I like Tom Mackell. I think he's a decent person. But you should know that his chief investigator is a man who got in trouble when he was in the Police Department. He was supposed to be a bag man for a captain out in Coney Island and he was caught off post a couple of times in bowling alleys—picking up collections. He was tried departmentally and eased out; Tom Mackell represented him, so Tom knew all about it. He was a damned fool to make that man his chief investigator.

"That office is . . . free and easy. Tom's an easygoing guy."

Hogan enjoyed telling the story because of what happened after Danzinger attended his first bureau chiefs' meeting in Queens. "Tom Mackell said to them, 'Oh, we're invited to have lunch tomorrow with the county leader, and he said he's picking up the tab.' Danzinger rushed right back to me and said, 'Jeez, could I come back to the office, Chief?' There was just that much, right at the outset, that told him what the office was like."

Few people knew how rigidly Hogan enforced Tom Dewey's housekeeping rules of thirty years before. Hogan could remember back when his old law partner, Anthony Liebler, was hired as an assistant D.A. Without permission, Liebler handled the probate of a will involving one of his in-laws. He also collected a fee. An irate Hogan suspended Liebler for a month, the loss of salary equivalent to his fee.

The years had worn on. Hundreds of young lawyers whose lives were touched by Frank Hogan had gone through their apprenticeship and moved out of the office. With so many of "his boys" working in the legal marketplace of bribe giving and taking, Hogan realized he might one day have to discipline one of his own. "Knock on wood," he would say, rapping his knuckles on the desktop. "It hasn't happened yet. Maybe we're lucky. Maybe it's just common sense. If anybody does anything wrong, why, they know I'm going to be after them faster than anybody else."

So far as is known, Hogan's faith in his men's incorruptibility was shaken only once. It was a hairbreadth escape from full-fledged scandal, perhaps the best-kept secret in the office. It involved onetime Homicide Bureau Chief Vincent Dermody, a fifty-five-year-old widower who had been struggling along on a senior assistant's salary for a number of years. Hogan had always liked Dermody. Vince was a little guy with a crewcut whose jibes and wisecracks kept the office laughing. His trial work was flawless: a solid record of murder convictions affirmed on appeal.

After 1969, Hogan noticed that the fiber of Dermody's work gradually seemed to lose its starch. Vince had grown despondent after his wife died of cancer. There were no more jokes, and Vince seemed to be letting himself go physically as well as mentally. He started hitting the bottle, lost weight, began calling in sick with "gastroenteritis" after blackout benders.

In 1970, Dermody's slipping world crashed. He was called as a character witness for his friend Deputy Chief Inspector Thomas Reneghan, who faced departmental charges of bribe-taking while head of the Police Department's Special Narcotics Unit. During cross-examination, a police lawyer elicited testimony that Reneghan and another man had met in a Third Avenue restaurant with Hugh Mulligan, a convicted bookmaker, to discuss "certain murder cases in the D.A.'s office." Then came the shocker: the third person at the dinner table had been Vincent Dermody.

Hogan paled when he heard the news, staring unseeingly at the telephone after a police official called from Headquarters. Hogan felt hurt, betrayed—victimized. One of his own! He called for help on the intercom: "Get me Joe Phillips."

Assistant D.A. Joseph Phillips, a ten-year veteran of the Rackets Bureau, was teddy-bear amiable. Ever since Burton Roberts had gone up to the Bronx, Phillips had been treated as one of the most important of Hogan's protégés. During the two-year ordeal of the Panther 21 trial, which Phillips prosecuted and lost, Hogan and Phillips developed an emotional dependence on each other, commiserating over the day-to-day humiliations of that highly disruptive legal battle. Hogan had confided some of his personal sorrows to Phillips—once, most painfully, Hogan's bitterness at being childless.

It was a resentment Hogan still nourished after all these years. Not against his wife Mary, but against the "drunken Irish surgeon" who had been recommended to the couple during Mary's first and only pregnancy. She had a miscarriage. The fetus was delivered prematurely and Mary had been "butchered," Hogan claimed. The stillborn infant was "a son . . ." Hogan began to sob. Phillips had found himself holding the old man's hand, realizing at that moment, the way he himself felt, that in a sense *he* was Hogan's son.

My God, Joe Phillips thought, that's really what Hogan's office was all about, wasn't it? Frank Hogan as *pater familias*. For such a man, corruption in his official family would cut to the quick.

Now, with Dermody in trouble, Hogan called Phillips in. The Chief broke the news calmly; he was very businesslike, trying to be dispassionate. Put a heavy tail on Dermody's movements around town. He lived in some fleabag hotel near the Third Avenue restaurant. Find out about it. Had any money changed hands? Find out about that, too. Until Vince was either cleared or convicted, no one else on the staff must find out.

Joe Phillips saw how upset Hogan really was. What alarmed Phillips was that Hogan spoke so often these days of his own mortality.

How deeply depressed was he? Phrases like "I'd rather shoot myself" kept creeping into his conversation. Now, pacing in front of the window ledges, Hogan flattened his palms to the glass and peered down eight stories to the street below. "Joe," he murmured, "if this guy turns out to be bad, I swear to God I'm gonna go right out this window."

When the news came back a few days later, Phillips prayed that the old man wouldn't have to kill himself to save face. Dermody had indeed taken money. Fifty dollars from the restaurant owner, who was a relative of Mulligan the bookmaker. Hogan winced—it wouldn't have made any difference if it had been a million dollars. What the hell was Vince doing being *seen* with such people? The time had come for Dermody to explain or face a grand jury.

The bureau chief was summoned to Hogan's inner office. There were no handshakes. No amenities. Just a curt "Sit down." Dermody, taking the chair next to Hogan's desk, sat fidgeting. Hogan toyed aimlessly with his pipestem cleaners. This was going to be an effort at salvation for both of them.

Hogan leveled the charge point-blank, one lawyer accusing another. "They say you took fifty dollars, Vince."

Dermody had an explanation ready. The check had come for dinner one night at the restaurant. Dermody had reached for his wallet and found it was empty. He'd forgotten to get a check cashed. The restaurant owner was a familiar face. Dermody was a regular customer. What could be more natural than for him to ask the owner, "Lend me fifty to cover the check and I'll pay you the rest back tomorrow." The owner broke out a wad, and that was that. "Chief, I had no idea who this guy was related to."

There was a prolonged silence. Hogan walked over to the window and gazed down at traffic. Then Dermody choked up:

"Mr. Hogan, I haven't been the same since I lost my wife. I guess you know that. My kids are away at college now and they really worship the old man. So I . . . I'm not looking for any . . . publicity."

Hogan shook his head. As a prosecutor, Vince should have known better than to go for the heartstrings. The innocent don't grovel. They fight back.

From then on, it was only a question of when and how—but Dermody was finished. Inspector Renaghan had already been indicted for grand-jury contempt after giving "vague and evasive" answers about restaurant conversations he had had with Mulligan and Dermody. Mulligan was also under indictment. Now Vince Dermody got his chance to tell his story before a grand jury.

Dermody repeated his version of the $50 misunderstanding to a New York County grand jury. The panel couldn't find anything to warrant a criminal indictment. Neither could Hogan. "You're excused, Vince," said Hogan, and that was the last he saw of him. Dermody dropped out of sight. A few days later, reporters called his office to ask some routine questions about a murder case. They were told that the bureau chief had taken an "early retirement" because of "personal problems."

Dermody's problems became known to members of the Knapp Commission, but how much this affected the panel's final report was an open question. The two-and-a-half-year work of the commission had come to an end. To Frank Hogan, it was one of the biggest "media ripoffs" in history.

The televised hearings had been a face-saving interlude for Lindsay while he prepared a primary campaign in Florida, where he was seeking the Democratic nomination for President of the United States. Everyone on the commission, it seemed, had come out ahead.

Chairman Knapp had been rewarded with a federal judgeship. U.S. Attorney Seymour had Leuci's blockbuster cases handed to him on a silver platter. Commission counsel Michael Armstrong was quietly arranging to take over as Queens D.A. Obscure commission attorney Nicholas Scoppetta would soon be head of the city's Department of Investigations, replacing former commissioner Arnold Fraiman, who had been ousted for his role in the Serpico cover-up.

By 1973, Serpico himself was on his way to becoming a multimillionaire. Patrolman Phillips could now afford *two* airplanes with the proceeds of *his* best-selling book, *On the Pad*. The royalties were augmented by a $15,250 salary Phillips continued to draw from the Department while under suspension. Xaviera Hollander, a Dutch prostitute caught paying Phillips $1,100 a month to protect her East Side brothel, also hit the publicity jackpot. The twenty-eight-year-old blonde, who looked like a dissipated Buster Brown, was fast becoming a talk-show celebrity. Xaviera had two writers at work on *The Happy Hooker*, her "memoirs" of sex with men, women, large guard dogs and a host of objects animate and inanimate.

Hogan had dropped prostitution charges against Xaviera in exchange for her testimony against Teddy Ratnoff. Ratnoff, a professional electronics snoop and blackmailer, had also worked as a Knapp Commission spy. He divided his time between the commission and the White House, selling his homemade bugging contraptions to the "plumbers" unit. Hogan's men caught him planting bugs under the beds in Xaviera's brothel (for obvious blackmail purposes). Ratnoff was indicted for illegal wiretapping. But he fled to England. Now, Xaviera was a source of zany amusement in the D.A.'s office as she undulated among the assistants, claiming she could tell by the length of a man's fingers and nose how well endowed he was below the belt.

The commission's aftermath exposed the very man who had seemed most successful in the investigations of narcotics payoffs. Detective Leuci, who everybody thought had a personal vendetta against heroin pushers, turned out to have a personal profit instead. The babyfaced narc had hoodwinked the Knapp Commission with his pretense of wholesomeness: he became the subject of a police dossier five inches thick. Hogan learned that Leuci had been stuffing his pockets with heroin bribes ever since he had joined the Narcotics Unit, sneaking literally hundreds of payoffs from pushers. Leuci must have known he was heading for a fall when he volunteered to work undercover for Knapp. But he also knew he would be granted immunity.

So, immunized to testify in the cases he brought to Seymour, Leuci had found a way to beat the rap. It was Leuci whom Seymour had posed as a "defendant" in Hogan's office. For reasons never made clear, the U.S. Attorney allowed the undercover narc to tell the story of all his undercover activities—as well as the crimes he'd committed—to *Life* magazine. The New York *Times*, which had been sitting on the same story for many weeks, learned that *Life* was preparing to hit the newstands with its "exclusive." In a fit of professional jealousy, the *Times* broke the story first. The published details of Leuci's undercover role blew his cover. Seymour's investigation into Hogan's office had to be called off, denying the D.A. an opportunity for self-vindication.

Most of the guilty slid off the hook, or even profited from their crimes. Their accusers were promoted one by one. Police graft remained pretty much what it had always been. And only one person stood diminished, bruised by the two-year purge—Frank Hogan.

On August 3, 1972, the Knapp Commission issued its long-awaited final report, a draft of which had been given to Hogan. Scanning the 380-page report, he found an objectionable passage—that corruption had been hinted at in "the D.A.s' offices," plural. Well . . . no specific mention of Hogan's own office, thank God. But the timing of the report bothered Hogan more than the content. The Phillips case was only a few days away from verdict. Now, the commission report would be plastered all over the newspapers and on TV. It was bound to influence the Phillips jury. Whitman Knapp had released his findings to the media on a Friday afternoon, with an embargo that would hold the news until Monday morning. Hogan immediately phoned Knapp. Couldn't he hold up the report until after the Phillips verdict?

"Frank, it's impossible," Knapp said. "The press already has it with a Monday deadline. Trying to suppress the report now would be the worst thing I could do."

Hogan interrupted. "You mean you *won't* do it!" He slammed down the receiver.

Mayor Lindsay called Knapp to plead Hogan's case for holding up the report. "Frank's got his Irish up," said Lindsay.

"Well, I've got *my* Irish up and I'm not even Irish!" Knapp shot back. "I have no more right to change a predetermined course for the sake of face-saving than *he* has."

To ease the suspense of that weekend, Frank Hogan did something unusual for him: he got out of town. He and his wife went for a nature hike in the Pennsylvania woodlands. Driving back from there on Monday morning, Hogan turned on the car radio and picked up a news conference: "This is coming to you live from midtown Manhattan where Governor Nelson A. Rockefeller has just announced that the Knapp report has been issued and that he intends to implement its chief recommendation." Then came Rockefeller's voice-over: "I am appointing a Special Deputy Attorney General with jurisdiction in the five counties of the city . . . to investigate and prosecute all crimes involving corruption in the criminal process."

Hogan glared at the radio. He was to be superseded—someone *over* him! Knapp had never told him anything about a special prosecutor. Nor had Rockefeller. It was a blow from behind. A wave of nausea rolled over him. Hogan's driver, looking in his rear-view mirror, nearly panicked. He braked and rolled the car off the road. The Chief looked in need of a resuscitator. In the back seat with him, Mary tried to steady her husband. Hogan flushed, doubled over, almost gagged. Then the anger surfaced, giving him strength:

"Christ Almighty, are we really living in America? What the hell are they doing to me? Am I not entitled to a hearing? What are the charges against me?"

The driver spun the car back onto the highway and floored the accelerator, speeding to the city. Hogan was in full sail by the time he reached his office. He tore into Rockefeller over the telephone. Whose idea was this—the Governor's or Lindsay's?

No, Rockefeller told him, "Lindsay was against it." Knapp had pleaded with the Governor for two days not to do it. It had been Rockefeller's own plan. He took full responsibility. Rocky explained that some sort of independent prosecutor was called for: "The target is Tom Mackell—not you, Frank."

Rockefeller explained that the Knapp Commission had uncovered a fraudulent get-rich-quick scheme operating out of the Queens D.A.'s office. To go after Mackell, Rocky was leaning on Section 63 of the Executive Law. The law made no provision except to supersede all five New York D.A.s at once.

"Personally," said Rockefeller, "I'm opposed to the form this thing took."

"Well, dammit," said Hogan, "if you feel that way, why don't you go public? You gave me no inkling of what you proposed to do." Rockefeller said he was sorry, he couldn't make his true feelings known. The Knapp Commission, after all, had somewhat "tarnished" Hogan's reputation.

Hogan was outraged. "*You've* done the most to tarnish it!" he yelled into the receiver. "We never, in my thirty-one years, *never* had any member of our legal staff in trouble that warranted criminal action. But now, a Special Attorney General—and his boss, Louis Lefkowitz—will exclude me. It so happens that we've indicted and convicted three or four assistant attorneys general.

"But I'm the one who's superseded. I'm the one who's humiliated—without due process. As an elected public official, I'm entitled to know the *charges* against my office. I'm entitled to a hearing. None of these were given to me."

"Hey, fella," Rocky humored him in that peculiar Froggy-the-Gremlin voice. "I'm not a lawyer. I'm an administrator. And I can't back down now."

Rockefeller hung up.

Hogan glowered. He was no different from many New Yorkers in his mistrust of Nelson Rockefeller. The sentiment had grown through years of antt-urban discrimination in taxes, state aid, judicial appointments and rural domination of a Republican-controlled Legislature in Albany. Beginning in 1958, when Rockefeller had entered the first of his four terms as Governor, there had been repeated Democratic calls for New York City to secede from the upstate "apple knockers" and declare itself a fifty-first state. The new city-state would then apply for federal aid under the name New York. The rest of the state would be rechristened Buffalo. Such secessionist talk was only half in jest.

Anti-Republican sentiment was so deep-rooted in 1965 that John Lindsay refused to run as the GOP candidate for Mayor. He won by pulling together a Liberal-Republican-Democratic fusion ticket in order to overcome the liabilities of running on his record as a Republican Congressman. This maneuver triggered a bitter feud with Rockefeller that had continued into Lindsay's second term as Mayor.

It has been said that every political party in New York seeks to hold itself up as the Party of Purity. Since the Democrats are usually in power—and Lindsay was a "radical Democrat" to the GOP conservatives—the designation of a Republican superprosecutor now gave Rockefeller a chance to purchase some Purity stock in the city.

Hashing over the Governor's motives with his aides later in the day, Hogan theorized, "I think Rockefeller made a decision, with Lindsay's permission, to put the ball in Lindsay's lap. Rocky would act in this way so the Mayor couldn't point a finger at him and say, 'I did *my* duty. I appointed this commission, which did a great job—but the Governor didn't follow through.'"

A few days later, on August 8, Hogan met for a final showdown with Rockefeller in the Governor's Fifth Avenue duplex. Hogan walked out red-faced and discomfited. Rocky would not retreat from his proposal. Indeed, he had already chosen a Republican to take over the duties of Special Prosecutor. And the new man was none other than Hogan's ex-assistant Maurice Nadjari—the man who had proclaimed that a guilty verdict gave him orgasmic ecstasy, the man whom Hogan had once cynically likened to Javert, the character in *Les Misérables* who relentlessly pursues Jean Valjean through the sewers of Paris because of the theft of a loaf of bread.

When the D.A. returned to the office entrance on Leonard Street, he was met by a radio news reporter who jabbed a microphone in his face: "Any comment on the Rockefeller meeting, Mr. District Attorney?"

Force of habit might have made the D.A. brush past the newsmen with a terse "No comment." This time, however, Hogan stood his ground and tore into Rockefeller all over again: "I defy him to name a case where we were reluctant to prosecute a complaint. I want him to give me a bill of particulars on that. If he means to say that I or anybody in my office has a reluctance to investigate crime, then I say he defames me and he defames my office!"

Hogan added that it was no mere coincidence that the Knapp Commission's findings were released just as the Phillips case was going to the jury.* Whitman Knapp was a "liar," Hogan declared. Then Mr. District Attorney shouldered his way past the reporter and went up to his secretary's office. There he sat down and scratched Whitman Knapp's name off the office Christmas-card list.

When Rockefeller officially appointed Nadjari Special Prosecutor on

---

* Three days later, when the Phillips trial ended with a hung jury, Hogan blamed Knapp for his early release of the commission report. Eventually, in the fall of 1974, Phillips went on trial a second time, and was convicted. He received a life sentence and will not be eligible for parole until the year 2000.

September 19, 1972, the Governor said it was the most important act of
his fourteen years in office. The public agreed. A newspaper poll taken
three and a half years later showed that among New Yorkers with an
opinion, 77 percent supported Nadjari and 55 percent thought he should
stay on the job indefinitely. People spoke of him as an honest crusader,
waging a frustrating battle against a brick wall of corruption in the courts
and political clubhouses.

Assuming the majority was correct about Nadjari's performance, what
had he actually accomplished in all this time? The superprosecutor and
his staff were lavishly ensconced in a suite of glassed-in offices high atop
the World Trade Center. The Nadjari crusade had gobbled up $11 mil-
lion in taxpayer money. Nadjari had busted a few court attendants and
broken-down patrolmen for petty crimes. But he was being paid to go
after bigger game. And the fact remained: not one big-name officeholder
had gone to jail.

Nadjari indicted a total of eleven judges, none on a direct charge of
taking money to influence the outcome of court cases. All but one of the
judges were acquitted or had their cases dismissed on flimsy evidence or
were never brought to trial during Nadjari's tenure. The only judge convicted later won a reversal of the guilty verdict on appeal. The Special
Prosecutor's most important case against a political bigwig—former
Queens D.A. Thomas Mackell—became one of several convictions reversed by the state's highest court, the Court of Appeals, which denounced the prosecutor's "illegal, outrageous and intolerable methods."

Nadjari specialized in the illegal wiretap, the grand-jury leak, the
broken promise, the duplicitous undercover agent. Overlooking the need
to establish a legal basis for his wiretaps, he unwittingly sabotaged many
of his own major prosecutions. Nadjari indicted countless policemen on
charges that were never brought to trial. On one occasion, he suckered
the New York newspapers into printing banner headlines with an announcement of "widespread corruption" in Mayor Lindsay's administration. In actuality, the "ongoing investigation" stemmed from a $30 brib-
ery charge against a lowly housing inspector. The case took sixteen
months to wend its way to trial, during which time no higher-ups were
implicated. And in the end, the defendant was acquitted. The headlined
"scandal" was thus reduced to a four-paragraph notice buried in the back
pages of the New York *Times*.

"The smear is on the front page and the exoneration is on the last page
in the bottom part of the corner," declared Bronx D.A. Mario Merola,
echoing the harsh criticism of the legal community against the role of the

press in Nadjari's crusade. "It's that kind of an era . . . It's the innuendo; it's the rumors; it's the climate. Watergate, you know, the whole bit . . ."

Overzealous to the point that one state official branded his tactics "Nazi justice," Nadjari outdid himself in the case of a former tax commissioner charged with fixing parking tickets. Nadjari's men knocked on the commissioner's door in the dead of night, arrested the man in his pajamas, and threatened to drag him from the house in handcuffs. The commissioner's wife and four-year-old daughter became hysterical. Neighbors were awakened to the spectacle.

All this for a ticket-fixing case in which the misdemeanor conviction was overturned and never put back on trial—presumably because Nadjari lacked proper evidence.

Meanwhile, Nadjari continued to equate all criticism of his methods with crookery. His opponents began to speak of a "Nadjari syndrome." Fearful that the prosecutor would ruin anyone's reputation to save his own political skin, his detractors kept silent, afraid of becoming the next victims to be paraded before a grand jury.

"Nadjari seems intent on carving a place for himself as a pathological example of prosecutorial misconduct," declared Ira Glasser, executive director of the N.Y. Civil Liberties Union, an organization never known to be "soft" on official corruption. In an effort to halt the abuses of the Special Prosecutor, New York Governor Hugh Carey announced on December 23, 1975, that he was removing Nadjari from office. Nadjari fought back. He refused to leave the World Trade Center and charged the Governor with a "cover-up" of alleged corruption in the Bronx Democratic Party. To back up his allegations, Nadjari belatedly filed an affidavit in open court charging that Patrick J. Cunningham, the state Democratic leader, was "at the center of the corrupt marketplace of judgeships in the Bronx." The skeptics couldn't help but notice that Nadjari made no move against Cunningham until after the attempted firing, when Cunningham was a "target of opportunity." But once again, the maneuver gained widespread public acclaim.

Nadjari's boss, State Attorney General Louis Lefkowitz, gave him six more months to finish his investigations. Nadjari's race against time produced a fluttering of indictment papers against judges and city officials of good repute. But the six-month deadline passed without a major conviction. On June 25, 1976, under intense public pressure to keep Nadjari on the job, Lefkowitz fired the Special Prosecutor.

Citing a 1974 study by the N.Y. Bar Association, Governor Cary noted that in twenty-five years, no prosecutor had been held in contempt for professional misconduct. Quoting former U.S. Attorney General Robert H. Jackson, Carey said that the "greatest danger of abuse" by errant prosecutors was in "prosecuting lies."

"The most that an overzealous prosecutor risks is losing a case on appeal," said Carey. "So who is to watch the watchman?"

In tones reminiscent of J. Edgar Hoover and Joe McCarthy, Nadjari went out snarling against a conspiracy to discredit him. Invariably, he linked his demise to "political reasons and political reasons alone." As in the heyday of superprosecutor Tom Dewey, the self-portrait of martyrdom, combined with assertions of his own infallibility, struck a sympathetic chord with the voters. People began to speak Nadjari's name as a potential candidate for governor. And like Dewey in 1938, Maurice Nadjari made no secret of his readiness to heed the call.

Perhaps the harshest criticism of the Nadjari debacle was directed not at Maurice Nadjari himself, but at the man who appointed him: former Governor Nelson Rockefeller.

Legal scholars pointed out that the prosecution of Watergate won respect not because it proved the undoing of Richard Nixon, but because it reaffirmed the ethical standards of men like Senator Sam Erwin, Judge John Sirica, and Archibald Cox. To restore the same measure of respect to the Special Prosecutor's office, Carey realized he needed a man of Frank Hogan's caliber to replace Nadjari. The Governor chose Assistant D.A. John F. Keenan, the former Homicide Bureau chief and Hogan protégé. After nearly four years of disdain, it seemed that Hogan's office had finally been vindicated.

10
DIFFERENT DRUMMERS

Hogan, laughing, mimicked the voice of a burlesque manager auditioning a new stripper: "Come on now—let me see those legs!" The young prosecutor standing before him, Assistant District Attorney Bennett Gerschman, stooped down and pulled up his trouser legs to expose his naked calves.

The setting for this strange performance was Hogan's private office. In the sports pages of the morning newspapers, Hogan had made an unexpected discovery: one of his own assistant district attorneys, Ben Gerschman, had been a top finisher in the twenty-six-mile Central Park Marathon. Hogan was delighted—a superjock, working right in the office! In terms of his work, Gerschman had already outdistanced all other assistants in Scotti's Rackets Bureau.

"You can run twenty-six miles on those skinny legs!" Hogan exclaimed in disbelief, reaching down to tap the young man's hardened calf muscles. "How the hell do you do it?"

Gerschman gave a modest grin: "Practice." The D.A. clapped the marathon runner on the shoulder: "Congratulations, son." Gerschman sensed that he might become a Hogan favorite: a bright career beckoned. He was halfway home.

A few days later, Hogan called Gerschman back for another chat. "I'm looking for a rookie-of-the-year," said Hogan, adding that he needed someone with spirit and dedication to go to work on thousands of disorderly-conduct arrest cases that were piling up on the complaint desk.

This was the season of America's discontent with the Vietnam War and the Selective Service System. Daily police busts on campuses, at induction centers, and at other anti-Vietnam convulsions had produced thousands of civil-disobedience arrests—and a mountain of paperwork. Facing charges were Dr. Benjamin Spock, Abbie Hoffman, Weatherman Mark Rudd, Conor Cruise O'Brian and a host of other controversial figures. Hogan outlined his plan to Gerschman: "I want to yank you off rackets assignments and designate you our house expert on political-demonstration arrests." Gerschman's mission was to get all these people to trial.

Gerschman did not welcome the assignment. He had traveled the ideological route of many young law students of the period. An NYU graduate and the son of a well-to-do lawyer, Gerschman's path to Hogan's office began on the Selma-to-Montgomery civil-rights march. He had stayed in Mississippi during the Freedom Summer voter registration drive of 1962. The following year, he was off to the Washington Freedom March to hear Dr. Martin Luther King, Jr., declare, "I have a dream!"

For Gerschman, the experience was akin to a religious conversion: the speech inspired his own dream. He walked away from the Washington Monument, surveyed the imperial granite of Capitol Hill, and decided on the spot to devote his life to one goal: becoming a fair and honest public servant. His Mississippi experience had taught him, he later recalled, that "the prosecutor has an infinitely greater ability to render justice than the defense lawyer, the Legal Aid attorney, or even the judge. The prosecutor has the discretion to decide what cases the judges will hear." The next logical step: an apprenticeship in Hogan's office. In 1966, he was appointed an assistant D.A.

One of Gerschman's early acquaintanceships was with Assistant D.A. Michael Metzger, the son and heir of a millionaire industrialist. Gerschman and Metzger were promoted to the Rackets Bureau together. The "Hoganesque" tone of moral rectitude was said to transcend the uncomfortable struggles of conscience in which his younger assistants labored toward a rough approximation of justice. But Gerschman and Metzger raised serious questions about the Chief's lofty outlook. There were really two Frank Hogans, they decided. One was the genial Irishman, regaling anyone who would listen with jovial "Dewey" anecdotes. The other was "Mr. Hogan," the self-righteous captive of his own Mr. District Attorney legend.

"Being a Hogan assistant, you know, is almost a religious calling," Metzger reflected when interviewed. "We're all Vestal Virgins when we come in here. We're fresh out of law school. We believe in all the court-house inscriptions and the chick with the blindfold. But there's a serious intellectual omission: nobody takes us aside and tells us that damn few cops are really honest. That judges are politicians. That government per-secutes as well as prosecutes. Hogan expects you to find out all of that for yourself. If he told you outright, it would be like telling a young priest: listen, there were Popes in history who had illegitimate children. We're all cherries. That's Hogan's master plan.

"There's a rarefied atmosphere here. Something almost incestuous, insular. You're twenty-five years old and you're given 30,000 police man-servants at your beck and call. You get power-crazed. You discover this is a scratch-my-back, scratch-your-back kind of town. Hogan has something on half of the judges and the politicians—like Huey Long with his little black book. The cops are terrified of him. City Hall is afraid of him, and so are the other D.A.s' offices."

Metzger spoke of the "muted panic" he could touch off simply by telephoning the city's most powerful politicians and suggesting that they pay the office a visit.

"They cry, beg, plead, and pull out all the stops to avoid the shame of being served a subpoena from Hogan's office. In the twenty or thirty min-utes it takes for their chauffeurs to get them down here, they've stewed long enough so that when we get to them they're ready to bury their mothers alive."

It didn't take long for Metzger to grow disillusioned at the way pros-ecutors were automatically assumed to share the reactionary values of cer-tain cops and judges. He once sent nineteen peace demonstrators to jail, and hated himself afterward. Not because he was overly sympathetic to the defendants, but because of something Judge Vincent Impelleteri whispered to him at a bench conference: "We'll teach these commie fucks!"

This from a man who had once been the Mayor of New York City!

Hogan, Metzger said, looked down his nose at all but a handful of defense lawyers in town. Most of the legal hacks were ignoramuses, the assistant D.A. felt, no better than the people they represented. Written motions were virtually unheard of—probably because the mouthpieces couldn't spell. The older men of the defense bar were Kentucky-colonel types who hated their clients and, according to Metzger, "just wanted to keep on the good side of the D.A."

By contrast, there was a peculiar asceticism in Hogan's office, according to Metzger: "A hint of implied excellence in not going out to fancy restaurants. Not buying a new suit or not having seen a Broadway show in years." Assistant district attorneys were so inspired by Hogan's own example that they accepted these hardships and imitated his work habits.

"Hogan hadn't been seen eating lunch outside his office in twenty years, and every one of us tried to follow his example by having ham and cheese sandwiches and milkshakes at our desks," remembered Metzger. "It was a big thing around here when we found out that Miss Delaney had been buying his sandwiches at Schrafft's. It was Schrafft's for the rest of us from then on."

Hogan's social friends were bankers, senior law partners, business tycoons; but new office recruits were often forewarned of Hogan's famous "casserole lecture." An exasperated assistant, earning $6,500 a year, had once gone to Hogan to ask for a raise. The assistant said he couldn't afford to buy hamburger meat for his wife and kids. Hogan's rejoinder was, "You should try more casseroles—more tuna fish." Then he sat the assistant down and tried to draw up a week's menu on the man's family budget. "It's not the money here that counts," said Hogan. "It's the learning experience."

"I appreciate the learning experience," the threadbare assistant protested. "But couldn't you either lower the tuition or increase the scholarships?"

The Columbia Students for a Democratic Society riot of May 1968 was Ben Gerschman's first glimpse of Frank Hogan as a man of principle, who stood still while the winds of change whistled past him. As assistant in charge of political-demonstration cases, Gerschman was now dealing with Hogan on a day-to-day basis. He saw, perhaps more clearly than others, that Hogan's ideals, by then, were engraved in stone. He wasn't about to take a sudden turn for the sake of revolutionary utopianism.

Approximately 600 Columbia students faced misdemeanor charges ranging from disorderly conduct to criminal trespass. Hogan angrily vetoed a recommendation by university officials that the charges be dropped. The decision pitted Hogan against a majority on the board of his fellow Columbia trustees. Night after night, twenty-three board members grappled with the problem in the Faculty Club board room. Angry voices reverberated behind closed doors. Hogan refused to sit in at the meetings. But his feelings were made known.

He bitterly castigated the university deans for "knuckling under" to amnesty demands. The board split. The hardliners who backed Hogan were in a minority. Among those favoring leniency was Federal Court Judge Frederick van Pelt Bryan. Bryan looked like a daguerreotype of a university trustee: the florid-faced jurist was never seen without his black Homburg and walking stick. But he was more contemporary in his outlook than many of the scruffy-haired political-science majors in the student body.

"We took the position that the big riot was, to a substantial degree, as much the fault of the police as the fault of the students," Bryan recalled later. "The cops overreacted and began cracking heads. The majority felt that prosecution would only keep the cauldron bubbling. But Frank couldn't be swayed. It was, I suppose, his integrity of spirit."

Gerschman felt torn apart by his role in the Columbia prosecutions. "I remember going to Hogan's office and making a recommendation that we go along with Columbia's request. I explained that these were not the kinds of crimes the office should be concerned with if there was a way out. Columbia was giving us a way out—amnesty. We'd probably look good from a public-relations point of view if we 'reluctantly' joined in the Columbia request and made a statement that while we condemned violence and asked for the rule of law, this was a unique situation.

"It wouldn't make any difference how we handled the case. If these people were acting out of conscience, they would continue to behave as they were behaving—as martyrs. The SDS people felt their behavior was civil disobedience, not criminality. I tried to compare it with Martin Luther King's case. I pleaded with Hogan. But he rejected my suggestions.

" 'Somebody,' he said, 'has got to stand up for the rule of law.'

"In retrospect, I may have been mistaken. I'm not sure that Hogan was wrong about establishing a bad precedent. If he had cracked down on Columbia, maybe all the subsequent campus riots could have been avoided."

Hogan was obviously traumatized at seeing his alma mater turned into a battleground. Because he was also a Columbia trustee, there were repeated calls for Hogan to disqualify himself and appoint a special prosecutor to look into the school disturbances. He refused.

Gerschman proposed a compromise: "Let me present all the evidence on both sides to a grand jury. Evidence of misconduct by the police as well as by the demonstrators." Said Hogan: "Too time-consuming."

"That's when the real disillusionment began to set in," Gerschman recalled later. "They key phrase seemed to be 'saving face.' Hogan was always saving face. The office couldn't take a dismissal because Mr. Hogan had to save face. It began to dawn on me that personal politics played a bigger part in the office than I had been led to believe."

In the months that followed, Metzger left the office and Gerschman's own disillusionment grew. "What kept running through my mind during that period was a Bob Dylan lyric: *The times they are a'changin.*' Mr. Hogan wasn't keeping pace with the times." Gerschman finally came to a wry conclusion: "The two things that seemed most important to him were the American flag and the penis."

The *penis?*

Frank Hogan couldn't stand to see the flag desecrated, much less made light of, and he couldn't stand to see a penis—period. Gerschman, smiling, remembers when the two elements were combined in a single comic instance.

Alerted to the existence of a chic porno-art gallery, the vice squad barged in at an entirely appropriate moment. A giant, torpedo-shaped sculpture was about to be unveiled. The *objet d'art* was draped with an American flag. While the police watched, the artist whisked away Old Glory, exposing an erect polyurethane phallus. The gallery clientele laughed. The artist beamed. The police served warrants. And Hogan blew his stack.

An appreciation of camp might have saved the situation, but Hogan never cracked a smile. "That case," said Gerschman, "was pursued with all the vigor attached to one of armed robbery or murder."

Hogan wanted to see the flag where it belonged: in a place of honor. If it waved inappropriately, Hogan came out marching to "The Battle Hymn of the Republic." Hogan's unequivocal rule-of-law stand in the Columbia campus disorders encouraged Gerschman to investigate what began as its resultant flip side: a reprisal demonstration to "Honor America" at City Hall, staged by a gang of construction workers who waved flags and pro-Vietnam placards. They made loud and suggestive remarks to women passersby and shouted, "Mayor Lindsay is a faggot!"

When a group of hippie-haired Pace College students happened by, words turned to blows. The hardhats lit out after the college kids with all the muscle they had. The students were outnumbered twenty to one. Police bystanders did just that—they stood by, watching the lunch-bucket brigade maul the longhairs in hand-to-hand combat.

"They really kicked the shit out of those kids," Gerschman recalled. "A number of students were hospitalized. This was about the time that the movie Z was playing. You couldn't fail to see the similarity between that film and what was happening in our streets . . . what might happen in any country when hysteria takes over. It was so graphic. We subpoenaed TV newsreel footage of the assaults. When we stopped the frames, we could identify John Birchites in business suits, inciting the construction workers with bullhorns. We had pictures of the cops just standing there, doing nothing to stop it.

"I went to my superior, Michael Juviler, and said, '*Something has to be done!* This is extremely serious and can't be condoned.' He agreed and went to talk to Hogan.

"Mike came back very upset. The Boss wasn't as troubled as we were. Mr. Hogan had said that the hardhats were 'provoked.' That the flag was important. And that the students were 'just asking for trouble' anyway.

"A lot of us agreed that if the office didn't take action, we would resign. So Hogan reluctantly did something. Eventually, one construction worker was indicted. But that case was nothing compared to what happened at Columbia. To me, *that* case was more political than any of the phony prison cases vanden Heuvel was yelling about."

Having served Hogan loyally for nearly six years, Gerschman now succumbed to self-doubts and a sense of spiritual malaise. Office morale slumped as Hogan pursued his personal pique in case after case. The word had gotten around. Prize recruits from Harvard and Yale no longer apprenticed in Hogan's office. The top graduates of the Ivy League headed to the other side of the fence to become storefront lawyers and radical activists.

Hogan couldn't be oblivious to the turnover on his legal staff. There were wholesale desertions. People ran out before the end of their four-year commitment. Hogan's chagrin turned to violent anger. Each time a young assistant appeared to give a month's notice, Hogan felt the chill of betrayal. Cries of "disloyal" echoed down the corridors. Hogan flung ashtrays across the room.

On December 29, 1972, after Special Prosecutor Nadjari had been installed in office at the World Trade Center, Gerschman went to Hogan and said, "I'm leaving. I'm going to join Nadjari. I suppose four weeks would be a reasonable time to dispose of all my cases—"

Hogan set down his pencil: "You'll leave *today!*"

"But, Mr. Hogan," Gerschman reasoned, "that would be unfair to the office. People inheriting my cases won't know anything about them—"

Hogan cut him off: "Nadjari may think he's going to raid this office—

but no one's indispensable. You're not indispensable. I'm not indispensable. We can do very well without you. You're disloyal!"

"Mr. Hogan, it isn't a question of loyalty—"

"Get out!" Hogan shouted, his voice breaking.

The young assistant who could run the marathon felt his knees buckle as he began to walk toward the door. By the time he'd reached it, Hogan was calmer. He spoke softly, almost soliloquizing: "It's not you. It's everybody. It's Knapp and Rockefeller and Lefkowitz and Nadjari and vanden Heuvel and everybody else who's been unfair to me . . ."

11
BUGGED

Once the Knapp Commission had shattered the myth of the D.A.'s invincibility, the press felt that it was at last open season in Hogan territory. And the message to editorial writers was clear: "Sic 'em." Anti-Hogan grievances had often been bruited about in pressrooms, but had never made their way into print. Responding now to the call of "Sic 'em," Paul Hoffman, a former courthouse reporter, began in the December 6, 1971, issue of *New York* magazine:

"Some see him and his office as too rooted in the patterns of the past, unable to cope with the revolution that has swept America in the past decade—not just in the law, but in mores, morals and manners. Some see the office as mired in the bog of its own bureaucracy, no longer aggressive and innovative, but tired and stodgy, and Hogan himself as too ready to pursue his own prejudices and preferences, too aloof and isolated, too concerned with maintaining the image of the institution. Some see it as part of the system, more interested in keeping the wheels of justice grinding than in what the mill is producing, unwilling to give the police and the courts the shake-up they need. Some simply wonder whether 30 years is too long for any one man to serve unchallenged, virtually unaccountable, in so powerful an office."

Hoffman's compelling case against D.A. Hogan produced a flutter of excuses among younger men in his office.

"It's true he's not St. Francis of Assisi," shrugged one long-haired assistant. "Hogan's only a human being who's made a lot of human mistakes. Anytime you render an important opinion, there's going to be an opposite opinion."

Other assistants pointed out that *any* D.A. would have been caught in the countervailing pressures alluded to in the article. Should Hogan constrict the law along the confines of decisional authority? Or capitulate on the prosecutor's function? Judicial bureaucrats had urged him toward the latter position. Their emphasis was on maximum disposition of cases to alleviate overcrowding in the Tombs. Manhattan night court seemed as hopelessly out of control as Dodge City in the 1880s. More than 100,000 arrests were processed each year; 5,000 felony indictments. The tendency was to move the traffic.

"What's your evidence?" a judge once challenged one of Hogan's men. "Unless you have a motion picture of this holdup, I'm throwing it out. We're too busy with serious cases around here tonight."

In his *New York* magazine article, Paul Hoffman charged that there was a slowdown in Hogan's rackets-busting:

"There has been relatively little in the past half-dozen years. No blockbuster investigation capturing headlines day after day, no sweeping scandal uncovered to panic City Hall or Albany, no unearthing of the underworld to send the mobsters fleeing to foreign shores, no probes of Wall Street wheeling-dealing to make the Big Board bounce."

In actuality, Hogan's rackets-busting was as relentless as ever—sixty-one major investigations under way and 175 cases pending. In response to the magazine attack, Scotti fired off an angry editorial reply, listing indictments against thirty-five crime kingpins in the previous five years alone. Among them: Joseph Colombo, the reputed boss of Brooklyn, later gunned down at a Columbus Circle "Italo-American Civil Rights Rally"; Aniello Dellacroce, described as Colombo's successor; Angelo Bruno, the reputed underboss of the North Atlantic region; gambling czar Hugh Mulligan; and a minor league of other "men of respect": Nicholas (Jiggs) Forlano, Vincent Napoli, Raymond Marquez, Charles (Ruby) Stein, Vincent Aloi. In one case alone, an intensive investigation into the killing of Crazy Joe Gallo in a Little Italy clamhouse, seven "caporegimi" had been indicted.

It was true that the rackets work still plugged along, but not in the spirit of the melodramatic 1930s and '40s. Gone were the gangbusters of Dewey's day, and the Public Enemies they pursued. The simplified stereotypes were outdated. By the 1960s and '70s, urban life had become so complex that an equally complex sociological approach was needed to cope with the new definition of criminality: "victims of society." The younger Hogan assistants could only laugh at "bad guy, good guy" maxims. They felt that perhaps not all that was illegal was necessarily evil.

At press conferences heralding police bonfires of marijuana stashes, the youngest Hogan disciples could hardly suppress their laughter. There were even jokes about gathering around the city incinerator for a "contact high."

Other televized demonstrations of law enforcement—the grinning prosecutor standing over a pile of confiscated weapons—struck the new young men as "oversimplified," a leftover from the Bad Guy comic book: "Look, we got their guns." This—in a city of 2,000,000 unlicensed hand guns.

And who were "they" anyway?

Some of the harshest criticism of the Rackets Bureau during this period came, not from the press, but from within the office—from assistants past and present.

Columbia Law Professor H. Richard Uviller, former chief of the Appeals Bureau, was among those who chafed over Hogan and Scotti's organized-crime tactics:

"Scotti's thinking was that underworld people were fair game. Hogan believed it. He believed—maybe Scotti persuaded him—that underworld people are the real cancer of society. The office article of faith was generated out of that atmosphere. There is something to be said for it: relentless, dogged harassment of underworld people is probably the only way you can have any prosecution at all. But on the other hand, what happens frequently is that nobody can agree on the source of the original belief that so-and-so is an organized crime member.

"He's got an Italian name, and some informant once told some FBI agent that so-and-so was friendly with somebody else, who went to somebody's funeral who went to somebody's wedding, and therefore they've got this guy all figured out.

"What 'family' he belongs to and everything else: when in point of fact, *nobody* has any hard evidence that this particular individual is involved in any illegal activity at all. One never knows how many innocent Italians may have been wronged."

Scotti himself once hinted that Rackets Bureau operations had about as much method as it takes to mix spaghetti: "We have a continuing interest in a number of underworld characters," he said. "It's like a large kitchen in a very big restaurant. Different pots come to a boil and that's when we take action."

Hogan did, however, make an attempt to keep the office from casting ethnic slurs, particularly against Italian-Americans. He stressed that the words "Mafia" and "Cosa Nostra" never be used, even in casual conversation. The expression Hogan preferred was "organized crime," not because he thought of it as a euphemism, but because the term accurately described the heterogeneous underworld syndicates.

Perhaps the best example of Hogan's new press policy—a low profile for the office and no sensationalism—was shown in the Vincent Rizzo case. During the two and a half years that the Knapp Commission had been capturing day-to-day headlines with its twenty-two corruption cases, Hogan's rackets-busters were quietly unraveling one of the most significant organized-crime schemes of the previous two decades.

Former Assistant D.A. Ronald Goldstock, who participated in the joint federal-state task force investigation, remembered what it was like: "When we started the investigation, Vinnie Rizzo was a big mob figure in the East Village. He wasn't well known. But everybody we picked up in that area always reported back to Rizzo. He was placed under surveillance and we put a court-ordered tap in his hangout, Jimmy's Lounge, on Avenue A.

"The first couple of days of the tap there were calls from Las Vegas and California. The wire produced evidence of Rizzo's ability to do a lot of things: there were indications of usury and stolen securities. Then we learned that Rizzo was going to Germany. He had once been involved with smuggling arms in South America. We came up with this theory that since Rizzo was going to Munich, where the Krupp arms works were, he might be working on arms to be sent to the IRA. It was pure speculation, but we felt the 'IRA plot' would convince Hogan to send a detective to tail Rizzo to Europe.

"It was obvious that Rizzo was in the middle of a lot of illegal activities. Whatever his reason for going to Germany, it was probably illegal. It would cost several hundred dollars to go over and watch him. Hogan was infuriated that the federal strike force didn't want to go. They had all the money. They took all our cases after we developed them. But Hogan finally sent over a detective from the D.A.'s squad."

The detective tailed Rizzo and his accomplices from Munich back to New York. One of these accomplices checked into a midtown hotel, the Summit. Hogan decided to plant a bug in his room. In charge of the court-ordered bugging operation: Detective Sergeant Robert Nicholson.

The next day, Nicholson reported back to the Chief: "Mission accomplished."

"Were there any problems?" Hogan asked routinely.

"Well, yes. The FBI was involved. They were supposed to keep a watch on the guy at a restaurant while the wire men were working. But the guy slipped away from them."

"Where did he go?"

"Back to his hotel room."

"Why did he go back?"

"To take a shower."

"How do you know that?"

"We called his room from a house phone in the lobby."

"And he answered?"

"No. He was in the shower. He didn't hear the phone. We assumed he was out, so we went up and picked the room lock with burglar's tools."

"Did you see him when the door opened?"

"Yeah. He was stark naked. He'd just got out of the shower."

"Did he see you?"

"No. We jumped back and tried to close the door."

"Why couldn't you close it?"

"He was trying to pull it open from the other side. He was trying to get a look at us."

"A tug-of-war?"

"Uh-huh."

"But you're sure he didn't see you?"

"The wire men ran to the fire exit and hid in a broom closet. The lock man and I hid in the shower stall of the room next door."

"Why were you in the shower stall?"

"The guy was hollering for the manager to search all the rooms. Our lookout man stayed in the hallway and pretended he was a guest. The target stopped him."

"What did he say?"

"He asked our man if he'd seen anyone running away from the scene."

"What did our man say?"

"He said, 'Yeah. I just saw two Puerto Ricans with raincoats running down the fire escape.' "

"What did the target do then?"

"He called the cops and ran for his gun—a .45-caliber automatic."

"How do you know he had a gun?"

"I saw it when he called the cops."

"He saw you?"

"Yeah. I got out of the shower stall, went over and flashed my detective's shield. I told him I was with the hotel burglary squad."

"There's no such squad."

"He didn't know that. Anyway, he had gotten dressed by this time, and that's when I saw his gun."

"Did you arrest him for carrying a weapon?"

"No. We hadn't put the wire in yet. I asked him if he got a good look at the perpetrators. He said, 'Yeah. Two Puerto Ricans with raincoats. I'll never forget their faces as long as I live.' I told him we've been looking for the same two guys. I said he'd better ride around the Times Square area in the car with me, and we'd try to spot them."

"Where did you take him?"

"The Stage Delicatessen . . . movie lobbies. I had to keep him occupied while the wire men went back to his room and finished the job."

"Did the hotel management find out about all this?"

"Nope. They reported it as an attempted burglary. The cops are still looking for us."

"All in a day's work," Hogan shrugged. The bug was installed and the investigation continued uninterrupted.

"It had to be one of the biggest cases the office ever had," former Assistant D.A. Goldstock recalled.

Indictments in the Interpol-assisted investigation came down in December 1972. Those indicted included Rizzo, who was a purported lieutenant in the Vito Genovese crime family; two bail bondsmen; a Japanese national; an Argentine cocaine smuggler; and twenty major U.S. figures in organized crime. The indictment papers, when stacked together, stood almost two inches high.

The stack presented a graphic picture of global crime operations: narcotics, counterfeiting, usury, extortion, attempted murder, the sale of stolen securities in Europe, conspiracy to sell stolen securities to the Vatican, stolen airline tickets. There were threats, beatings, people being hurled through windows. There was even a movieland scenario: men traveled from three continents to meet with Rizzo at his five-acre estate in upstate New York, an estate protected by Doberman pinschers and an 8-foot electrified fence.

"Every one of the twenty-five persons we indicted in the case was convicted and they are all in jail," said Goldstock. "I would say that it was the biggest organized-crime case within the last twenty years. Maybe even longer. It wasn't like your usual big case which meant only a big name.

This case had to do with people and crimes in five states and Canada, Japan, Germany, Argentina, Italy and other countries. Rizzo was in the middle of the most elaborate crime network imaginable. He brings a securities expert in from Europe who looks at some stolen stocks and says they are too hot for Europe, but that he would try to unload them in Argentina. Rizzo says, fine, and while you're down there see if you can make a narcotics connection. The guy says OK and goes to Argentina and makes a connection and arranges to have six kilos of cocaine delivered. Meanwhile, counterfeit money is being sent down from Canada to cover the purchase.

"The investigation lasted eighteen months. Any other prosecutor would have announced the indictments a few days ahead of time, so there would be big headlines each day and lots of publicity afterward," said Goldstock. "Hogan refused to do it that way. He had only one small press conference. Period. The newspapers hadn't been prepared for anything spectacular—so they treated it as routine. A few twelve-paragraph stories and that was that."

It was in support of the Rackets Bureau that Hogan spent years defending the controversial technique of wiretapping. He was, of course, confronted by an onslaught of Supreme Court decisions restricting the practice as an invasion of privacy. Between 1934 and 1966, an anomalous situation existed under New York State law. In state courts, Hogan was permitted to admit wiretapped recordings into evidence. But the very act of divulging the same conversations in federal court was a federal crime.

Hogan went before a Justice Department hearing panel in Washington to plead for a relaxation of the federal law. He explained that organized crime was, by definition, "indoor crime," unobservable by uniformed police. Wiretapping was the only "investigative tool" able to uncover it. Hogan asked for *carte blanche* approval to wiretap.

"Without it," he testified, "I do not think that our office would have convicted Lucky Luciano, Jimmy Hines, Louis (Lepke) Buchalter, Jacob (Gurrah) Shapiro, Socks Lanza, George Scalise, Frank Erickson, Johnny Dio and Frank Carbo."

Celluloid echoes of all those dead gangsters could still be heard in Hogan's ninth-floor "wire vault." The tape-storage vault was a vacuum-sealed, double-locked chamber guarded by police officers. A self-activating humidifier-dehumidifier kept the room temperature at an even 70 degrees. Thousands of tape spools were stacked floor to ceiling within the vault; some of the material contained thereon was so sensitive that Hogan ordered it permanently sealed off—a time capsule for criminologists of the millennium to listen to and ponder.

These secret tapes were said to incriminate scores of politicians, judges, entertainers, sports figures and other prominent individuals—men and women who escaped indictment only because Hogan lacked enough cor-roborative evidence to convict them. In New York State, corroborative evidence can't be given by an accomplice, so it's hard to develop a good case.

"If we could put on a Kefauver kind of circus without having to pro-duce corroborative evidence," Hogan once said, "we could blow the town open wide."

For years, it was rumored around City Hall that Hogan had evidence in his vault that stopped just short of putting Mayor O'Dwyer behind bars. Each time First Deputy Fire Commissioner Moran picked up his building-inspection collections in Brooklyn, there was evidence that he went straight to the porch of Gracie Mansion, the Mayor's residence.

When Moran finally landed in jail, Hogan himself went to the ex-Commissioner's cell, hoping he would open up and talk about this "funny coincidence." Moran, refusing to divulge information on O'Dwyer, said: "Mr. District Attorney, I came into this world man and I'll go out of this world a man."

Although the D.A.'s office depended on breaches of such loyalty, Hogan betrayed a grudging admiration for Moran's moral code. When Scotti wanted to know the outcome of the jail-cell meeting, Hogan told him: "Moran could have saved himself ten years in prison, but he re-fused. God, I admire that!"

Scotti recalled that none of the fire inspectors realized they were doing anything immoral or illegal: "City Hall said it was OK." In light of O'Dwyer's political double-cross during the Hogan-for-Mayor fiasco of 1948, nothing would have pleased Hogan more than seeing his old enemy O'Dwyer in the can. But since Moran never talked, O'Dwyer was never charged.

As the years wore on, Hogan was often accused of maintaining his "near-miss" files in order to keep certain New York judges and district leaders in line. At the same time, he was praised for refusing to divulge noncorroborative information that he knew would ruin lives and careers, without serving a constructive purpose.

The underworld suspected the presence of Hogan's wiretappers on the line as far back as 1938, when Dewey first introduced the FBI technique into the Special Prosecutor's office. Dutch Schultz felt so certain the line was bugged that he ended every conversation with the aside: "I know you're on there, *schmuck*. I hope your ears rot off!"

The public learned of Hogan's wiretapping in 1943, following the political assassination of Carlo Tresca, a friend of Mayor Fiorello La Guardia's. The sixty-eight-year-old Tresca, the scholarly Italian editor of *Il Martello* ("The Hammer"), was an anti-fascist, radical activist; with his pince-nez, neatly trimmed goatee and floppy black sombrero, he was a familiar folk hero to thousands of strikers in the Pennsylvania coal fields, the New Jersey silk mills and the Colorado copper mines. During a turbulent career, Tresca had been bombed, bludgeoned and kidnapped; he was finally gunned down by a hired assassin. Friends of Tresca's said the "contract" had come from Italy and that the assassin had acted on Mussolini's orders.*

Detectives seized a suspect, Carmine Galante, identified as the driver of the murder car. Galante, an ex-convict who gave his occupation as "pushcart peddler," stuck to his alibi—that he had been at the movies with his girlfriend when the murder occurred.

Then Frank Costello entered the picture. The silk-suited mobster was, at the time, a forty-seven-year-old hoodlum who had risen to power during Prohibition as a bootlegger and slot-machine czar. Suspecting a connection between Costello and Galante, Hogan ordered his wiretappers to listen in on Costello's unlisted Central Park West apartment phone.

Wiretapping wasn't very sophisticated in those days; tape recorders were still in the developmental stage. Detectives clamped on earphones and tediously took down every Costello phone conversation in shorthand. The information Hogan sought on Galante never materialized. But the months of patient eavesdropping paid off in a quite unexpected way. On August 24, 1943, Costello's phone rang and detectives heard the following conversation between the gangster and Magistrate Thomas A. Aurelio, who had just received a bi-party nomination for Supreme Court Justice of the State of New York:

---

* Hogan: "All these persons, professing to have 'inside' knowledge about the murder, were questioned by this office in the hope that they might be able to provide some hitherto unknown information, and all were required to testify under oath before the grand jury. One theorist not only identified the instigators of the crime but even 'knew' the price paid for its execution. In every instance it was discovered that the explanation of the murder, advanced with such assurance, had no more substantial basis than hearsay."

Aurelio: "Good morning, Francesco. How are you and thanks for everything."

Costello: "Congratulations. It went over perfect. When I tell you something is in the bag, you can rest assured."

Aurelio: "It was perfect. [Congressman] Arthur Klein did the nominating—first me and then Gavagan and then Peck. It was fine."

Costello: "That's fine."

Aurelio: "The doctor called me last night to congratulate me. I'm going to see him today. He seems to be improving. He should be up and around soon and should take the train for Hot Springs."

Costello: "That's fine."

Aurelio went on to discuss a nomination outside New York County, and arranged to have dinner with Costello and his wife.

Costello: "Well, well, we'll have to get together with you and your Mrs. . . ."

Aurelio: "That's fine, but right now I want to assure you of my loyalty for all you have done; it's undying."

Costello: "I know. I'll see you soon."

The phone clicked. Four days later, Hogan startled the city with an announcement that New York's best-known mobster had proved powerful enough to swing a Supreme Court nomination.

Aurelio's explanation—"I knew Costello to be a businessman of good repute"—only made things worse for him. Tammany leader Michael Kennedy repudiated the nomination. Aurelio refused to eliminate himself from the race, however, and he did win at the ballot box. But even as a judge, he was a dead horse politically. Aurelio soon stepped down from the bench to become a virtual recluse—hounded to his grave by that less-than-sixty-second "courtesy call" to "Francesco."

Hogan's pursuit of Costello was eventually frustrated because the racketeer shifted his one-armed bandits from New York to legal slot-machine states such as Louisiana and Florida. This was too far away for Hogan's reach—and so the reputed boss of the entire U.S. underworld, being totally legit in New York State, could enjoy living in The Big Apple as a businessman of "good repute"—for a while.

In 1950, Hogan's wiretap files on Costello provided the Senate's Kefauver Crime Committee hearings with 90 percent of the information that astounded a nationwide television audience. Costello starred in his real-life melodrama: tapping his buffed fingernails on the witness table and reeling off tales of gambling and bookmaking operations that took in millions.

Hogan's only face-to-face talk with Costello came when the mobster was called before a grand jury to testify about having the Aurelio nomination in his pocket. The two men chatted briefly and seemed to understand each other fairly well. Hogan felt that Costello was at least a sincere witness.

"He talked straight, anyway, and it was a relief to hear straight talk after watching some of the yellow politicians who were in that mess up to their ears squirm and squidge all over the place, giving maybe a teaspoonful of truth to every bucketful of lies. He didn't tell everything, and there wasn't any way we could force him to, but when he laid a fact out on the table, he didn't try to dress it up any and make it look better than it was. As soon as it was over, Costello came up to me and said:

" 'Well, how did I do in there?'

"I said, 'Pretty well. You did pretty well. I noticed that every now and then you cut some corners sort of sharp, but to tell the truth it was a lot better than I thought it would be. Not bad at all, not bad at all.'

" 'You're right about cutting the corners,' Costello said, 'I guess I know plenty you'd like to know, but you understand how it is—I'm a legitimate businessman now, but I've still got to protect my boys. They've done a lot for me, and you wouldn't think much of me if I didn't protect them.'

"He started telling me how badly he'd been brought up," Hogan recalled, "what a rotten neighborhood he'd lived in, how his family always needed money, and what bad associations he'd had from the beginning. It was quite a tidy little lecture. Just before he left, he looked around the room—kind of enviously, I thought. 'Maybe if things had been different,' he said, 'I'd have become an honest lawyer and worked on this side of the street.' "

Throughout the 1950s, Hogan activated as many as seventy-five taps each year. The mob was now skittish about using telephones. But without phones, horserace "wire rooms" would have gone out of business. Hijack deals would have had to be negotiated on street corners from city to city, requiring expensive jet travel rather than long-distance phone rates. In the hands of a racketeer, a telephone receiver could be used as a blunt instrument for blackmail, extortion, conspiracy. The mobsters tried to set up safe phones—unlisted numbers, pay telephones. Hogan had the numbers traced. The hoods spoke in Sicilian, but so did Scotti. More and more of the mob's lifelines began to go dead: they used the phones less and less. Rackets convictions dropped off slightly.

Then, in 1962, a scientific breakthrough: Hogan discovered the crime-fighting possibilities of the bug. One of the first bugs he experimented with was a miniature German microphone transmitter, attached to a portable wire recorder. An East Side bar owner, Ralph Pansini, had come to the D.A.'s office in January 1962, complaining that he was being shaken down by investigators of the State Liquor Authority. Pansini refused to pay a $3,500 bribe for a liquor license. He obtained the license anyway. Then, SLA investigators returned to demand a $1,000 payoff. The bar owner went to Hogan.

The D.A.'s office fitted Pansini with the new wire recorder, gave him marked money, and sent him off to gather evidence. In so doing, Pansini uncorked the single most inflammatory corruption scandal in the history of the Empire State. The State Liquor Authority scandal, with its Cecil B. DeMille-sized cast and jigsaw puzzle of interlocking conspiracies, took Hogan seven years to unravel completely. In the process, one state official committed suicide by throwing himself under a subway train. The right-hand man of Nelson Rockefeller, then Governor and Presidential aspirant, was indicted, tried and convicted for bribery. The law firms of some of the state's bigshot Republican politicians were sullied by charges of impropriety for doing business with the SLA.

And there was more: secret tapes in Hogan's vault alerted the District Attorney to an attempted cover-up of the liquor scandal by some of the highest Republican figures in Rocky's inner circle. These top politicians talked of getting Rockefeller to supersede Hogan in the liquor investigation (". . . take this out of the D.A.'s hands") by appointing a commission under the Moreland Act to investigate the liquor laws. A month later, Rockefeller *did* appoint such a commission. Because there was no evidence on the tapes that the cover-up plan was directly discussed with the Governor, Hogan never released the actual recording transcripts during his own lifetime. But information developed from the tapes stayed with Hogan's office, and in fairness to the Governor, the District Attorney waited until the day of Rockefeller's 1962 reelection victory before announcing word of the liquor scandal to the press.

The saloon scandal was an outgrowth of the system of liquor licensing that still persists in many large U.S. cities today. In 1962, in New York City, there were 9,513 bars and liquor stores, grossing millions a day. But their right to sell drinks hinged on the five-member board that governed the State Liquor Authority.

The $25,000-a-year chairmanship of the SLA had been given to a Brooklyn political hack named Martin Epstein. Epstein was a bosom pal of Johnny Crews, the Republican boss of Brooklyn. The two men lived in the same apartment building. After Rockefeller's initial victory in 1958, Crews had asked as his reward that "my boy Marty" be made SLA chairman. Rocky had acceded.

Once Epstein got into office, doing business with the SLA became a nightmare for saloon owners in the city. Their liquor licenses cost $1,200 legitimately. But under Epstein, the under-the-table cost escalated to roughly $10,000 to $12,000. The graft involved a kind of secondary licensing that hinged on both greed and the archaic state liquor laws. One law, for example, was that drinks could be served only on premises where a fulltime "chef" was ready to prepare food. Another law: if a prostitute solicited trade in a bar, the operator could lose his license. The same fate awaited him if he got caught serving a minor—even if the teenager used a fake ID card to claim drinking age. Competing bar owners paid SLA investigators bribes in exchange for winking at such violations. Many bar owners complained, saying that it was common practice, for instance, for an investigator to plant a prostitute in a bar and then "accidentally" find her there—as a reprisal against an owner who refused a payoff.

To expose such practices, honest bar owner Ralph Pansini, equipped with the D.A.'s German "Minifon" and a battery pack hidden in a shoulder holster, bugged the two men who had tried to shake him down—two SLA investigators, Ernest Moss and Maurice Bernstein. Both men were indicted. Two days later, Moss hurled himself under a subway train.

Hogan and Scotti then sent Pansini, posing as the prospective buyer of a bar on 45th Street, into SLA headquarters. Pansini was told to see Albert Klapper, managing clerk of Martin Epstein's Wall Street firm. The portable recorder caught Klapper saying: "If I speak to the chairman [Epstein] you don't have a thing to worry about . . . I can't get you any closer than that. . . . It may cost you about ten thousand."

Pansini: "Above ten? Gee, that's a lot more than I figured."

Klapper: "Fifty-fourth Street, about three weeks ago, cost much more than that . . . I don't mind telling you that if I want to I could have a million guys at the door outside . . ."

Klapper went on to explain that he only did business through his lawyer, Harry Neyer: "When Harry walks in, it has a certain value . . . It's no use talking. I don't have to tell you."

Pansini went as directed to Neyer's office on West 48th Street and recorded conversations with the attorney. On the basis of these tapes, Hogan obtained a court order to plant a bug in Neyer's office. From that eavesdropping evidence, he was able to get another order to bug the office of theatrical agent Harry Steinman. And on the basis of those recordings he received authorization to install a hidden mike in Martin Epstein's hospital bed. The SLA chairman, a diabetic, was in New York Hospital having a leg amputated.

On October 6, 1964, the logs of all these tapes were placed in evidence in the trial of Ralph Berger, a Chicago public-relations man charged with conspiracy to bribe Chairman Epstein in order to obtain a liquor license for the Playboy Club in New York. Playboy empire builder Hugh Hefner had already invested $3.5 million in his sex-and-status Valhalla for the worn-out businessman. Dozens of cocktail bunnies had been scouted up and fitted for their cotton tails. Thousands of monogrammed Playboy keys had been peddled to Hefner's leisure-time clientele.

The key club was scheduled to open with attendant hoopla when Hefner suddenly got the word: there wasn't a single bottle of liquor on the shelf. The SLA took a dim view of key clubs, it seemed, unless Hefner could cough up an "extra-legal" fee for a private club liquor license. A figure of $100,000 was suggested. The man who did the suggesting was none other than Nelson Rockefeller's top aide: Republican State Chairman L. Judson Morhouse.

When one of the Playboy officials balked, Berger said, "I wouldn't complain if I were you. The Gaslight Club paid sixty thousand and they're not out of the woods yet." Hefner applied a businesslike solution to the matter. He hired Morhouse to double as both legal and public-relations counselor for Playboy Enterprises, Inc. Eventually, a payment of $60,000 did wing its way from Chicago to New York. Morhouse's "fee" was $18,000. The jam of liquor trucks in front of the Playboy Club on opening day looked, in the words of *Life* magazine, "like the invasion of Normandy."

When a grand jury called Morhouse to answer questions about the $18,000 fee, his reaction sent a gasp of disbelief through the Albany Legislature. "Jud" refused to waive immunity. He quit his party post and went into seclusion.

According to testimony at his bribery trial two years later, Morhouse was under the impression that Republican party leaders had been given the State Liquor Authority for their personal use in return for campaign efforts in getting Rockefeller elected. The pattern of SLA operations became clearer as wiretap evidence was introduced during the Berger trial. The only way to obtain a liquor license, it seemed, was to hire an "in"

Republican lawyer, then pay him a staggering fee in exchange for an introduction to Morhouse.

The list of lawyers with a history of successful operations before the SLA included some interesting names and alliances. A liquor store owned by A&P heir Huntington Hartford found itself dealing through Court of Claims Judge Melvin Osterman, a former GOP leader. Osterman had been recommended through Eric M. Javits, nephew of the state's Republican senior Senator, Jacob Javits. And Eric Javits had been referred through Seymour Alter, a liquor-store manager, who got his information from Charles (Bebe) Rebozo during a trip to Paradise Island.

The man described as "the biggest liquor lawyer in town" was Hyman D. Siegel, who inherited his title when his law partner, Louis J. Lefkowitz, became Attorney General in 1957.

This was the same Louis Lefkowitz who admitted he had "heard stories" about SLA payoffs when he held the "best liquor lawyer in town" title, but declared that he hadn't listened to the stories. "After becoming Attorney General, I completely divorced myself from my practice," said Lefky. "Before that, I'm ashamed to mention . . ."

Siegel was among the seventeen persons eventually indicted in the SLA investigation, but the six-year statute of limitations had run out since Lefkowitz had "divorced" himself from the liquor business. There was a savage irony in the situation. Louis J. Lefkowitz's office of the Special Prosecutor, in 1971, would supersede Frank Hogan in Manhattan corruption cases.

Hogan could never bring Epstein to trial because even on his "wired" hospital bed, the SLA chairman never spoke—out loud, that is. He used sign language. Osterman would ask how much a liquor license was worth. In reply, Epstein would hold up his fingers: One. Two. Three.

When the hidden microphone failed to produce evidence, Hogan ordered Epstein to appear before a grand jury. The seventy-year-old patient pleaded that he was too ill to appear: besides being diabetic, he suffered a serious circulatory ailment. Hogan ordered the dying witness to appear anyway, "just so he knows we mean business."

Epstein's reluctant grand-jury appearance was a strange spectacle indeed. Hogan dismantled the revolving doors of the Courthouse so that Epstein could be brought in on a stretcher. The chairman was wrapped like a mummy in blankets. An ambulance attendant hovered over him, mindful of intravenous bottles. Clamoring newsmen pressed forward and almost knocked the stretcher to the ground. Microphone wires got tangled in the intravenous tubes that ran in and out of the patient's body. Upstairs, in the grand-jury room, hostile questions were directed at the dying man.

Eyes heavily lidded, lips sealed tight, Epstein refused to waive immunity. He escaped prosecution briefly by moving to Florida, but then was rolled back in a wheelchair to a New York courtroom, where he was indicted for taking unlawful fees and filing false state income tax returns. An interesting charge: at the time, there had been only one other case in state history of a person indicted for evasion of *state* taxes. Hogan made this particular charge because he lacked enough corroborative evidence to nail Epstein for bribery. Epstein was free to return to Florida, where he lingered in poor health over the next ten years, submitting regular hospital affidavits to prove that he was too ill to stand trial. When the patient's condition became "terminal" in February 1974, the charges were finally dismissed.

Osterman pleaded guilty to conspiracy and bribery charges in November 1964. He was stripped of his judicial robes and trotted off to serve a one-year term on Riker's Island. Ralph Berger, the go-between in the Playboy payoff, was found guilty of the same charges, but fought his conviction all the way to the Supreme Court. The high tribunal reversed the conviction on June 12, 1967, in a landmark decision that severely restricted U.S. prosecutors, including Hogan, in their future use of wiretapping.

At the time Morhouse came to trial, there were reports that Joseph Carlino, the Republican speaker of the Assembly, and State Senate Majority Leader Walter J. Mahoney were also representing clients before the SLA. If Morhouse had cooperated with the grand jury or taken the stand in his own defense, these and other names might have come out at the bribery trial. Morhouse was convicted of bribery in 1966, after he refused to testify on his own behalf.

Why did "Jud" refuse to take the stand? According to testimony at Rockefeller's 1974 Senate Rules Committee confirmation hearings, the Vice President admitted being informed by Morhouse in 1959 of a $100,000 cash gift in a shoe box. Rocky said he discussed the shoe-box money during a huddle with Attorney General Lefkowitz and then Lieutenant Governor Malcolm Wilson on the dais of a Waldorf-Astoria fundraising dinner in June 1959. Rockefeller described the gift as an "attempted political contribution" for the state committee. He ordered the shoe box returned. Wilson later said he had no recollection of the dais discussion. Lefkowitz refused any comment at all.

But Rockefeller's account differed from a sequence of events established at the 1965 trial of Assemblyman Hyman E. Mintz, accused in an alleged racetrack bribery scheme. Hogan believed Mintz had been an errand boy, delivering the shoe box to Morhouse from license-seeking sponsors of a proposed racetrack in the Finger Lakes region of New York. Scotti was sure the $100,000 was bribe money, and for a while, the Lieutenant Governor himself was a target of the racetrack investigation. Mintz was later convicted for trying to bribe one of Hogan's detectives. The assemblyman had wanted the detective to tell him how far the investigation had "moved up the ladder."

In spite of the SLA scandals, Rockefeller's 1966 reelection campaign succeeded. Returned to office for a third term, he pardoned Morhouse, in 1970, for reasons of severe illness. The pardon seemed justified: Morhouse was suffering from cancer as well as Parkinson's disease. His life would almost certainly be shortened if he went to prison. Accordingly, Morhouse spent only three days behind bars. Out of jail, "Jud" became a forgotten man. By 1974, everybody assumed he was long dead and buried.

It came as quite a shock, then, when the House Judiciary Committee discovered that Morhouse was still very much alive in 1974. Moreover, a committee investigation showed that physicians' affidavits on Morhouse's condition back in 1970 had been doctored by Rocky's staff to strengthen the argument that Morhouse's life would be threatened by a prison term. A short time later, Rockefeller had loaned his sick friend $100,000. Then the loan was "forgiven"—even though that money had earned Morhouse $500,000 in real-estate interest by 1974.

The liquor scandal that had been bottled up on the shelf for nearly eight years spilled open again when the District Attorney's office released transcripts of the secret SLA-Morhouse tapes. In one of the recorded conversations, a Morhouse business partner, Aleer J. Couri, tells Walter E. Bligh, former secretary of the GOP State Committee:

". . . it was on my insistence Jud went to the Governor and [George] Hinman [Republican national committeeman] and told them, 'Look, I've told you my situation because I want the Governor to know and be protected. . . . The Governor appreciated it, but I think you ought to take it out of Hogan's hands. It's too late for me to benefit, it's for the Governor I'm thinking about.' "

Hogan's secret tapes, heard in the context of Rockefeller's Vice Presidential confirmation hearings, left a lot of people in New York convinced that the $100,000 Morhouse loan was nothing more than hush money, and that the biggest corruption scandal in state history was essentially a Watergate that worked.

12
ENTOMBED

Mornings in the Manhattan Tombs tended to be indistinguishable from one another. Each day, metal benches, hinged to the wall, unfolded at the same angles before a communal television set, tuned to the same soap operas. The breakfast of Spam and oatmeal tasted much like last night's dinner of canned ham and bean soup. There were no real windows—only those translucent glass bricks, so that prisoners could tell that it was day, not night, in the outside world. They called their painted blue ceiling "the sky."

The morning of March 9, 1972, began, as usual, with the rhythmic clang of metal breakfast trays against iron bars. The flush of toilets. An ocean's roar of voices: shouts back and forth, obscenities, catcalls.

Despite the noise, the prison was following routine—except for one trouble spot, Cellblock F, on the sixth floor. Prison commands blared through the static of a loudspeaker: "General population. Sixth floor. Keep it down!"

But the noise did not subside on Cellblock F. Arms snaked out between the crossbars. Prisoners greeted their keepers with the universal prison salute: "The Finger." Everyone on the cellblock—prison deputies and inmates alike—sensed that this morning was going to be different, one of the rough ones.

Almost at random, the prisoners began acting out—kicking, punching, spitting at the guards. "Hey, officer!" an inmate sniggered. "I can't wait to hump your missus when I get out. Ver-r-ry nice!" The guard's rage became the next prisoner's hysteria. The anger swept, in a soundwave of hoarse taunts, from cell to cell.

The torpor broken, it would be hours before order could be restored. Hours before the violent chain reaction could be quieted down with the aid of tranquilizer injections. Hours before the men would lie on their iron cots again, gazing, stupefied, at the fly-specked ceiling, the cockroaches crawling in the toilet bowls beside their beds, or at their *Penthouse* "pets" Scotchtaped to the walls.

High-potency drugs like Thorazine and Dilantin had largely replaced blackjacks as the prison guard's first line of defense. And the chemical restraints zapped inmates much more effectively. Still, on the rare, mean morning such as this one, people could get hurt. Some prisoners balked at taking "their medicine":

"Whazzat?"

"Hundred and fifty milligrams. Spansules. Swallow 'em."

"I'm allergic, man."

"Swallow them or we're gonna crack your cell and shove 'em down your throat!"

"Stick 'em up your ass!"

There were various ways to pressure a man into taking his medication. Like ordering him to double up with someone else in a single cell. Or depositing him for punishment in the Bing—the only place in the Tombs worse than the seventh-floor "bull pen" where homosexual rapists were locked up together. Nobody knew why they called it the Bing, just as nobody has ever been certain why the Manhattan House of Detention for Men is called the Tombs. Prison officials called the Bing "punitive segregation." Guards called it a "strip cell": a solitary iron box where the prisoner was stripped to his undershorts and fed a diet of soda and white bread, except for a single square meal every three days.

In places like the Tombs, official imagination must be exercised to keep inmates in line. The Bing was the end product of that imagination: no toilet paper, no sink for washing, no mattress for the steel-spring cot hinged to the wall.

This particular morning, another disciplinary measure was imposed on Cellblock F. "Lock-in, feed-in," announced the loudspeaker. To which the prisoners screamed back a chorus of "Shit" and "Fuck." "Lock-in, feed-in" was a form of solitary that meant inmates would stay behind their cell doors all day, mopping up. No volleyball. No outside meals. No soap operas. Prisoners would not be allowed to mingle in the communal center of the cellblock, as they usually did after morning head count. Roll call was taken promptly at 8:00 A.M. The tour commander hesitated as his eyes fell on two names: Timbuk and Sonni Pyles. The commander knew today's problem would concern the Pyles brothers. They had been the instigators of much of the trouble on the sixth floor this week.

On Monday and Tuesday, they had refused to leave their cell and face robbery charges in the dismal courthouse that adjoined the Tombs. Wednesday, they obtained an adjournment. Today was Thursday, and Criminal Court Judge Myles J. Lane had run out of patience: "Use all necessary force," he directed the Corrections Department. "I want to see these defendants in my courtroom."

The Pyles brothers had a date with the judge at nine o'clock sharp.

At 8:25 A.M. the correction officer in charge of Cellblock F climbed the catwalk over two tiers of meshed cages and unlocked a switchbox. He checked for the master control number of the Pyles brothers' cell and yanked the lever for "lower" F-5. The cell door "cracked" open. The men in the surrounding cells tensed and pressed their faces against the bars, craning to see and hear the rumble they all knew was coming. Someone yelled for Timbuk and Sonni not to let those "mothers" push them around. There was a clangorous echo as the iron cell gate slid all the way open and locked into place.

The guard looked inside. The brothers sat on their mattresses, top and bottom bunk. Timbuk and Sonni were twins. At twenty-six, they had magnificent bodies, developed from Mississippi field labor. Six-feet-four, they weighed nearly 200 pounds. Lying down in the 6-by-8-foot cell, they looked too large for the bunks. Their faces bore identical, watchful expressions, eyes narrowed, full lips parted, ready for retort.

It was exactly 8:30 now. The Tombs guard knew his responsibility: to get the two men into court by the nine-o'clock deadline. Any way he could. "Gentlemen," he announced to the two immobile hulks, "let's move it. Outside!" For a few seconds, neither prisoner moved a muscle. Then Timbuk, still resting on the bed, spoke loudly and deliberately in his deep South drawl. "The onliest way we leavin' is iffen you kill us first."

Catcalls and cheers rang through the cellblock. The officer followed procedure: he alerted Warden Albert Glick, officially in charge of the Tombs. Glick summoned Dr. William Kimmell, the house doctor, instructing him to pack his emergency kit and hurry to the sixth floor, where two black inmates were holed up in the F section. Other prisoners were threatening to riot. How far it would go (the riots of October 1970 were still fresh in the warden's memory) was anyone's guess. The entire floor might have to be tear-gassed.

In his courtroom across the Bridge of Sighs that connected the Tombs to the Criminal Courthouse, Judge Lane donned his black robes—he was, as yet, unaware of the action taking place in that gray cement monolith just a few hundred yards away.

A seven-man guard detail was ordered to report to Cellblock F. Riot-squad Captain Constantine Mellon and his men donned bulletproof vests and steel helmets and then ran for the sixth-floor elevators. Warden Glick and Dr. Kimmell reached the cell just as Mellon and the other guards arrived. Seeing themselves so outnumbered, the Pyles twins rose up, grabbed the crossbars with locked wrists and braced themselves for whatever might happen.

Warden Glick tried to read them the judge's order, but his voice was drowned out by the shrieks and shouts of the hecklers. The noise level was incredible. The officials, unable to make themselves heard, communicated with each other in sign language. Captain Mellon motioned to one guard to bring a tear-gas "duster"—powdered CN gas in a 9-inch-long CO_2 cartridge. The aerosol can worked in much the same way as an ordinary insecticide spray, sending out a direct *pouf* of acrid chemical mist. The aim was supposedly direct, so that gas masks weren't needed. But when Mellon stepped into cell F-5 and pressed the nozzle, the noxious spray backfired, dousing his own face and eyes. Mellon sank to the floor, blinded and gagging.

Gas masks were called for. Another guard stepped inside, this time scoring a direct hit on Timbuk and Sonni. Sickened by fumes, they loosened their grip on the bars and reeled back into a corner of the cell. Their shoulders hunched, they slumped forward over the toilet, gasping for air, and tried to vomit.

The Pyles brothers were temporarily blinded, but though retching and sick, they struggled by body instinct: grasping, punching, kicking to the groin of the nearest man attacking them. Eventually, the six guards threw the two men to the blood-stained cement and managed to clamp on handcuffs and leather leg shackles. Trussed up in this fashion, the twins were being dragged down the corridor to the elevator when that door opened. The Pyles' attorney, Daniel Sheehan, stepped out and intercepted the guards.

"Mucus was pouring from their noses and Timbuk was apparently saying he just wanted an adjournment," Sheehan described the scene after he returned to Judge Lane's chambers. "The guards were calling the defendants cocksuckers. The warden kept saying, 'Please, stop, don't hurt them.' Timbuk had his hands cuffed in front of him and his feet tied with a nightstick between the handcuffs and they were carrying him like a lion out of there, with his head dragging on the floor."

Sheehan described how Warden Glick ordered the guards to "stop what you're doing" and strap the prisoners in chairs—"Carry them out that way." This idea did not go over well with one of the correction officers, a hardliner who complained, "This motherfucker keeps asking us not to hurt them when they're just lying here refusing to come. And he calls himself the warden!"

Sonni was totally unconscious by then. Timbuk was semi-conscious. Both inmates were uncuffed and strapped into chairs, their arms dangling. They were dragged through the cellblock again in bloodied T-shirts. Timbuk's left shoe was yanked off. His head banged up against the "slop sink," where the inmates shaved, washed underwear and sometimes urinated. The brothers were paraded before the other inmates, who screamed obscenities at the guards and rammed clenched fists through the crossbars. One of the prisoners hurled his shoe at the warden. An addict inmate on the upper tier, who was "de-toxing" on Methadone, still found enough energy to set fire to his mattress. A black inmate taunted several black guards: "Electronic niggers! The white man push a button, you jump—slave niggers!"

Timbuk Pyles, his eyes puffed shut with tears, regained consciousness long enough to murmur, "My ribs. My ribs . . ." The doctor stopped the guards—"Put them down"—and dug his fingertips under Timbuk's ribcage: "Possible fracture. I won't know for sure until we get him to stand up. It may be soft-tissue damage."

Both brothers were hustled, in chairs, to the seventh floor. Belts were strapped around their waists. They were rehandcuffed to the belts. Timbuk's other shoe had been dragged off his foot. He was still murmuring something about an "adjournment." One of the guards answered, "I couldn't give a fuck about your fucking adjournment."

Sheehan was so repulsed at what he was witnessing, he told the judge later that day, that he began sobbing in full view of the other men. "I couldn't talk with him [Timbuk] because he couldn't hear anything I was saying to him. He just kept saying—that's when I started crying. He said he just wanted 'due process' . . ."

Meanwhile, about twenty other officers had crowded into the room.

The doctor was checking Sonni's heartbeat with a stethoscope. The physician turned away just as the patient went into convulsions and slid off the bench onto the floor, banging his skull. While the guards struggled to lift Sonni's limp torso back up on the bench, Timbuk fell off. Gas burped out of him; mucus oozed onto the concrete.

A younger guard shook his head: "I shoulda been an insurance broker."

Frank Hogan's hot line rang while he was eating his tea-and-rye-toast breakfast. The call came from his office, alerting him to the emergency in the Tombs. Listening to the details, Hogan winced in anticipation of the next day's newspaper and TV editorials. Professional libertarians would see in the Pyles brothers' revolt a repudiation of ghetto conditions in America and give them a moral license to defy the court. Law-and-order conservatives would cheer the guards' get-tough tactics. And Hogan would be caught in the crossfire once again.

Within twenty minutes of leaving home, the Chief was at his desk. One of his rookie assistants, Kenneth Gribetz, a Phi Beta Kappa graduate of City College and New York University Law School, waited in the outer office. Gribetz had been inside Hogan's private domain only once before, when he had been interviewed for the job.

Executive Assistant David Worgan appeared at the door and signaled Gribetz to step inside. The rookie stood more or less at attention until the District Attorney offered him a seat. Then Gribetz began to review the morning's bloody skirmish. He told Hogan that the twins had been gassed out of their cell, and that two guards had been injured in the scuffle on the sixth floor. An ambulance had just screeched out of the receiving yard, rushing Timbuk Pyles up to Bellevue Hospital's emergency room for X-rays.

Hogan listened intently as Gribetz told him more about the Pyles brothers, who had been known to New York police for some time. A flamboyant pair, they lived in a penthouse and sported custom-made Afro hats of leopardskin. Although they flashed large wads of bills and bragged of their exploits, the brothers were obvious, sloppy muggers. They were certainly in the lower echelons of crime when they were arrested in March 1971. A New York County grand jury returned a series of indictments that month charging them with seven hotel robberies and related weapons offenses. The indictment alleged that the twins had held up hotel clerks with a sawed-off shotgun. Before their arrest the brothers had lived in the Hotel Webster, on West 45th Street, where they rented an eleventh-floor penthouse. There, they had grown overconfident, or perhaps they were just lazy—twice they robbed the place next door, the Hotel Seymour, a geographic convenience which eliminated the problem of a getaway car. Once before they had been arrested in a getaway car, but they beat the rap by convincing authorities they had been forced into the auto at gunpoint. The driver was later identified as a resident of their small hometown in Mississippi.

The brothers were bottom-rung hoodlums, working their way up from street muggings to bigger heists, when, on the evening of March 5, 1971, they tried something different—ripping off a shopkeeper who was making a $1,100 night deposit in a bank vault. This was their biggest haul, and their biggest blunder. Next day, the victim provided an eyewitness identification of the twins, noting their bizarre African hats. Detectives raided the Pyles penthouse and arrested the brothers. The shotgun was seized along with $445 cash from a dresser drawer.

The Pyles had been maintaining their innocence ever since. But during the intervening year, they skipped a scheduled court appearance and were indicted for bail jumping. They were recaptured and returned to the Tombs. As Kenny Gribetz related all this to the District Attorney, Hogan reached over and flipped through a manila folder containing mug shots of the brothers. The belligerent twins stared back from a police lineup: Sonni, beneath a bushy Afro, sported a goatee. Timbuk was clean-shaven. They were both dressed in conservative suits and ties, their shoes shone all spit-and-polish.

Pulling out the twins' "yellow sheets," their arrest records, Hogan scanned the list of arrests made, charges dropped, court appearances postponed, bench warrants outstanding, parole violations. A bench warrant was out for their arrest in the Bronx at the time they were picked up in Manhattan. They were considered armed and dangerous, with no real roots in the community. On the arrest reports, the brothers claimed they worked as musicians at a cocktail bar-and-grill called the Club Monterray. But the manager of this establishment had said that the two men were short-order cooks; the Club hadn't featured live entertainment in years. Bearing in mind their previous bail-jumping record, the judge had set bail at $30,000 each.

The brothers were unable to post bond after being remanded to Cellblock F. Instead, they began to write letters to Congressmen.

A torrent of mail began issuing from the Pyles' cell. There was really no theme to the letters, Hogan noticed, just an unending scream of protest that they had been denied "due process." One of these letters found its way onto the desk of Representative Seymour Halpern, a liberal Democrat from Queens County, who read into the Congressional Record next day "serious questions of due process" posed by the Pyles case.

Hogan certainly understood Halpern's charge that the present bail system discriminates against the poor and denies them due process. The D.A. opposed as both unconstitutional and unworkable the White House-sponsored experiment in "preventive detention." He felt the plan had backfired when it was tried out in Washington, D.C.; all it did was burden the courts with still another pretrial motion. Similarly, Hogan wanted to do away with the cash bail system, which was intrinsically unfair to the dispossessed, he believed. The system put political pressure on judges appointed by a liberal mayor to be lenient in granting parole and nominal bail. The result under a liberal Mayor John V. Lindsay: more than 31,000 defendants had absconded while on parole in the past few months—or jumped bail. As for finding any one of them, "You have only to move six blocks in New York and you're lost," Hogan muttered. "You don't even have to take a different name."

The Police Department assigned thousands of policemen to write up daily quotas of parking tickets, Hogan griped, but the department allotted only six cops to follow up on thousands of arrest warrants in the city. Prohibitive bail, in Hogan's view, seemed the only rational alternative for "protecting the city," the only way to make certain that alleged offenders would show up in court. He had the satisfaction of knowing the higher courts agreed with him. Kenny Gribetz had scanned the Pyles' appeals on bail reduction, heard at four judicial levels up to the Federal District Court. All of these appeals had been denied. "We were ready to proceed to trial within two months after the arrest," Gribetz told the Chief, who nodded sympathetically. The Pyleses had proved remarkably effective jailhouse lawyers since then. Hogan supposed they had been in trouble often enough before to know all the delaying tactics that renegade defense lawyers exploit to frustrate the court system.

In their letters, the Pyles twins clamored for a "speedy trial." Yet each time their names had appeared on ready lists, they developed a sudden change of heart.

This was a familiar ploy. By turn, the Pyleses got rid of eight qualified lawyers—state-funded "Section 18-B" attorneys, men specially selected by the court's Appellate Division for their competence and brainpower.

The ease with which the defendants fired these lawyers and obtained adjournments was enough to make anyone wonder why New York law didn't provide a deadline for the filing of pretrial motions. On the eve of four separate trial dates, the brothers had filed various motions to sever their cases, reduce "excessive" bail, or get rid of their latest team of lawyers. The motives for these delaying tactics were clear. With the passage of time, any criminal case goes stale. Witnesses get scared off, or killed off, or move to distant cities. In the past, it had paid the Pyles twins to delay: they had succeeded in putting off their day in court for an entire year, until the first anniversary of their arrest—March 6, 1971. When they were finally brought into the courtroom, they filibustered—talked, talked, talked, and talked until neither Judge Lane nor the prosecutors nor their own defense team (the fourth set of lawyers to represent them free of charge) could get a word in edgewise. The brothers ordered their chief defense counsel, Daniel Sheehan, then volunteer legal advisor to the Tombs, to remain silent while they harangued the bench for hours with gibberish that was meant to sound legal. (Sample: "Now, Your Honor, if I may go on further, to bring out this point, the Criminal Procedure Law, article 30 gives the A.D.A. C.H. 996, effective September first, nineteen hundred and seventy-one, in the year of our Lord, Your Honor—I don't speak sometimes too clearly, I'm from Mississippi, and my words sometimes get hung up . . . but we know there is no way in the world we can win this case without a defense . . .")

They befriended a faith healer called Sister Marlene who wore crotch-high miniskirts, spiked heels and two tiers of false eyelashes. She claimed to be the daughter of silent film star Barton McLane. She had obtained consent forms to visit the Pyles brothers as a "spiritual advisor" in prison and claimed she could "heal them with my body" by parading her 38–24–36 measurements inside the counsel room. Somehow, Sister Marlene had also gotten hold of Judge Lane's unlisted phone number. She began to harass the judge's wife with crank calls, complaining about the way the case was being handled.

These antics had reduced the court to judicial slapstick, a kind of "Here Comes De Judge!" routine on *Laugh-In*. Hogan shook his head dejectedly: at one point, the brothers actually stuffed cotton in their ears to avoid hearing the accusations made against them. Meanwhile, their game of charades had wasted five days of precious court time and taxpayers' money. And even the light-hearted moments in court had overtones of pathos: the Pyles twins were black, but hardly militant. They were the eldest of eleven children born to an illiterate sharecropper, who relied on Sonni and Timbuk to help feed nine other hungry mouths in their Mississippi Delta family. Nothing about their case could be construed as the prosecution of a "political" crime. In court, the brothers denounced "black power" radicals and swore undying allegiance to the American flag. They suffocated Judge Lane with courtesy and respect. They just wouldn't shut up.

It became impossible to try the case in any traditional fashion. Patience exhausted, Hogan's office provided Judge Lane a legal device to cope with the dilemma and at the same time protect the defendants' constitutional rights.

Judge Lane accepted Hogan's suggestion and ordered the defendants tried in absentia. They were to be placed in a special detention pen outside the thirteenth-floor courtroom. The cage was equipped with electronic gear and a loudspeaker system. That way, the Pyles twins could hear the testimony against them in the courtroom. But by the time the microphones were set up and ready on Thursday, the brothers refused to leave their cell in the Tombs. The prison disturbance ensued.

When he heard the news, Judge Lane ordered Gribetz to go over to the Tombs and take depositions from the corrections officers who had been involved in the melee. Gribetz returned from the prison with a stack of sworn affidavits under his arm and proceeded to tell Hogan what had happened.

According to the guards, the Pyles brothers had been coaxed out of their cells on Tuesday morning, two days before the disturbance, but refused to go to court. They agreed to be taken to the counsel room on the ground floor of the Tombs to meet their lawyer, Daniel Sheehan, but wouldn't budge one step farther. Instead, they insisted on talking to another man who was very interested in their case. That man was William vanden Heuvel, chairman of the Board of Corrections, the watchdog group that acted as a collective ombudsman for complaints of abuse from within the city's prison system.

The depositions told how Sheehan had telephoned his friend vanden Heuvel from the prison and "Vandy" had rushed over immediately. Captain Mellon and his men were standing by as vanden Heuvel requested permission to pass through three iron gates leading to the lawyer's room.

Mellon began unlocking and relocking the gates, his heavy keys rattling. As they moved through the middle gate, vanden Heuvel asked what was happening with the Pyles brothers. Mellon explained that although the guards had been ordered to bring the defendants to the courtroom that morning, the guards feared a riot if they used physical force on the brothers. So for the time being, the guards were permitting the prisoners to continue their protest and speak to whomever they wished.

Vanden Heuvel nodded approvingly: "Well, it's about time you people started to defy the court."

Until Gribetz had related this part of the story, Hogan's face had remained passive. He sucked on his pipe and seldom took his eyes from the window. Now, the blue eyes narrowed.

"What was that, again?"

Gribetz glanced down at the affidavits in his lap and reread, " 'It's about time you people started to defy the court.' "

Hogan, flabbergasted, dropped his pipe on the desk blotter. The blood drained from his jowls. He sat bolt upright in his swivel chair.

"You mean he was ordering them to disobey the courts?"

"Well," Gribetz suggested, almost apologetically, "Mr. vanden Heuvel has no official powers—"

"Disgraceful!" Hogan exclaimed. "Mr. vanden Heuvel's conduct is . . . he has no right . . . I want this brought to Judge Lane's attention immediately. He may want to start contempt proceedings, or order a grand-jury probe—obstructing governmental administration. Go back and get sworn statements from more corrections officials. Judge Lane may want to handle this through the Bar Association—"

"But, Mr. Hogan," Gribetz said, "this was just a general statement. You couldn't prove anything by it." Gribetz braced himself for an angry reprimand for such backtalk. Instead, there was a lengthy silence while Mr. District Attorney regained his composure.

Hogan fidgeted with a pipe cleaner as Gribetz went on talking, then interrupted to buzz Ida on the intercom: "Bring me the vanden Heuvel file, please."

Ida tiptoed in and placed a thick dossier on the desk. Hogan flipped through it for a few moments. When he finally spoke, he seemed to weigh each word.

"What did the guards say about this?"

Gribetz, referring again to the papers in his lap, related what Captain Mellon had told him: "We just looked at Mr. vanden Heuvel with blank expressions. We were stunned. We didn't feel we were trying to defy the court. As a matter of fact, we were trying to con the Pyles into going to court. We didn't want a riot on our hands."

There was an awkward silence as Hogan gazed out the window. Then Ken Gribetz rose to excuse himself from the office. He walked as far as the door before Hogan swiveled around in his big upholstered chair and said angrily: "This is not the *first* time Mr. vanden Heuvel's acted disgracefully. I have an entire dossier of acts I consider improper."

"Yes, Mr. Hogan," Gribetz answered before he shut the door behind him.

The manila folder on Hogan's desk contained a great deal that was already known about the Corrections Board Chairman. Then forty-two, William Jacobus vanden Heuvel had long been one of the Beautiful People of the Eastern liberal Establishment.

Despite a record as a two-time political loser, vanden Heuvel's image as a man with an unlimited political future remained intact. He had run a losing race for the U.S. Senate in 1958, but the defeat was offset by his successful work in helping Democratic State Controller Arthur Levitt get elected in New York. That victory was all the more remarkable because it happened in the midst of the Republican landslide led by Governor Nelson Rockefeller. Vanden Heuvel's second defeat in 1960, to then Republican Congressman John V. Lindsay of Manhattan's chic Silk Stocking district, did neither man much harm. Lindsay went on to become Mayor. And Vandy made enough friends in the Kennedy camp to go to the Justice Department under Attorney General Robert F. Kennedy in 1963.

The New York lawyer had first met Hogan in 1958, the year he applied for a job as an assistant district attorney. Vanden Heuvel was then a law associate of New York's Republican Senator Jacob K. Javits, and six years out of Cornell Law School, where he had been editor of the *Law Quarterly*. After graduation he had spent a year in Thailand with his political mentor, the legendary William J. (Wild Bill) Donovan, the most decorated citizen-soldier of World War I, whom Eisenhower sent as Ambassador to Southeast Asia. Vanden Heuvel had never tried a criminal case, but his youthful experiences were so impressive that Hogan offered him a position on the legal staff.

When vanden Heuvel heard of Hogan's hiring policy—everybody starts at the bottom in the Complaint Bureau—he turned the offer down. Hogan was chagrined. He liked the young man's combination of brashness and urbanity. "Now there's a decent fellow," the Chief had told his closest aides.

Twelve years later, the two men were still on friendly terms. Bill vanden Heuvel even came to Hogan for advice on whether to seek the 1970

Democratic nomination for Governor. Hogan encouraged him to "go after it," which vanden Heuvel did—unsuccessfully.

Of modest origins—his parents were poor Dutch immigrants in Syracuse—vanden Heuvel had married Jean Stein, the *Esquire* magazine editor and television producer. Her millionaire father, Jules, was founder of Music Corporation of America. The marriage elevated vanden Heuvel into wealth and social prominence, and he developed a patrician manner in keeping with the aristocratic sound of his name. Still part of the Kennedy family entourage in the 1970s, he shuttled between Manhattan and Hyannisport with the ease of liquid assets. He was a partner in the prestigious Manhattan firm of Strook & Strook & Lavan. In October 1970, following the worst jail riots in the city's history, Mayor Lindsay named him unpaid Chairman of the Board of Corrections.

The first task vanden Heuvel assigned himself was to investigate prisoner suicides in the Tombs: there had just been three deaths in as many weeks. The chairman recruited a staff of young Wall Street lawyers to investigate the events surrounding the suicides. Most of these young attorneys had never been in a prison before. Inside the skyscraper dungeon on Centre Street, they were stunned, repulsed at what they saw—cells with open toilets, fevered unrest, the hostile atmosphere of desperation and defeat. Later, Hogan's defenders claimed that these youthful investigators would have been equally shocked inside *any* prison in America. Never having been in a prison before is like never having been in a slaughterhouse before, or visiting an embalming parlor for the first time. The institution is *intrinsically* upsetting.

One of their committee reports, distributed to the media under the title "Shuttle to Oblivion," created a crisis within the city's penal system. Among some New York constituents, there had long been a reflex reaction to allegations of prisoner mistreatment. News stories of beatings, killings, homosexual rape or suicide in prison always had a dramatic impact. It was tempting for officialdom to find a scapegoat for such atrocities. And the temptation had been irresistible in the case of Raymond Lavon.

The twenty-five-year-old black inmate, labeled a "homosexual psychopath" by prison psychiatrists, was locked into a solitary Bing cell on November 1, 1970. There, two days later, his half-naked corpse was found dangling from a strip of twisted bedding. Lavon's final act of defiance, after slashing his wrists, was to dip a finger in his own blood and scrawl across the wall: "I am that I am!"

Lavon's "shuttle to oblivion" included five stopovers at Bellevue Hospital for mental observation and twenty-four separate court appearances on charges of assault, reckless endangerment, and illegal possession of a weapon. The official prison report stated that the prisoner began "acting out" in his cell on November 1 and refused to take medication when it was brought to him by a guard. Lavon claimed he was allergic. The guard ordered him to swallow the pills anyway. The prisoner reacted by ramming one of his shoes through the crossbars and smashing the officer's face with the heel. Blood spurted from the guard's nostrils. He reached up and felt that his nose was broken. Other guards were immediately dispatched. After a bloody wrestling match that lasted several minutes, they forced Lavon into a Bing cell. There, after a paper-plate dinner on the evening of November 3, he hanged himself.

Vanden Heuvel rejected the official findings and called for a new investigation, implying that Hogan—who routinely investigated every death in the Tombs—had been derelict in his responsibility.

A Tombs guard, having read vanden Heuvel's report, went directly to the Corrections Board Chairman and told him a remarkable story. The deputy said he had been an eyewitness to Lavon's death. The officer swore he saw four deputies blackjack Lavon, then string him up. Instead of taking his story to the police or the District Attorney, vanden Heuvel went straight to the newspapers with it. Hogan read all about it in the Sunday *Daily News.*

The next day, vanden Heuvel began seeking "subpoena powers" to investigate the death on his own. Searching for the prisoner's alleged weapon, his shoe, vanden Heuvel asked to see the inmate's personal effects. He found only one pair of shoes: size 10½, black imitation leather, width M, ankle high. Vanden Heuvel went to the cell and tried to stuff the shoe through the bars. "Impossible," he declared. He pressured Corrections Commissioner George McGrath into suspending the four guards on suspicion of "foul play."

Immediately after the death, Hogan had assigned one of his ablest Homicide Bureau assistants, Terence O'Reilly, to the case. The young attorney was built like a furniture mover, but his talents as a criminal investigator had won him the grudging respect of defendants as well as their lawyers. (O'Reilly would later develop such devastating evidence in the case of Black Panther Richard Moore, accused of machine-gunning two policemen in front of Hogan's apartment house, that during a break in the trial, Moore laughed, "Man, you're too good to be on the side of the reactionaries. Why don't you join the revolution?")

To satisfy himself with the veracity of the official prison report on Lavon's death, O'Reilly had also gone over to the Tombs after the incident and stuck his own size 9½ shoe through the bars, with the door in the same position it had been during the assault. He found he could do so with room to spare. He then checked the official autopsy report. The report stated that Lavon's head lacerations and skull fracture were inflicted after death. The skull had cracked when the body was cut down and the head struck the floor. While researching the victim's medical background, Terry O'Reilly made an interesting discovery: vanden Heuvel's "eyewitness," Arthur Blake, had a lengthy history of psychiatric disorders himself.

In January 1971, O'Reilly called vanden Heuvel before a New York County grand jury investigating Lavon's death. Under cross-examination, the chairman's version of the death amounted to "quadruple hearsay," according to some of the jurors. O'Reilly provided them with measurements proving that a shoe size larger than Lavon's could be shoved through the cell bars with ease. As other witnesses reconstructed the death, Lavon was alone at the time of his suicide. He was fed dinner on the evening of November 3. Afterward, he used a paper pie plate to cover the overhead light in his cell. The guards had ripped up his mattress the previous day, looking for "pigstickers," makeshift weapons that Bing prisoners had started improvising out of twisted-off bedsprings. Some time after 7:30 P.M., Lavon ripped the torn cloth from the mattress and braided it into a hangman's noose.

An observation officer on the four-to-midnight shift approached the cell about 10:55 P.M. He saw a body silhouetted against the dimness of the paper-plate lampshade. The guard aimed his flashlight inside and saw the body, clad only in jockey shorts, hanging from the bars of a rear window. The guard yelled, "Hang-up!" and ran around to the rear catwalk. Using a penknife, he cut the body down. There was a dull thud as the head hit the floor. Other guards came running with a resuscitator. They unlocked the cell door and frantically massaged the victim's chest. Ten minutes of oxygen and external heart massage failed to revive Lavon, and one of the guards announced: "He's dead."

The grand jury found no criminal responsibility on the part of the four officers and decided they should be reinstated with back pay.

The next day, O'Reilly telephoned Frank Hogan: "Vanden Heuvel's gone bananas. He's calling this a 'whitewash.' He wants a federal investigation." Frank Hogan shook his head. He couldn't condone the nightmare that had tormented Raymond Lavon to his death in the Tombs. But prison reform was a social problem, not one, he thought, that ought to be dumped in the criminal courts. Certainly the problem didn't justify condemning four guards, without evidence, on charges of first-degree murder.

Vanden Heuvel didn't give up. A few days later, he got the victim's father to order an independent autopsy. The new results showed that some of Lavon's injuries had occurred before death. Frank Hogan was chagrined, but feared that the Lavon case was becoming "politicized." "Political" trials were undermining the judicial process, Hogan felt, and fighting them was like fighting a Hydra-headed monster: as each new suspicion was laid to rest, another would rear up to take its place.

For weeks, New York political activists were breathing down the neck of U.S. Attorney Whitney North Seymour, Jr., pressing him to initiate a federal inquiry into the Tombs suicide. Congresswoman Bella Abzug called it a "lynching." Greenwich Village Democrat Edward Koch lined up two other liberal representatives in a cheering section for vanden Heuvel. Seymour, when he saw what he was up against, reluctantly agreed to look into the matter.

The former Republican State Senator was heir to a great legal tradition in New York. His father, Whitney North Seymour, Sr., was an authentic Brahmin of the Blue Chip Bar: past president of both the New York and American Bar Associations, the senior partner of Simpson, Thacher & Bartlett, a giant among corporate law firms, with tentacles reaching inside foreign governments as well as into the former Nixon Administration.

Not unlike his friend Frank Hogan, the elder Seymour's image was that of a gentleman with Tory manners who was followed everywhere by an entourage of briefcase-toting junior partners—the quintessential Wall Street lawyer. His son "Mike," before becoming a federal attorney, had also worked for Simpson, Thacher, headquartered in an ultramodern skyscraper overlooking New York Harbor and the canyons of Manhattan's financial district. The very foundations of the $1,000-per-square-foot money district were built on farmland once belonging to his wife Catryna's ancestors. Her father was wealthy, aristocratic Barent Ten Eyck, a descendant of Manhattan's original Dutch settlers. The career of Seymour Jr.'s deceased father-in-law had linked Hogan to the Eastern legal Establishment as far back as the 1930s and '40s, when Barry Ten Eyck was an assistant district attorney under both Dewey and Hogan. U.S. Attorney Seymour risked destroying this family friendship of two generations when he went over Hogan's head and used the catch-all "violation of civil rights" clause to gain jurisdiction in the Lavon case—because there were really no federal grounds at all. Hogan objected bitterly—but only in private. Over the years, jurisdictional disputes had built up a wall of enmity between Hogan's office and the U.S. Attorney for the Southern District of New York.

Then, in 1970, U.S. Attorney Seymour, a bald, babyfaced man, over six feet tall, threw protocol to the wind and went to Hogan's office personally to negotiate a policy of *détente*. The agreement reached, as Seymour later recalled it for the author, was that the struggle for recognition between competing law-enforcement agencies is the sorriest "waste of energy" in government. Henceforth, the two men determined they would work together to yield jurisdiction, depending on whose office could make a better case.

As Hogan viewed the Lavon case, Seymour appeared to be backtracking on that agreement. The credibility of the D.A.'s office was on the line. A thirty-year reputation for integrity seemed in danger of dissolving into the old vaudeville lament: "You're only as good as your last act." Seymour had initiated a totally independent investigation. He refused even to look at Hogan's files on the case. The FBI also began looking into Lavon's death, and a federal grand jury took up its own probe.

Frank Hogan thumbed through dozens of reports in the thickening vanden Heuvel file: letters, notarized affidavits, sworn statements, all representing hundreds of man-hours he felt could have been better spent. Hogan thoughtfully re-examined a sheaf of typescript from the folder. This was his ace in the hole. He could never forget Terry O'Reilly's bringing this statement into the office one wintry day while Seymour still had the case. "Chief," O'Reilly blurted out, "Arthur Blake just walked into my office and told me that he lied in the grand-jury room."

The Homicide assistant told how he had looked up from his desk earlier that afternoon and had seen Corrections Officer Blake standing there, his eyelids reddened from crying. "I lied to you," Blake said, losing control of his lower lip. "Those guys never did that to Lavon."

O'Reilly felt his own pulse quicken, but he tried to stay calm and keep his voice soothing. "Why did you wait this long to tell us?"

"It won't leave me alone . . . it's been bothering me." Blake began to sob. "I can't sleep. . ."

O'Reilly interrupted, "You gave up four fellow officers—just like that?"

The Tombs guard dug his fingers into his scalp. "I was mad at them

. . . at the department. They knew about my problems. They promised me . . . I asked them for help, for psychiatric help. They refused to get it for me."

"Are you willing to sign a statement that you lied? To swear to it?" challenged O'Reilly.

Officer Blake nodded, and O'Reilly called for a stenographer. The guard dictated his confession.

The District Attorney studied the document in front of him now, a confession signed and notarized. How Terry had pleaded with him to release the statement to the press! Especially to TV and radio. Hogan had said no. He had helped formulate the "Fair Trial–Free Press" guidelines that forbade premature release of confessions.

O'Reilly gritted his teeth: "There are two kinds of Irishmen, my father used to tell me. The fighting and the smart." His remark drew no response from Hogan. "Chief," O'Reilly tried again, "vanden Heuvel's been going on radio and TV saying that we railroaded the case through the grand jury. That we misled the jurors. Now here's something to slap back with."

Hogan arranged his pipe and Brindley's Mixture tobacco on the desk blotter and gazed past O'Reilly's shoulder as the younger man spoke. Then the D.A. repeated, "No. We'll send this over to Mr. Seymour and let him do with it what he pleases."

O'Reilly risked getting in the final word. "Mr. Hogan, you're too ivory tower-ish. These days you have to say more than you want to—you have to fight to get your ideas across."

It was one of the few times O'Reilly remembered Hogan's looking directly at him as he spoke. "This office has never had to defend itself before and I'm not about to start now!" Hogan kept his word: the confession was never leaked.

By contrast, vanden Heuvel was playing buddy-buddy with the press. Hogan fumed over an article in the *Times* on April 14, 1971, in which vanden Heuvel criticized the state grand jury for failing to indict the four Tombs guards. Vandy commented: "It's difficult to get a conviction out of Hogan's office."

The article no sooner appeared than the D.A.'s telephone rang. "I didn't say it," vanden Heuvel declared. "I never said anything approximating the words attributed to me."

"Bill," Hogan said, "you're *quoted* as saying it."

"But I didn't."

"Well, I'm glad to hear that."

"I'm going to insist on a retraction," vanden Heuvel went on. "I'm very close to Sulzberger—I'm going to call and ask him to put in a retraction."

It was an intriguing proposition: the world's mightiest newspaper kingdom printing a retraction as a favor for a friend of the ruler. Hogan was skeptical that it could be done: the *Times* editorial board seemed to take an adversary position in any controversy involving the District Attorney. But it would be interesting to see how hard vanden Heuvel *tried*.

Hogan was casually acquainted with Sulzberger; they served together on the board of Columbia trustees. At a meeting the following month, the D.A. asked the publisher if he'd seen or heard from vanden Heuvel recently.

"No, I haven't," said Sulzberger. "I ought to have him up for lunch. Glad you reminded me."

"Did he ever talk to you about what he said about me in the Lavon case?"

The curly-haired publisher looked mildly surprised. "Nope. Never spoke to me about it."

With that conversation indelibly in mind, Hogan wasn't surprised when vanden Heuvel later rejected the findings of the U.S. Attorney's office—Seymour reached the same conclusion as the Corrections Department, Hogan's office, the state Grand Jury, the FBI, and the opposing medical examiners, who reconciled their professional differences and agreed with everybody else that Lavon's death had been suicidal.

Vanden Heuvel lambasted Seymour ("I'm surprised at you") and continued harping about the "whitewash" investigation by the D.A.'s office. Patience exhausted, Hogan finally sat down and wrote a "Dear Bill" letter to vanden Heuvel:

". . . thus far, you have rejected the findings of five separate bodies. Your refusal to accept these findings, in large part, is based on your total commitment to the veracity of Arthur Blake who, tragically, has exhibited symptoms of mental illness. Moreover, *sua sponte*, Mr. Blake recanted the version of the incident he supplied to you. Is there no limit to your omniscience!"

Vanden Heuvel's political aspirations had crystallized around the Lavon case. The aftermath of the suicide probe, with Hogan's own Homicide Bureau coming under investigation by the FBI, convinced people in the D.A.'s office how far—and to what lengths—the watchdog chairman was willing to go to "impugn the integrity of the office." To Hogan's bureau chiefs, vanden Heuvel was an opportunistic, inexperienced hip-shooter who was aiming at the D.A.'s job for himself—as a launching pad to higher office. The reasons for keeping a dossier on his activities seemed both clear and logical to Hogan's inner circle.

The office had already monitored a tape of vanden Heuvel making "political noises" on a radio talk show. He was careful to praise Hogan as a living monument to his profession, the personification of integrity in a nonpartisan office. Then vanden Heuvel began to chip away at the living monument by characterizing the man behind the "Mr. District Attorney" legend as too old and too out of touch.

Vanden Heuvel's insinuations that the office had become a haven for civil-service deadwood—a little bureaucracy overcome by inbreeding—left the District Attorney stricken. Clearly the times had overtaken Frank Hogan when an iconoclast like vanden Heuvel could attack the office. The office was more than an office—it was an institution, with a tradition to defend.

Hogan liked to describe his policies as a continuation of Dewey's. Modesty never prevented assistant D.A.s from giving Frank Hogan the lion's share of credit. It was Hogan, they said, who transformed the scandal-ridden office Dewey inherited into a "quasi-judicial" institution.

Tom Dewey the fusionist had been a shrewd political opportunist, they said. He held the job only four years and used it mainly as a springboard to the Governor's mansion. (Dewey's absentee record while running for President made some people wonder whether "administrative assistant" Frank Hogan hadn't been running the show all along.) It was Hogan who kept the office truly nonpartisan.

Even the Mafia paid tribute to Hogan's integrity. Juries in at least two federal racketeering trials heard wiretapped conversations of mobster voices discussing whether bribes should be attempted in cases before the Manhattan D.A.'s office. Each time the question came up, it was dismissed with snorts of derision by other voices on the line: "Nah. That's Hogan's office."

The vanden Heuvel dossier translated everything the "Candidate" did and said into the context of a Democratic Primary race the following year. His involvement in the Lavon case was interpreted as an attempt to line up support from the party's liberal faction.

Memos were fed into the file on the date, time and place of vanden Heuvel's movements around the prison and courthouse. One example:

On Sunday, June 13, 1971, William vanden Heuvel visited the Manhattan House of Detention for Men for the purpose of talking to Michael Molese, an inmate. Accompanying him was a man whose name did not appear on the list of approved visitors. He told the correction officer assigned to the Register that the man was his secretary and that he was there to take notes on vanden Heuvel's conversation with Molese. Actually, the man was a newspaper reporter. William vanden Heuvel gave false information to the officer, and knowingly participated in a violation of the Department's rules.

Eventually, of course, vanden Heuvel was tipped off to the office dossier. "If that's his mentality," the board chairman told friends, "it's the sort of thing that J. Edgar Hoover represents—the misuse of files of angry nonsense by a vindictive official."

William vanden Heuvel looked more and more likely to win the upcoming 1973 Democratic Primary. After sewing up the support of the new Democratic coalition, he had gone on to win, by a two-to-one margin, the endorsement of the county executive committee. The six months that he spent lining up backers—from September 1972 until February 1973—marked an agonizing period of limbo for Hogan and his office staff.

When—and how—would he relinquish this preserve and trade his desk for a park bench on Riverside Drive? For almost four years, Mary Hogan had been egging him into retirement. Only weeks before, the couple had returned from a Florida winter vacation at The Breakers, *grande dame* of Palm Beach hotels. The resort suited Hogan's taste: Tropical Tudor elegance. He had enjoyed it all—swimming and dining in the sun-ripened splendor of the place, watching men and women his own age set out in spiked shoes for the golf links, where electric carts awaited them. But back in New York, Golden Age brochures and shuffleboard trophy goals symbolized defeat to him. He regarded his age as theoretical, having nothing to do with his ability. Old age wasn't an alibi, an excuse to quit working. Old age was nothing but a wrinkled false face. Underneath, he felt like a kid—healthy, lean, his memory intact, invigorated by new challenges each day.

Discussing the vanden Heuvel challenge with an assistant on one occasion, Hogan jumped up from his chair and emptied his pockets. Keys and coins jangled onto the desk. He next tore off his jacket and poised himself for a moment in the center of the room. Then, while the assistant looked on in amazement, the District Attorney dived to the carpet and landed on his hands. He came up from the handspring a little woozy and short of breath, but that was all right. The old man's ego had been satisfied.

"The newspapers used to call me 'Frank Hogan,' " he said. "Now they call me 'Frank Hogan, age seventy-one.' I feel younger than that. I had a checkup last week and I'm in perfect health. If this guy calls me an old man one more time, I'm gonna challenge him to a wrestling match at Madison Square Garden."

Hogan's attitude distressed his chief supporters during this period. Many senior men privately felt that the Chief should have stepped down a year earlier and arranged with the leaders of both parties for a mutually acceptable successor. There was no doubt whom Hogan had in mind for any takeover that might come—Chief Assistant Alfred Scotti. But Hogan couldn't sell Scotti to the Democratic leaders. At sixty-seven, Scotti was unelectable, they said; it would be one old fogey replacing another. Rockefeller, too, turned aside the Scotti recommendation after consulting with Lieutenant Governor Malcolm Wilson (coincidentally the man Scotti had fingered in the SLA-Morhouse-Mintz scandals of the 1960s). On Wilson's advice, Rockefeller told Hogan: "Look for someone dynamic, youthful-appearing and universally loved."

Scotti too got the message: among political leaders in Albany, he was universally unloved. "I guess I just stepped on too many toes," he said.

Hogan's next choice was his one-time protégé Burton Roberts. But the Bronx D.A. had just been elected to a sixteen-year term on the State Supreme Court bench. The judgeship was a lifelong achievement, too important to sacrifice in a risky primary battle with vanden Heuvel. Roberts decided not to run.

On February 7, 1973, vanden Heuvel, flanked by his supporters Coretta Scott King, former Attorney General Ramsey Clark, and Harlem Congressman Charles Rangel, made his opposition official. From his posh fourteen-room campaign headquarters on West 57th Street, vanden Heuvel cleared his silver throat and formally announced that he was a candidate for Manhattan District Attorney. Tossing his thick shock of Kennedy hair, he delivered his Kennedy message: "It's time for a change." His own appearance asserted the kind of change he had in mind. A time for youth, not age. A time for style, not stodginess. A time for fun, not fogeyism.

A packed house of newspaper and television reporters had gathered for the announcement. The candidate's staff, many of them Kennedyites, had been blitzing the media with press releases for weeks. The vanden Heuvel machine, with a $250,000 campaign budget to draw on, was running as slickly as a well-oiled Mercedes. The fair-haired boy with cheek was already hotfooting it along the radio-TV talk-show trail.

Downtown, in his cement monolith, Frank Hogan had nothing: no campaign, no headquarters, no money. It wasn't even clear to him that the home team *had* a candidate. Could he, should he, run for his own office? Or should he clean out his Dewey-desk and head for Riverside Drive?

At last, on Friday, March 2, Hogan called a special staff conference and faced his key bureau chiefs at a polished conference table.

Theirs was a mood of expectation. They needed a definite answer— someone, anyone, who could beat William vanden Heuvel. Hogan began. He hadn't decided yet whether he would run against vanden Heuvel in the primary. If he decided not to, he wanted to find the proper candidate to succeed himself: "It's not that we don't like Bill vanden Heuvel," he said. "It's pretty hard not to like the guy once you meet him socially. He's a pleasant fellow. But as District Attorney, I think I'd rather have Kunstler."

Everybody laughed. A few assistants couldn't resist wisecracks at the image of radical lawyer William ("I cannot defend anyone I do not love") Kunstler as District Attorney.

"Free all the crooks and lock up the judges!"

"Cops carry guns. Why not the Black Panthers?"

Hogan turned serious again. There was nothing "venal or immoral" about vanden Heuvel. But his "lack of savvy" in running the criminal-justice system bothered Hogan. In point of fact, vanden Heuvel had never tried a *single* criminal case.

"He talks out of both sides of his mouth on plea bargaining," Hogan said. "One day he's knocking it. The next day he says we've got to clean out the jails." It was "vulgar," Hogan said, the way vanden Heuvel had insulted him in the Pyles case, calling the D.A. a "persecutor." The word itself troubled Frank Hogan; he never even referred to himself as a "prosecutor" because that had such an inquisitorial sound.

Hogan's hostility to the candidate had its roots in the Pyles case. But that wasn't the only reason for the D.A.'s disapproval. If vanden Heuvel ever got elected, Hogan said, he'd be off and running for higher office.

Hogan's paramount concern was for the continuation of a professional, nonpartisan D.A.'s office. He was torn, he said, between the anxieties of Mrs. Hogan, who wanted him to retire, to travel and to write his memoirs, and the personal responsibility he felt for upholding the Dewey-Hogan tradition. And so he was assembling everybody in the "family" to consider a possible successor. The first name he mentioned was that of John Keenan, then chief of the Homicide Bureau.

Except for a thinning hairline, the forty-three-year-old Keenan bore a strong resemblance to the young Frank Hogan. Hogan had hired him fresh out of the Army in 1956 on the strength of a strong recommendation from the dean of Fordham Law School, Keenan's alma mater.

"John," said Hogan, as all heads swiveled, "I've been going through everybody's assets and liabilities and I've decided I wouldn't have any trouble endorsing you for a run in the Democratic Primary."

Keenan looked astounded, and then laughed. "Great," he said. "But after sixteen years, don't you know I'm a Republican?"

Hogan slapped his forehead like an idiot. "Good God . . . I *didn't* know that!"

Laughter from around the table: they had gotten off to a hopelessly amateurish start. The suggestion of sending in a player from the wrong team—talk about Hogan's independence from political organizations!

With Scotti, Roberts and now Keenan eliminated, the possibilities in Hogan's mind were narrowed to two: himself or former Assistant District Attorney Richard H. Kuh. Kuh had resigned in 1964 and gone into private practice. Since leaving the office nine years before, however, he had been itching to return. Kuh wanted to come back, not to his old job as a bureau chief, but to Hogan's job as Manhattan D.A. Kuh had spent the last six months soliciting political support for a possible race against vanden Heuvel, but Kuh had pledged not to announce his candidacy unless Hogan retired. The consensus around the Hogan conference table on March 2 was that Richard Kuh shouldn't run at all. From a purely political standpoint, he had an ineradicable blot on his résumé. Since leaving the office, Kuh had been branded "the man who crucified Lenny Bruce."

No one could say, then or now, at what point Hogan's popularity began to decline. But the Lenny Bruce case was probably the first in which the D.A.'s office stepped across the line that separates honest prosecution from official harassment. The 1964 Lenny Bruce imbroglio, which reflected more than poor judgment on Hogan's part, was bound to be exploited by vanden Heuvel as a campaign issue. From the strategic standpoint of the conference table, it would be necessary to shift the blame away from Hogan as much as possible. This *realpolitik* notion coincided with a genuine staff hatred of Mr. Richard Kuh, who, everybody said, had given Hogan bad advice on the Bruce case. It had been Kuh who insisted on bringing Lenny Bruce to trial. Even the moralistic Al Scotti had opposed the prosecution: "How can you accuse a cabaret performer of offending people who've paid money to hear what he has to say?"

From the very beginning, Kuh distinguished himself as a grind in the D.A.'s office. After his appointment as an assistant in 1953, he shot to the head of Hogan's class. By 1959, Kuh had been named head of the Criminal Court Bureau, responsible for all misdemeanor cases. A legal perfectionist, Kuh trusted no one's abilities more than his own. "If you disagree with him," said a colleague, "he feels you're either inaccurate or corrupt." Kuh's arrogance grated on the staff. Hogan recognized the problem, but attributed most of the resentment to sour grapes. Hogan had often said that Richard Kuh possessed one of the most brilliant legal minds in the office. Kuh was a Columbia Phi Beta Kappa (Class of '41) and editor of the Harvard Law Review (Class of '48). A tough customer in court, Kuh could wither a witness with a single glance from his deep-set eyes, and his sharp tongue could cut testimony to ribbons. His '50s crewcut and horn-rims pegged him with an image—Jack Webb, the hardassed, clean-cut cop on *Dragnet*. Kuh was also like Sergeant Friday—uptight, Puritanical, pro-death-penalty. A stop-and-frisk advocate. And a real go-getter. Preparing a case, Kuh knew no clock or calendar. He worked until the early hours of the morning, then unrolled an army cot and caught some sleep in his office. There was evil out there, and Kuh was all for cornering it and then locking it up.

His hard-line approach did not endear him to liberals, or to anyone else, either. The first friction occurred early in Kuh's career with Hogan. The case seemed insignificant. A Columbia football player, staggering back to campus after a fraternity beer blast, felt an urge to take a leak. It was 2:00 A.M., the street was dark and deserted. The player teetered out between two parked cars and urinated in the street. During this blissful release, a patrolman happened by and ordered the jock: "Freeze!" The youth was placed under arrest and charged with indecent exposure.

When the case reached Kuh, he insisted on throwing the book at the player. The office underlings reacted in disbelief. Why not just tell the kid to keep his fly zipped? There was no suspicion that the player had any deviate intentions.

Al Scotti rushed to Hogan. "What is this nonsense? For Christ's sake, we're going to ruin this fellow's reputation for life. Throw the case out!"

Hogan fidgeted, then said he was tempted to dismiss the charge, but that it was important not to let his personal prejudices interfere with the discretion of a senior staff member. Then, too, Hogan was a Columbia trustee—any action on his part might be construed as favoritism. Scotti was overruled.

But so was Kuh. He no sooner had read off the charge in court the next day than the judge turned to the defense lawyer: "Make your motion to dismiss." Kuh's "piss in the puddle" case was literally laughed out of court. The staff breathed a collective sigh of relief.

Then Lenny Bruce entered laughing. Hogan had never even heard of Bruce in March 1964, when a Department of Licenses inspector, Herbert S. Ruhe, bought a ticket to see Lenny's act at the Cafe Au Go Go. Bruce came on stage at the Greenwich Village cabaret, getting lots of yuks and titters with words like "cocksucker" and "tits." Ruhe scribbled the dirty words furiously onto his notepad. The next morning, he carried his official complaint to Hogan's office. The complaint entered the files—and the mass of conflicting data on "obscenity." The legal definition of obscenity was still evolving. It would be two years before the U.S. Supreme Court considered whether to lift an obscenity ban on *Fanny Hill*. Then, the case was still winding its way through appellate review.

Meanwhile, two of the Hogan men assigned to obscenity cases received Inspector Ruhe's complaint. One of the assistants was Nicholas Scoppetta. The other was Richard Kuh.

"Dick Kuh knew I had seen Lenny Bruce performing at the old Loew's Theater on Second Avenue," Scoppetta recalled afterward. "Lenny was doing the same act at the Cafe Au Go Go. Kuh knew I was a Lenny fan. Kuh hadn't seen the act. He asked me what I thought of this complaint from the license department. I said I didn't think it would be sustained, not on the basis of the act I saw, based on the test of redeeming social value. I said *Fanny Hill* is running into problems, and that book has nowhere near the social significance that Bruce's performances have. Dick said, 'Don't you think that's a determination for a grand jury to make?'

"I suggested that we all go to the Cafe Au Go Go and watch the performance. He said maybe we'll do that. Nobody suggested that Hogan go, because no one thought it was likely that he would."

In the meantime, Kuh took the complaint to Hogan and strongly urged him to investigate. Kuh noted that the act contained "blasphemy" against the city's highest priest, Francis Cardinal Spellman, and that Bruce had made "sick jokes" about the Kennedy assassination, accusing Jackie Kennedy of trying to "haul ass" when shots rang out in Dallas. Hogan was doubtless offended. He ordered the D.A.'s squad to monitor Bruce's act that same night. But would Hogan have pursued Lenny if Kuh had warned him away from a sensitive case?

Whitman Knapp later maintained: "If an assistant convinced Hogan that an obscene performance couldn't be sustained as a matter of law, he wouldn't care who was yelling for Lenny's scalp, he wouldn't have pursued it. Labels meant nothing to Frank Hogan."

The Lenny Bruce performance, according to Knapp, was not the first "blasphemy" case brought to the Chief's attention. Way back in October 1947, the Catholic Archdiocese had complained of a Robinson Jeffers play entitled *Dear Judas*. Knapp vividly recalled the Jeffers version of the Greatest Story Ever Told:

"In his plot, the Virgin Mary was a prostitute. Jesus Christ didn't have a father, so he picked God as his father. Judas, contrary to the original text, was Christ's *favorite* disciple. Jesus himself was a political visionary, exploiting the fervor of the Passover to stage a revolution. Judas realized this would be suicidal. In order to save Jesus from himself, Judas made a deal with the high priests to take Jesus into custody. But the high priests double-crossed him and ordered the crucifixion.

"Well, the Powerhouse [the Archdiocese] came down and wanted the play stopped. All the monsignors and bishops were crowded into Hogan's inner office and they wanted to know what I thought of *Dear Judas*. Jeffers should have sued me—I said it was dull. The playwright was so afraid of his theme that he talked it to death.

"That wasn't what the Powerhouse wanted to hear. They wanted to know, wasn't there an old statute that made it a misdemeanor to portray the Almighty on stage? I said, yes, I had looked it up, and I thought the law would be unconstitutional. The bishops started yelling 'sacrilege' and turned on Hogan. They demanded he close the show. I'll never forget it. Hogan stared one of the bishops right in the eye: 'Knapp says it's unconstitutional. End of discussion.' "

By the 1960s, it was well known that Hogan always resisted the pressures of moralistic clergymen. But the Lenny Bruce performance involved obscenity more than sacrilege. And Hogan's priggishness about dirty words had been longstanding—it was especially evident back in the days when

Knapp insisted Hogan couldn't be swayed into prosecuting a weak First Amendment case. In the 1940s, Knapp had played the same advisory role that Richard Kuh did in the 1960s. As chief of the Appeals Bureau, Knapp might have persuaded Hogan not to prosecute Doubleday & Co. for publishing Edmund Wilson's *Memoirs of Hecate County*. But Hogan, acting on a complaint lodged by the New York Society for the Suppression of Vice, *did* prosecute, and got a conviction.

Knapp argued the obscenity appeals all the way to the Supreme Court, delivering the shortest argument ever heard before the high tribunal:

"The record justifies the finding of obscenity. The finding justifiably made under valid statute raises no constitutional problems."

Knapp was correct in assuming that the prosecution could be justified as a matter of law. The Supreme Court affirmed the conviction, and to this day, a major literary work by the departed dean of American letters is still banned in New York State. The brevity of Knapp's argument, written by Hogan, didn't do much to clarify New York's archaic obscenity statute. The very wording of the law betrayed a Victorian reticence to describe the sexual imagery it condemned: "indecent," "immoral," "impure." The sweeping vagueness of those adjectives had never been clarified by litigation.

Hogan and Kuh each took the position that the Lenny Bruce prosecution would help establish, at least for the time being, how far the tide of moral license had extended in the contemporary arts since *Hecate County*.

In his excellent analysis of the Lenny Bruce case, Columbia professor Albert Goldman, author of the best-selling biography *Ladies and Gentlemen—Lenny Bruce!!* wrote:

"The men who conceived and executed the New York prosecution of Lenny Bruce were not foolish bigots. Hogan and Kuh were moral conservatives who could see the future clearly—probably a lot more clearly than Lenny Bruce and his befuddled liberal allies!—and were determined to offer it all the opposition they could muster.

"Theirs was a perfectly understandable and respectable aversion to change: the pity of it was that the man they selected for their test case was the last person in the world whom they should have treated as the bellwether of the avant garde. Lenny Bruce was, in his own terms, just as moralistic, conservative and 'uptight' as [presiding] Judge [John] Murtaugh and Assistant D.A. Kuh. From the very beginning of the trial, he felt a secret affinity with these men and a secret aversion to his long-hair hippie and short-hair libbie supporters . . . Lenny Bruce was a man with an almost infantile attachment to everything that was sacred to the American lower-middle class. He believed in romantic love and lifelong marriage and sexual fidelity and absolute honesty and incorruptibility—all the preposterous absolutes of the unqualified moral conscience."

Every day of the Bruce trial, a liberal-intellectual audience gathered in Judge John M. Murtaugh's courtroom—poet Allen Ginsberg, cartoonist Jules Feiffer, novelist Philip Roth, dozens of composers, critics, entertainers. Performing for these egghead spectators, prosecuting attorney Richard Kuh was maddeningly brilliant. Unlike the clumsy, finger-pointing prosecutors of Bruce in other cities, Kuh raised solid legal arguments. He made mincemeat out of "obscenity experts" for the defense. And he twisted the opinions of articulate critics such as Richard Gilman of *Newsweek* and Dorothy Kilgallen of the New York *Journal-American* into babbling contradictions.

Kuh's talents were wasted on the pro-Lenny crowd, which thought the whole sideshow was a futile exercise in official harassment. As the trial droned on over the muggy summer of 1964, the spectator benches thinned out. Bruce's supporters stayed away in droves, sickened by the courtroom spectacle they now dubbed the theater of the absurd.

Assistant defense counsel Martin Garbus was seated beside Bruce when License Inspector Ruhe was called upon to recollect the performance that had offended him. This outraged Bruce: he had appealed constantly to Judge Murtaugh to "let me do my act." The requests were repeatedly denied. Instead, Ruhe was permitted to "do Lenny's act" from memory, assisted by his handful of "tits and ass" notes. As Ruhe warmed to the task, he lost his initial embarrassment over saying the dirty words, and soon he was mimicking Bruce with grinning abandon. He even began to get a few laughs—not just from Lenny's fans, but from some of Hogan's younger assistants, sneaking down to the courtroom between cases to get in on the fun.

Upset by Ruhe's performance, Bruce hissed into Garbus' ear: "Just listen to him! He's giving a lousy performance and *I'm* gonna be convicted for it."

Hogan himself walked into the courtroom one day and took a seat on a front bench. In his book, Albert Goldman described what happened next:

"A professor from his own university, Columbia, was on the stand comparing Bruce with Rabelais and Swift. Daniel Dodson, associate professor of English and comparative literature, was cool, crisp and clear-headed in his appraisal. He concentrated on the sense of moral outrage in Lenny's work—precisely the point that rebutted most strongly the accusation that Bruce was a vulgar, cheap laff-grabber.

"Hogan was visibly upset by the caliber of the witness and the character of the testimony. Looking around from his seat, he saw that the rows behind him were full of young men from his own office—his prize recruits from Harvard and Yale, sitting at the feet of this renegade professor and taking it all in. Tossing them a peremptory signal, Hogan stalked out of the courtroom. He rounded on the young men in the corridor. 'What are you doing here?' he said, and he was livid. 'Is there anyone here who doesn't have work to do? If so, tell me and I'll *find* things for you to do!' "

By 1966, Bruce was, in effect, exonerated. But technically, he was convicted and sentenced to four months in the workhouse. He would never spend a day in jail. He refused to take the advice of his lawyer and appeal in the proper form. His co-defendant, Howard Solomon, did appeal properly and eventually beat the obscenity rap—as Bruce would have done, if he had not taken a self-destructive path. Lenny had lost his cabaret card, so he couldn't work in New York. Other obscenity raps had frozen him out of a performer's livelihood in Los Angeles, Chicago and San Francisco. Toward the end of the summer, he was heavily into heroin. And on August 16, he was found dead in his California home, either a deliberate suicide or an accidental heroin overdose victim.

The New York cultural community found it more agreeable to blame the death of a fallen idol on Hogan than on heroin. By turning Kuh loose on Bruce, Hogan had "hounded Lenny to death," the critics charged. Hogan disagreed: "He hounded himself to death. Lenny Bruce was a narcotics addict. That was his trouble."

But by 1973, it was impossible for Hogan to try to justify that prosecution without sounding like a cold fish. New York City had changed along the lines of sexual permissiveness and political awareness that Bruce had prophesied. Life's ironies being what they are, Richard Kuh had made himself over in the Kennedy image. He had once written anti-smut articles in periodicals like the *Ladies' Home Journal*: "Wake up, America!—A Plan to Keep Pornography Away from Children." Now he took to writing libertarian-sounding articles on plea bargaining for intellectual magazines like *The New Leader*. Kuh got rid of the horn-rims. He sprouted sideburns. At age fifty-two, he had a full head of hair, untouched by gray. A dye-job? Whatever it was, the effect was incredible.

Kuh had turned the clock back. He now looked younger than his Harvard yearbook picture. He was an attractive political candidate of 1973.

There were still a few people in the office who preferred him to vanden Heuvel. But the consensus around the conference table on March 2 was that Kuh had already been defeated by the ghost of Lenny Bruce. Kuh should divorce himself completely from any Hogan-office campaign. The Friday afternoon meeting broke up with the realization that there was only one person in the room who stood a chance of beating vanden Heuvel: the incumbent Hogan. If the Chief didn't feel like "sacrificing himself" in the campaign, he should let Scotti try. Hogan would have to decide. Meanwhile, the "boys" would get together and draft a "position paper" on the Lenny Bruce case. They would acknowledge that the Lenny Bruce crusade was a mistake and that contemporary sexual mores had changed. If Hogan had it to do all over again, he wouldn't prosecute Bruce in 1973. "Isn't that right, Chief?"

Hogan cleared his throat. "Well, I'm sure we wouldn't prosecute him today. After everything we've tolerated on Broadway and in *Screw* Magazine and *Deep Throat*, I guess we've out-Lenny Bruced Bruce himself. I still say he was spewing filth. Is there nobody to say that this offends? I thought Lenny Bruce's act was vulgar and filthy. It was prurient by definition. It was without redeeming social value. It was obscene.

"The only reason I wouldn't prosecute him today is the difficulty we'd have getting a conviction."

The position paper on Lenny Bruce was never written.

13
PRIDE AND PREJUDICES

With a flair for the obvious vanden Heuvel concentrated most of his criticism of Hogan on a popular "issue"—the elimination of plea bargaining. That practice, unfortunately, was a day-to-day reality in administering the world's busiest prosecutor's office. While Hogan and his young assistants struggled to keep from going under in the surging caseload, legal hacks loitered around the courtrooms, attaching themselves to criminal flotsam. Bewildered by courtroom procedure, the ignorant defendants usually went along with the defense lawyer's advice: plead guilty to a charge one rung down the ladder from the act charged in the indictment—assault, say, instead of armed robbery. Then offer the plea to the assistant D.A. ("He'll go along with the deal"). For this service, the hack would charge a $25 to $100 fee.

The process took place dozens of times a day, a perversion of the law by lawyers that reinforced the underworld's contempt for law enforcement. The criminal lawyers knew perfectly well that the assistant D.A. had no choice but to go along with the deal if he wanted to keep his head above water. Some of the disreputable hacks even added a $200 or $300 extra charge to the fee, "so I can put in a fix with the District Attorney's office." The swindle, known as "rainmaking" in the D.A.'s office, usually ended up seeming a bargain to the fleeced defendant. When he went to court, he received a sentence of ninety days for assault rather than three to five years for armed robbery. What else was there to conclude except that the criminal lawyer had successfully bribed the District Attorney?

"Never shake hands with a defense lawyer," was one of Hogan's standard directives to new prosecutors. "The defendant might interpret it as a deal."

Most indigent defendants were represented by Legal Aid lawyers, free of charge. In that case, the plea-bargaining process transformed the public defender into a prosecutor, the assistant D.A. into a judge, and the judge into an auctioneer—or worse, a spectator. For although our legal textbooks and law schools pay lip service to an advocacy system (a Perry Mason system) of trial by jury, with each side presenting its side of the case, what we really have in urban America is an administrative system of justice in which only a few of the most heinous or sensational crimes are ever argued in court—assuming they do not dissolve in the welter of pretrial motions to suppress evidence.

Inspired by Hogan's reputation for excellence and integrity, his young assistants were free to apply their own standards and value judgments in screening and siphoning off weak cases, reducing felonies to misdemeanors, and deciding when there was enough evidence to go before a grand jury. In 1972, this winnowing process left 6,324 felony cases out of 33,285 felony arrests, plus a backlog of 2,563 pending cases with nearly half of the defendants out on bail. This screening process was necessary because cops, always bucking for promotion, generally exaggerated the seriousness of any arrest.

One could understand the Pyles brothers' reluctance to come to court in view of the large number of indictments that would culminate with a plea or jury verdict of guilty. Hogan's screening system produced a conviction rate that had remained fairly constant at 95 to 97 percent from 1942 through 1967.

"I ask a question whenever there's an acquittal," the D.A. said in 1967, "because it means the jury thinks we brought an innocent man to trial, and I think a jury is usually right."

By 1972, the conviction rate had begun to drop off slightly, along with Hogan's prestige. And before that year was out, he would say something he'd regret for the rest of his life. Frustrated and demoralized by a verdict of not guilty in the case of three ringleaders who had taken hostages in the October 1970 riot in the Tombs, Frank Hogan could no longer restrain himself.

"This is a hideous miscarriage of justice," he declared while being interviewed by a black reporter, Gerald Frazer, of the New York *Times*. "What we face in this type of case is jurors making political statements . . . and not returning a verdict based on evidence. It's something new in my experience. It happened for the first time in the Panther 21 case. Jurors no longer abide by the instructions of the court."

Hogan's outburst was a shock. He was launching an all-out attack on the American jury system he had spent a lifetime defending. Hogan was, in effect, politicizing controversial cases that he had heretofore insisted were "strictly criminal." The hyperbolic vanden Heuvel jumped on the D.A. with both feet: "We are left to view the ruins of a criminal justice system when it is administered by those who have lost their sense of balance, of equity, and of justice itself."

The challenger's scattershot approach missed the essential question posed by Hogan's lament: when is a crime political? Hogan recognized that history abounded with immoral heroism—unconscionable acts later regarded as praiseworthy. Unfortunately, history does not show its alternatives. One could only speculate on what might have happened back in 1969 if Hogan had ignored police undercover reports of a Black Panther plot to dynamite several department stores at the height of the Easter shopping season. On April 2, twenty-one Panthers were indicted in the bizarre conspiracy allegations. During many of the hearings, the defendants were not present. When they did appear in November and December, they put on quite a show. Testimony was frequently interrupted by their outbursts. Fistfights broke out in the courtroom. Spectators were dragged away by policemen. Defendants screamed at presiding Judge Murtaugh:

> The Court: Do the defendants want to enter pleas?
> A Defendant: You can take the indictment, you can take the entire Nixon Administration and stick it up your ass.
> Another Defendant: This is toilet paper.
> The Court: Be seated.
> Another Defendant: You white-haired racist pig.

The loudest defendant was Panther Richard Moore, who jumped bail later in the trial and for a while was said to be hiding out in Algeria.

> The Court: The weapon is offered for identification, not in evidence.
> Defendant Moore: You are a liar.
> The Court: And it will be so marked.
> Defendant Moore: You want to know why black people don't dig this racist mother-fuckin' country. You can understand it. When

you get in the car in your commuter train and go back out in your convertible suburbs, and when them black people go up in there, they're going to have M-14's for your ass.

(Spectators applaud)

Defendant Moore: . . . If you can't give black people justice in this courtroom, don't bring us in here. All we ask for is justice. That's all we ask for. For hundred and fifty mother-fuckin' years we ask for justice. And you got this punk calls us terrorists and you got the Gestapo in our community murdering us; because of punks like that we got guns.

Admissions such as these, made by the defendants in court, convinced Hogan that the Panthers were mouthing more than "the ghetto rhetoric of violence," as their defense lawyers claimed.

Night after night, prosecuting attorney Joseph Phillips would return from the vexing courtroom battle to the serenity of Hogan's inner office. As the trial progressed, and Hogan studied the transcripts, he conceded that the conspiracy indictment had been too broad. The charges should have been broken down to individual cases of arson, weapons possession, attempted murder. By hastily combining them in one conspiracy indictment—aimed at thwarting an imminent plot to bomb the Bronx Botanical Gardens—Hogan had strayed into a nebulous area of the conspiracy law.

"Mr. Hogan impressed me during that time as a man qualified for the Senate of ancient Greece or Rome," Phillips recalled. "He saw the Panther case not in terms of months or years, but in terms of centuries. He talked about the roots of that case in the Civil War riots. He brought up Eugene Debs, Hamilton and Burr, Jefferson and Burke. When the jury reported back after deliberating only ninety minutes, the courtroom attendants were preparing for a riot. Everybody in the office was congratulating me on a conviction. The evidence was so overwhelming. There had really been no defense. We produced all the evidence, all the guns and hand grenades and explosives. The defense lawyers anticipated a conviction. The press anticipated a conviction. When the jury acquitted, it was a shock to everyone. I couldn't believe that the American system of justice could be so perverted. When I reported back to Hogan, he said, 'Joe, don't be depressed. The jury didn't decide that case on the evidence. They decided it on the sins of the slave traders.' "

What had gone wrong? Why had the integrated jury become radicalized? (They celebrated the acquittal at a jubilant cocktail party with the defendants.) By what convoluted reasoning did liberal-intellectual whites seek to justify the Panther verdict in terms of compensatory bigotry? Why were black jurors unwilling to convict black defendants?

Part of the answer was contained in the U.S. Census tracts for 1970, showing that the Manhattan that voted Frank Hogan "Attorney for the People" in 1942 was only geographically the Manhattan of 1972. Who were "the People" that Hogan represented now? Population figures for 1970 showed that the inhabitants of Manhattan island were actually fewer by 300,000 than the year he took office. The 1970 population total of 1.5 million also reflected a "white exodus" of nearly a half-million persons who had fled to the safety of the suburbs while a corresponding influx of blacks and Puerto Ricans strained the inner city's economic and social resources.

There was a well-founded feeling among Hogan's assistants that black jurors were not what they used to be—especially when they deliberated over black defendants. What Hogan couldn't seem to grasp was that previously, black jurors tended to be petit-bourgeois, working-class people; their names would not otherwise have appeared on jury lists, which are drawn up from voter registration lists.

In the past, black jurors had tended to be hostile to black defendants—they probably identified more strongly with law enforcement than they did with the ne'er-do-wells of their own race. Then the Black Power and Black Pride movement of the 1960s developed in jurors a stronger identity with skin color than with economic class. Assistant D.A.s began reporting case after case—especially in the Homicide Bureau—in which black jurors had rather irrationally hung juries or contributed to acquittals—even when the defendant confessed. This was a cause for much sadness in the office because none of his black assistants had ever detected—in the most offhand remark, raised eyebrow or ethnic joke—any racial prejudice in the District Attorney.

Frank Hogan had been dealing with racial tensions longer than any prosecutor in U.S. history. Back at the end of his second summer in office, the scorching summer of 1943, racial tensions were, as they say, ignited. The sparks were there, twenty-five years before Stokely Carmichael and his cry of "Black Power!" Black "impotence" was obvious. Harlem was ruled by the city's lily-white police force, which looked glaringly like an army of occupation.

The summer of '43 did not become famous as a time of racial violence. Its pages in black urban history were never written; newspapers did not bother much with the story.

On August 2, 1943, the black ghetto and its Italian enclave near the East River were clamped under martial law. Governor Dewey mobilized the National Guard. Police and U.S. troops rushed in with loaded rifles to quell rioters. It was the first black riot in the nation since 1935, and perhaps the last authentic *race* riot in the nation's history.

The Burn-Baby-Burn conflagrations of the 1960s in the inner cities of Watts, Detroit and Newark were more desperate rebellions in comparison, pitting blacks against white-owned property, blacks against police. The Harlem '43 skirmishes were blatantly racist: blacks against whites. The human toll: five persons shot and killed, 503 rioters and forty policemen injured. One night alone, there were 484 arrests and arraignments in Criminal Court, a record. Most of those arrested were black. A few hours later, broken bodies were carted off to hospitals. The looters went to jail; the looted storefronts were boarded up. Damages were estimated at over $5 million.

There was no Presidential commission formed to investigate the self-destruction. No social emergency was declared. The press obliged City Hall, without being asked, by keeping the disturbances contained to a few paragraphs on the back pages. The ostrich mentality prevailed in city government. Society—or at least that part of society which reads newspapers—was not even permitted the privilege of learning from its mistakes. The future would not benefit from the past.

The devastation was revisited on the city in July 1964, after a trigger-happy police lieutenant, Thomas Gilligan, shot a black schoolboy to death on Manhattan's East Side. The shooting touched off six nights of looting and rioting in Harlem. Gilligan testified to the grand jury that he was off-duty at the time of the incident, and had stepped in to break up a street fight. He said he flashed his police badge and ordered the youth, James Powell, to drop a switchblade he was holding. Instead, the youth lunged at him with the blade. The lieutenant insisted he had fired only in self-defense. But that was not the way other witnesses called it.

A teenager who had given Powell the knife said the victim dropped it as soon as Gilligan drew his service revolver. The officer then fired three shots at point-blank range, killing the boy instantly. When the witness asked Gilligan why he had fired a third time, the lieutenant replied, "This is why," taking from his pocket the badge, which he pinned on his shirt. He then turned the boy's body over with his foot and directed the witness, "Go call an ambulance."

When an autopsy revealed that two slugs from Gilligan's gun had been fired into the boy's stomach and lungs from two feet away, while his arm had been grazed by an initial bullet that Gilligan called a "warning shot," the Manhattan ghetto exploded.

Hogan took the evidence before a grand jury in September. He returned with a vote of "no bill," the first such report in anyone's memory. The jurors said they absolved Gilligan of any felony because they did not believe the witnesses. The boy's death was therefore "justifiable homicide." The jury's refusal to go along with militant black leaders, who wanted Gilligan tried and convicted, was descried as a "whitewash." And in some quarters, Hogan was branded a "racist" for not pressing harder on the case.

Was Hogan a racist? He most certainly did not want to be one, but he also seemed to have exhibited some degree of unconscious fear of blacks. Whenever a case involved black militants, Hogan became noticeably tense. He feared a massive black terrorist attack of some kind. This was evident during the Panther trial, but even more dramatically demonstrated when fugitive Angela Davis was captured by the FBI in a New York motel room. Hogan's responsibility: arrange her extradition back to Marin County, California, so she could stand trial for murder.

Hogan was ready to ship her back when the police sent word of a black assassination plot against the Communist soul sister. Hogan's agitation peaked. Remembering his experience in prosecuting the Black Muslim assassins of Malcolm X, the D.A. bit his nails and warned the FBI that Angela would be "worth more to her supporters as a dead martyr than as a live college professor." Despite every assurance of adequate FBI protection for Davis on a scheduled passenger flight back to California, Hogan couldn't be talked out of his paranoia. He devised a fail-safe plan of his own, and ordered the Traffic Department to go along with it.

On the day of Angela Davis's scheduled takeoff, an airline flight number was announced to the press. Reporters and TV crews scrambled out to Kennedy Airport, only to find themselves looking at each other like idiots. Miss Davis was nowhere to be found.

Meanwhile, traffic helicopters were beaming back reports of one of the worst traffic jam-ups in the city's history. Instead of taking Miss Davis to Kennedy, Hogan's men spirited her through the Brooklyn-Battery Tunnel in an unmarked police van. Angry motorists were left honking their horns at the mouth of the tunnel for two hours. Hogan had ordered roadblocks set up so that no vehicle could follow the van to its destination, a remote government airstrip called Floyd Bennett Field. There, at Hogan's request, a U.S. Air Force transport plane was fueled up and waiting for its only passenger. Angela was safely returned to California—and freedom following her acquittal on the murder rap.

Frank Hogan was distinctly out of place in a changing world of sympathy for the anti-hero—a world he could neither alter nor control. It became steadily more difficult to maintain his professional detachment in the endless, shrieking psychodrama of black community-control protests, prison riots, Black Muslim assassinations, Black Panther shootouts with the cops. The new legal conflicts involved a new breed of political criminal among young whites, too: campus vandals who occupied administration buildings, terrorist bombers, psychedelic messiahs.

Crime was no longer just breaking the law, but had become "civil disobedience," an act of witness against the Establishment. Hogan prided himself in being one of the firmest pillars of that Establishment, a defender of the American faith. And he was now pitted against forces so deep within the structure of society that neither side could change the other—except at the expense of the intellect and the human values they sought to preserve.

14
HOMESTRETCH

From the mammoth corporate law fraternities of Wall Street and Park Avenue, an unofficial Hogan Alumni Association rallied in the first week of March 1973. Senior partners who had once graduated from Hogan's school set up a telephone alert: "Mr. Hogan is in trouble—vanden Heuvel is leading in the polls." A number of the Establishment names—labor mediator Theodore Kheel, Simon Rifkind, Bernard Botein, Bruce Bromley—met on the weekend and called Hogan at home, urging him to run.

On Monday morning, March 5, Governor Rockefeller called the D.A.'s office. Unable to decide on a successor, Hogan was now the only man strong enough to run with Republican endorsement in the November election. It would be "a sad day for Manhattan," Rockefeller told him, "if Mr. Hogan was no longer Mr. District Attorney." Rockefeller said he had already been in touch with Alex Rose, the Liberal Party boss: "Alex will call you later in the day."

Rose telephoned that afternoon, promising Hogan the Liberal Party designation. Having learned from Rockefeller that Hogan also had the Republican designation if he wanted it, Rose was certain that Hogan would now pick up Conservative Party backing.

The senior bureau men scrambled back into executive session. Okay: Hogan was now assured the position of home-team candidate on three ballots. But the voter registration of New York County was heavily Democratic. It would be suicide to concede the Democratic ticket to vanden Heuvel. Hogan should go into the Democratic Primary.

The Chief resisted. The staff meeting went on for hours. They sent out for sandwiches and Cokes (fruit salad and coffee for Hogan). Long after most of the office force had gone home for the night, the chief made his decision: "If I'm going to do it at all, I shouldn't just go halfway. If I beat this guy, we can get back to running an office instead of a political campaign."

On Thursday, March 8, reporters and TV cameramen were called in. Facing a thicket of twenty-three radio and TV microphones, Hogan cleared his throat and began. After "the anguish of indecision," he *would* seek an unprecedented ninth term as "Attorney for the People" of New York County. Whatever else he had brought to the office—be it honor or dislike—"Our record for diligence in protecting the innocent and bringing the guilty to justice is unmatched. I am running on that record." The following morning, Hogan's first primary battle in thirty-one years as Manhattan prosecutor kicked off.

He called an office meeting, inviting anyone who wanted to join the campaign. The Bar Association ethics committee had no prohibition against using staff people to circulate nominating petitions in their free time. "It's strictly a personal decision," Hogan said, "and nobody can expect a gold star."

The day after that, a carload of assistants rode with him to 355 Lexington Avenue. Hogan stepped out of his limousine and entered a deserted storefront. The room, vacant except for litter, had a sad, hollow feel. A lone wastebasket was the closest thing to any scrap of furniture. Up-ending the can, Hogan sat down, looked around and shook his head: "Look what you've gotten me into!"

The campaign proceeded as amateurishly as it had begun. None of the staff had ever met Ted Kheel, who had been named overall campaign chairman. On their own, senior assistants mapped out and assigned special tasks—to recruit wives and secretaries to ring doorbells, to write up position papers, to dole out the budget. The staff printed up a handbill with the inspired and inspiring message

INTEGRITY   ABILITY   COURAGE

centered over a faded photograph from the Hogan-for-Senate campaign of 1958. The photograph bore no resemblance whatever to the Frank S. Hogan of 1973. Manhattan pedestrians didn't even recognize their District Attorney as he passed out these old-fashioned handbills on the street. A typical voter would take one look at the Hogan flyer and toss it to the curb. Instead of trying to shake hands, Hogan spent all his time stooping over to retrieve the throwaway literature—and complaining that no one knew who he was.

Later in March, Hogan sat still for a series of rambling, tape-recorded interviews with reporters Mike Pearl and Fern Marja Eckman of the New York *Post*. Hogan spoke candidly of his changing attitudes on sex, drugs, women's liberation and a host of other media issues. The old gentleman showed that he was not altogether a cold fish. Mrs. Eckman later described him as "charming, whimsical, literate, courteous, aloof, fond of reading Dickens and Thackeray aloud to his wife, given to using words like 'hearken' and 'gee' and 'heavens' in an age that vents its verbal spleen in four-letter expletives, widely regarded as a man of integrity, the kind you'd rush to buy a used car from . . ."

These interviews were full of surprises. Hogan admitted, for instance, to a certain enjoyment of erotic literature, provided it had a civilized veneer. After all these years, it rather amused him that the cover of each copy of Doubleday's *Memoirs of Hecate County* was still stamped "Not for Sale in New York State."

"They'd laugh us out of court today on that one," Hogan chuckled, adding with a genuine twinkle that he loved the book. Hogan spoke with a lilt as he recalled the "offensive" chapter, "The Princess with the Golden Hair." "It described a . . . uh . . . love encounter that was beau-ti-fully done—*artistically* done. Edmund was a great master of language. The fellow was titillating, but the nuances were *lovely*."

Then, why, in his discretion, had Hogan gone after Doubleday?

"I wasn't [laughing] sophisticated enough," Hogan replied.

"Are you more sophisticated now?" asked Mike Pearl.

"Yes, I am, I think, in that I wouldn't do *that* again . . . but I despair of making a contribution to the morality of the community."

(Later, Pearl learned of a behind-the-scenes episode in which Hogan had already forsaken his role as guardian of public morality, heralding a new era of sexual permissiveness in the arts. During the theatrical season of 1968–69, Hogan received a telephone call from London. The caller was Kenneth Tynan, the eminent British drama critic and stage director. Tynan said he was rehearsing an all-nude comedy revue, scheduled to open soon in Manhattan. Accustomed to dealing with the Lord Chamberlain, Britain's official theater censor, Tynan offered, at his own expense, to fly one of Hogan's assistants to London to witness rehearsals of the show. The assistant could delete any "objectionable material."

Hogan refused the offer.

Well then, Tynan suggested, would Hogan like him to send a copy of the script for approval? Hogan again refused. He explained that in America, such approval constituted prior restraint, the legal term for censorship.

Another question: what did Hogan think of the show's working title, *An Unhurried Night of Erotica?*

"Too suggestive," the D.A. said. Two years before, he told Tynan, the U.S. Supreme Court had upheld the conviction of *Eros* magazine publisher Ralph Ginzberg not on the basis of the magazine's content, but because the publisher's lurid advertising promotions had constituted "pandering." Hogan said he had no objection to Tynan's alternate marquee title, *Oh, Calcutta!*

The nude show opened on Broadway with glittering accompaniment—a chic first-night audience, mink stoles, limousines, and ticket scalpers pocketing $200 apiece for front-row seats. No one complained. In fact, everyone applauded. Hogan let the jubilant, naked actors do their thing. Police were never summoned. Tynan had the last laugh: at a cocktail party some time later, a judge drew Hogan into a corner and whispered that had his French been better, he'd have understood the *double entendre* of *Oh, Calcutta!* The title was a pun—"*Oh, quelle cul t'as!*" or, freely translated, "Oh, what a lovely ass you have!"

The *Post* interviews brought out the fact that Hogan had improved his civil-libertarian image as a critic of Governor Rockefeller's "Get tough with the pusher" drug law, making life sentences mandatory for second offenders. Across the span of thirty years, Hogan had never backtracked on his "Typhoid Mary" theory of heroin addiction as a communicable disease. It was as necessary now as it had ever been, he said, to "quarantine addicts in treatment centers, not behind prison bars."

Out-of-state District Attorneys who modeled their office policies after Hogan's would have been happier if he had cracked down harder on marijuana. But Hogan, who cheerfully identified himself as a "square," preferred to concentrate more on the hard stuff. As early as 1943, he accepted the findings of the long-forgotten La Guardia Report—that marijuana smoking was nonaddictive. (Hogan's tolerance of pot smoking was later influenced by talks with Assistant D.A. Samuel Yazgur, son of Max Yazgur, the upstate dairy farmer who became a counterculture hero after he leased out his cow pasture for the epochal "Woodstock Festival.")

"We've probably taken liberties with our policy," Hogan explained to

the *Post* interviewers, "but on any felony indictment involving marijuana, the accused had better be an inveterate seller with pounds and
pounds of the stuff. I'd refuse to indict anybody for having forty or fifty
cigarettes . . . I'd rather just give the kid a warning: 'Go and behave
yourself . . .'

"What set me to thinking about this policy was the experience of my
own junior assistants. I'm sure some of them have experimented along
the way. I'm afraid to ask them whether they smoke marijuana because
they're probably honest enough to admit it."

The entire subject amused Hogan, and he warmed to an anecdote con-
cerning his good friend Dr. William J. McGill, then president of Columbia University.

"President McGill is a very charming person who thinks it part of his
job to meet with students in their dorms and residences. So on a particular afternoon, he was invited to a student tea party. He went to the party
and sat crosslegged on the floor with twenty or thirty students, chatting,
and somebody next to him said, 'Mr. President, will you have a puff?' "

Hogan pantomimed McGill sucking on a reefer. Hogan sniffed, imitat-
ing the university president: "What is it?" The District Attorney's blue
eyes gleamed with amusement, and he looked as if he were about to split
his sides laughing. His words blurred and tears ran down his cheeks.
"Imagine! If I'd raided the place just then, there would be Dr. McGill
squatting on the floor—passing a . . . what's the word I'm thinking of
. . . a joint. Yes, that's it. Dr. McGill smoking a joint!"

One early campaign morning in April, Hogan strolled from his apartment across the Columbia campus quadrangle to the university's law
school, where Professor Richard Uviller, the former chief of the Appeals
Bureau, was waiting for him. Hogan took the stairs two at a time and
seemed hardly out of breath. Uviller was reassured. The law professor
had heard disturbing rumors lately that the campaign was "taking too
much out of Mr. Hogan," that the chief wasn't "feeling himself" on certain days. "Sometimes I can't get my words to match my thoughts,"
Hogan had told John Keenan.

On this particular morning, April 28, Hogan looked in the pink. The
two men sat down to rehearse Hogan's scheduled appearance at a meeting of the powerful Women's Political Caucus, led by the heavy-
breathing Congresswoman Bella Abzug. Uviller anticipated a question
uppermost in the minds of the women's liberationists: "What is your policy, Mr. Hogan, with respect to prosecuting johns as well as prostitutes?"
Uviller tape-recorded his session with the D.A.

Hogan: Well, let me say preliminarily, I'm not sure this group would be interested. This is a *women's* political caucus.

Uviller: Prostitution is one of their first issues.

Hogan: Really?

Uviller: Oh, yes. This is not like the League of Women Voters. This is a militant group. They want to know who is immunized and who is prosecuted in prostitution arrests.

Hogan: Well, both of them are out hunting. They're equally guilty. Traditionally, we made the case—probably wrongly—in favor of what the john could tell us, since theoretically, at least, he was the one approached.

Uviller: Well, that's not the women's view of it.

Hogan: No?

Uviller: The women's view of it. . .

And so it went over the next three hours, Uviller explaining the feminists' demands for legalized prostitution, and Hogan conceding that there was a "forceful argument for that kind of change," preferably through voter referendum.

Mulling over that meeting later in the campaign, Uviller seemed impressed at how fast a man of Hogan's breeding and paternalism caught on to the spirit of the women's movement. "I tended to think of him as an old-fashioned gentleman with an old-fashioned courtliness that used to be called gallantry and was now being called male chauvinism," Uviller reflected.

In public, Hogan always tipped his hat to women. In the office, his assistants were under strict orders to get up from their desks and put on a suit jacket when a woman entered the room. Profanity was forbidden in a woman's presence. In the early days, he hired special male stenographers to take down testimony of lurid sex crimes, rather than embarrass any of the girls in the regular steno pool. And he once refused to hire a qualified young attorney after learning that the job applicant's "roommate" was his fiancée.

If it was unfair to suspect Hogan of maintaining a subconscious "quota" of blacks and women on the legal staff, the suspicion was borne out by actual numbers. On a staff of 175 in 1973 there were six black and eleven female assistant D.A.'s. "I'm breaking my back to get more," Hogan told Uviller, "but what can you do when blacks and women still constitute such a small percentage of the legal profession?"

Over three consecutive summers, Hogan sent two of his black assistants, Richard Lowe and Edward Dudley, son of the Administrative

Judge of Criminal Court, on recruitment missions to Howard University and Harvard. Hogan's missionaries returned empty-handed each time. It seemed that the highest-paying Wall Street firms were beating Hogan to the punch—snatching black law seniors out of the middle of the class before they even looked at a white *Harvard Law Review* man.

"I don't think Hogan did everything he could have to recruit more blacks," said Dudley. "The majority of the people in court were black, and if they saw more black faces at the prosecutor's table, they would feel that there was justice and not merely a repressive system. Dick Lowe and I wanted to set up a more active program to recruit blacks, but Hogan declined. He just said, 'You can't get them.'

"I wanted to set up a committee that would recruit blacks at Harvard and Yale, but he said that was an insult to him. He had always felt that he was a liberal person. If he went to Harvard just to recruit blacks, he said, that would be a discriminatory thing and he would be subjected to criticism by other ethnic groups who would want to know why he didn't recruit more Italians or Chinese."

As for the token number of women prosecutors on staff, Hogan began by keeping them, in effect, "barefoot and pregnant"—restricted to the household drudgery of writing appeals briefs and indictment papers. Women were not permitted to try serious felonies in court, and Hogan maintained that they were "too squeamish" for work in the Homicide Bureau. He flatly asserted that a man would never confess a sex crime to a woman.

But behind his back, there were frustrated females on the legal staff who ridiculed Hogan's paternalism in four-letter expletives that made men's-room graffiti sound like love sonnets. Also unbeknown to Frank Hogan, women prosecutors were trying misdemeanor sex offenses in Criminal Court every day—cross-examining obscene phone callers and flashers, men caught exposing themselves or masturbating in public. Several rapists had confessed their crimes to female assistants.

Assistant D.A. Leslie Snyder, a women's activist who joined the staff in 1968, eventually became the rape expert of Hogan's office. The ravished victims found her more sympathetic than cynical detectives in precinct houses, and so gave her more information on their attackers.

Many rape cases are even more horrendous than one would expect, involving incest and the anal rape of small children. Hogan was pleased when he learned that somebody on his staff took a special interest in the problem. Mrs. Snyder made him aware of the traditional skepticism and the arched eyebrows that greeted many rape victims at the stationhouse, so Hogan assigned her to lecture on the problem at the Police Academy. She also spoke to women's groups, and as word of her crusade spread through the media, more and more rapes were reported to police—and more rapists were caught and punished.

Hogan rewarded Leslie Snyder with a position as trial lawyer in the Supreme Court Bureau. She became the first woman permitted to try major felonies in the history of the office. More female lawyers were encouraged to apply for jobs on the legal staff. Hogan began to hire more women lawyers, though he persisted in being somewhat protective of them. When Mrs. Snyder requested reassignment to the Homicide Bureau, Hogan reluctantly agreed—but only after she had brought in a note from her husband to say it was okay with him.

Hogan had come a long way, baby. But not far enough to satisfy the fire-breathing Women's Political Caucus, which convened on May 9 to hear Hogan and vanden Heuvel.

Seated alongside his challenger at a symposium table, Hogan was forced to answer cries of "sexism" from the Furies of Women's Lib—a loose-knit coalition of feminists who ranged from moderate types to radical Lesbians.

Hogan kept his cool while attorney Brenda Feigen Fasteau harangued him for more than an hour. The tirade ended with an ultimatum: Hogan must instantly hire ten female assistants. Hogan responded forthrightly:

"I don't pick a woman if I can get a man who's better, and I don't pick a man if I can get a woman who's better."

"What if the man and woman are equally qualified?" Fasteau demanded. The question was put first to vanden Heuvel.

"I'd hire the woman," he said.

Hogan smiled wanly: "I hope that I could hire both of them."

To the assembled women, vanden Heuvel's reply sounded suspiciously pandering—Hogan got bigger applause. But he departed the meeting in a state of battle fatigue: "I don't think I can go through this sort of hippodrome again."

The staff cut back on his appointment schedule over the next few weeks. The Chief was complaining more of headaches and buzzing noises in his ears. Mrs. Hogan was troubled by her husband's weakening health.

Some nights, Hogan could be coaxed into campaigning at senior-citizen parties, where he even danced with septuagenarian ladies. The Social Security set gave him a hero's welcome wherever he went. Hogan would respond with a private joke at vanden Heuvel's expense: "I am delighted to be here with so many people who remember Pearl Harbor."

The Hogan record was already familiar (and dear) to New York's population of a million oldsters. Though he was preaching to the already converted, the District Attorney reiterated his grand-jury presentments against substandard nursing homes and shady operators who bilked funds from Medicaid and Medicare.

Hogan also told them of his success against another crime that struck terror into the hearts of the city's defenseless elderly: mugging. He could boast a 93 percent felony-conviction rate for robbery indictments in the past year. Of those convicted muggers, 53 percent had been sentenced to state prison. His conviction rate, even after the bum arrests were thrown out, was still among the highest in the United States: "More people are mugged in Detroit."

As for New York's large kosher-meat contingent, Hogan reminded them that he had indicted unsavory Department of Agriculture inspectors and money-hungry executives of the Merkel Meat Co. "Merkel" must not be forgotten: how millions of dollars had been made by selling the contaminated meat of dead horses and diseased cattle and calling it "Kosher Prime." Thanks to the D.A., New Yorkers were no longer eating horsemeat frankfurters or kangaroo burgers.

Hogan was cajoled into a few speaking engagements at testimonial dinners and clubs like the Rotary and Kiwanis, but he refused to circulate among the tables afterward. "With my record, why should I go around with my hat in my hand?" As the crowd began to thin out, Hogan would scoop up the floral centerpiece from a deserted banquet table (for Mary) and head home to Riverside Drive.

In the midst of what was for him a hectic campaign schedule, nights at home together were Frank and Mary Hogan's most enduring pleasure. His rather musty asceticism was reflected in the library bookshelves. Among other collections, he owned a number of valuable editions of the works of Charles Dickens. Hogan would touch the volumes lovingly in turn, then, puffing thoughtfully on his pipe, choose a well-worn favorite for the evening.

In the quiet of their home, Hogan would read aloud by the hour to "Miss Mary." Sometimes she drowsed off, nodding in her rocker. Hogan, chuckling, would tell friends of the ritual exchanges he would have with his wife at these times.

"Yes?" Mary would cry, snapping back to wakefulness as Hogan reached an emphatic line ("But, Pip, you must believe!")

"You've been asleep for half an hour," her husband would chide.

"Oh, no. I remember. Please, go on . . ."

It was incongruous, somehow: the most feared crime-fighter in America (well, perhaps second to J. Edgar Hoover) fortifying himself with quotations from *Great Expectations* or *The Pickwick Papers*.

Frank Hogan had become something of a Dickens scholar over the years, secure in his opinion, for example, that Dickens' "Child's Story," from an 1850 collection of Christmas stories in *Household Words*, surpassed in literary value the ever-popular *A Christmas Carol* (1843). Hogan had read every biography of his favorite author and rejoiced, too, in Dickensian letters, notebooks and essays. He could quote at length the writer's observations after a visit to the sordid Manhattan Tombs of 1842: "What? Do you thrust your common offenders against the police discipline of the town in holes such as these?" And he knew exactly how, in a letter to an English friend, Dickens had contrasted American courtroom procedure with the powdered-wig rituals of the British law courts. Despite its lack of pomp, Dickens wrote, the American system "managed to hang a man just the same." Hogan himself envied the British their law courts. They seemed to show what Hogan considered the proper regard for form, for precision in language, for courtesy and eloquence in debate.

Hogan's apartment windows did not face urban decay: the rotting tenements, street stands and fleabag hotels were tucked behind his building at 404 Riverside Drive. The Hogan apartment looked west, across the slate-blue Hudson River to the wide shelf of the Jersey Palisades. By day, he could see sun-dappled water, soaring gulls, an occasional tugboat or a palatial yacht. At night, his windows framed even more dazzling pictures: the firefly lights of boats, moving out on the river, and, closer in, the West Side Highway turned into a spectacular streak of neon, the taillights of cars aimed like tracer bullets at the suburbs beyond the city. To the north, crowning this light show, was the diamond coronet of the majestic George Washington Bridge.

The rent-controlled apartment at 404 had been decorated by Mary Hogan to give her husband the mood he wanted: the peace and solace of an earlier age. The antique furniture gleamed with polish. Hogan's rocking chair, his mahogany pipe racks, his well-stacked library shelves. Green tendrils of ivy curled over the ornate marble mantle; needlepoint pillows were nestled into the couches. Hogan's own oil portrait gazed somberly back at him from one wall.

The twelve-story building was itself an Old World anachronism. When the building had first opened its doors in 1909, the doormen wore white gloves, the lobby was baroque, the furniture gothic. The ambience had survived. People of refinement lived there. Among the seventy-five tenants were university professors, City Hall administrators, musicians, publishing executives, professionals.

Hogan was a regular bridge partner in the men's foursome that rotated around the building on weekends. The players nibbled cheese and sipped Scotch. After a game, they held forth as a discussion group called "The Occasional Saturdays," debating philosophies of life in the manner of wing-collar characters out of *The Forsyte Saga*. With literate discourse, good music, and their own companionship, the neighbors were never bored with themselves. Well-kept and supervised, 404 remained a civilized bastion in a neighborhood that had largely deteriorated into dingy welfare hotels and hangouts for pimps and pushers.

Security was tight: a depressing sign of the times. Frank and Mary Hogan had lived in their ninth-floor apartment for nearly thirty years, protected only by the doorman, who announced all visitors from the lobby. But now, every night of the campaign, the District Attorney could peer out the apartment window and see two policemen leaning on the fenders of a radio squad car parked diagonally to the soaring canopy of the apartment house. Searchlights concentrated starkly on the front door, blinding anybody who entered or left the building.

The Sixth Division had ordered round-the-clock police protection for Hogan in the aftermath of the Panther 21 trial. During the one-year trial, the longest and costliest in the state's history, the house belonging to presiding Judge Murtaugh had been firebombed. Snipers murdered four policemen. A purported assassination attempt against Hogan was thwarted when police intercepted a cache of hand grenades in a locker at the Port Authority bus terminal. During all this commotion, Hogan refused to be bothered with bodyguards. Then, on May 19, 1971, a patrol car cruising near Hogan's home was ambushed by two armed men in a passing auto. Two police officers were badly wounded by .45-caliber machine-gun bullets. The fusillade shattered one man's spine, crippling him for life. Hogan's mistrust of the Panther jury verdict was borne out. Panther Richard Moore, who had jumped bail and was acquitted *in absentia*, was now under arrest as one of the passengers in the getaway car. He was later tried and found guilty of attempted murder.

Against Hogan's wishes, the Department put the District Attorney's apartment house under guard and installed a special-frequency two-way radio in his limousine so that Toby could alert headquarters to any suspicious "tails."

Meanwhile, Hogan's attitude of peace-above-the-tumult reaffirmed Alexis de Tocqueville's theme of the Bar as the only possible American aristocracy. Hogan's equanimity was so impressive to his staff during this dangerous period that the Chief seemed to function as a sort of legal "Godfather."

One incident early in the campaign demonstrated the feelings of affection, admiration and loyalty that Frank Hogan inspired in his staff. It happened while he was on the reviewing stand of the annual St. Patrick's Day parade along Fifth Avenue.

Hogan stood through a four-hour drizzle. Mayor Lindsay and other dignitaries had waited to get their pictures taken and then ducked away to the dry warmth of their limousines. At the end of the parade, Hogan stood alone on a platform of official deserters. A solitary figure in rain-drenched overcoat, he coughed and sneezed, but held his ground, determined to salute the last bedraggled marching band. As the Immaculate Conception High School Drum and Bugle Corps passed in review, Hogan doffed his hat and turned to leave.

Suddenly, a cheer rose up from the last stragglers of the parade. Hogan squinted into the rain. What was this? More than sixty of the D.A.'s own men and women were bringing up the rear. They whooped and hollered and held up V-for-victory fingers. The band joined in applause for Hogan. Majorettes broke ranks and ran to plant wet kisses on his cheek. Bugle boys rushed over to shake his hand. Then Hogan's loyal sons and daughters sang out in unison, and the windswept mob of strangers picked up the refrain:

It's a long, long way to Tipperary
Tip-per-aryyy-y-y . . . my home!"

15
THE UNHEARD
HURRAH

Toward the end of April, voter-opinion polls showed vanden Heuvel leading by 8 percent. He had received the editorial endorsement of the New York *Post* and was picking up support among liberal Democratic assemblymen.

Mayor John V. Lindsay offered the underdog the services of a political gun for hire, a professional campaign strategist named Richard Weston. Weston, a Brooklyn Law graduate, had worked as an advance man for Lindsay and Rockefeller. Slick, successful and handsome, he seemed as if he were being played by movie actor George Hamilton. Hogan mistrusted him on sight.

"I was the outsider, the stranger," Weston later recalled. "Everything I did in that office was monitored—dozens of eyes were on me. The staff was offended that I didn't address 'Mr. Hogan' with reverence. I called him Frank—to show these guys that you had to deal with Hogan as a human being and not let the 'Mr. District Attorney' myth get in the way."

Before he agreed to work for Hogan, Dick Weston solicited advice from his friends in the liberal-radical legal fraternity:

"I wanted to prove I wasn't a hired gun. If politics is the art of the possible, I wanted to see if it was possible for me to live with the Hogan ideology, or sacrifice principle."

Weston discovered that support for Hogan came even from those who most fiercely opposed him in the courtroom. Curly-haired Gerald Lefcourt, the shrewd radical attorney who had successfully defended the Black Panthers, expressed a grudging admiration. "You can't buy the guy," Lefcourt told Weston. "Despite his faults, Hogan runs the best damned D.A.'s office in the country. His kind of integrity isn't easy to come by in this day and age." Several ACLU lawyers echoed Lefcourt's appreciation of Hogan the man. Perhaps the Manhattan D.A.'s office was out of touch, or even ossified, they conceded, but at the bottom line the man in charge gave you a fair shake. Hogan couldn't be accused of prosecuting anyone to advance his own career. He had forsaken political ambition.

After Weston met with the D.A. in person, the younger man came away with two strong impressions: "One: I was impressed with his analytical ability and his vitality; he was like a man in his fifties.

"Two: I felt I was talking to a foreigner. His lack of political knowledge was incredible. He didn't know how many districts there were. He didn't know who the district leaders were. He knew nothing about the county committee and how important it is. I thought for a while that he might be putting me on . . . trying to convince me he was really nonpolitical. Then I realized it was all true. Politics was an unknown world to him."

Weston junked the two-bit "Hogan for D.A." handbills and put to work all the merchandising techniques of the Madison Avenue media manipulator. He rigged up a computerized statistical survey of Manhattan's 1.5 million Democratic electorate. Six hundred carefully worded questionnaires were distributed. What did the Democratic voters think of their District Attorney? What was Hogan's reputation for integrity and ability? Then the subtle question: "There are those who say Frank Hogan has been around too long and 'it's time for a change.' What is your opinion?"

The computer analyzed the questionnaire in terms of each respondent's age, sex, religion, ethnic neighborhood, and income bracket. Ordinarily, this sort of feedback presents a number of socioeconomic factors which the campaign manager must take into account when trying to sway people toward his candidate.

The Hogan feedback reduced the entire campaign down to one simple issue: age. The voters—black, white or Puerto Rican—would rather vote for a young William vanden Heuvel, however "opportunistic," than an old Frank Hogan, however honorable. Hogan came across as a hero to everybody—Italians, Jews, Germans, the Irish—but time had apparently passed him by.

The average American voter may regard most old people as out of touch with the rest of society, but in Congress, and to a lesser degree, the courts, American government remains essentially a gerontocracy. In the Senate in 1973, seventeen regular committee chairmen were over seventy, four others over sixty-five. In the House, three committee chairmen were over seventy, four more were in their late sixties.

So, the "elder statesman" was still venerated at the ballot box, Weston knew, but only if the candidate communicated an aura of strength and paternalism. Weston went to work on Hogan's age problem with the help of motivational research experts from a TV advertising agency. Together, they developed a two-pronged strategy. To accentuate the positive, nonpolitical aspect of Hogan's reputation, the agency came up with a double-edged, when-did-you-stop-beating-your-wife-type campaign slogan:

"You can't play politics with people's lives."

This message was linked to a crucial second phase of the strategy: saturation exposure of Frank Hogan on a carefully modulated, thirty-second TV spot commercial. "People don't know Frank Hogan. All they know is the Frank Hogan legend," Weston asserted. "We have to show them that there really *is* a Frank Hogan. He walks. He talks. He's alive and well and living in New York City."

With considerable reluctance, Hogan agreed to appear at the TV agency's studio and videotape the political advertisement for himself. The day he arrived, a Hollywoodish stage setting had been erected. Hogan was ushered into a cardboard "courtroom" and posed in front of a mock jury box. A makeup artist arrived to beautify the D.A. by daubing at his wrinkles, outlining his tired blue eyes, and powder-puffing his jowls.

Sound technicians tested their microphones. Hogan squinted into the Tele-prompter and began a runthrough of the rehearsal script, written by Tony Isadore. Isadore, a million-dollar idea man in the ad business, had several successful TV catchphrases to his credit, including the Urban Coalition slogan, "Give a Damn."

Hogan recited:

"I'm no politician.

"I've never had to go to coffeeklatches or kiss babies.

"I'd be a flop on the *Johnny Carson Show.*"

Hogan hesitated. The Johnny Carson line disturbed his vanity. "*Why* would I be a flop on the *Johnny Carson Show?*" Tony Isadore and Weston said okay, they'd take that out.

Hogan continued:

"You can embarrass the Democrats.

"You can embarrass the Republicans.

"You can go after the Mayor's man.

"You can go after the Governor's man."

Hogan stopped in midsentence. "I've never 'gone after' anyone in my life," he protested. "If they committed a *crime*, I prosecuted them." Isadore smiled weakly as Hogan went reluctantly on with the rest of the script.

"You can take on a labor union. You can take on all of Wall Street. You can go after the head of organized crime, a borough president, or the Mayor himself. You can do all of these things when you run a nonpolitical D.A.'s office. But there's one thing you can't do.

"You can't play politics with people's lives."

Hogan read through the last line and shook his head. "That's a terrible thing to say, 'You can't play politics with people's lives.' "

"Why is it so terrible?" asked campaign chairman Ted Kheel.

"Because it implies that vanden Heuvel *does* play politics with people's lives."

"Well, don't you think he does?" asked Kheel.

"Yes, I believe that would be the effect of his conduct," said Hogan, "but I'm not going to say it *in public*."

Kheel and Roberts argued that this was the message they were trying to get across: Hogan would be saying it without really saying it.

The D.A. retreated to a corner of the studio and began scribbling his own script: "Politics has no place in the District Attorney's office. My job is to administer justice vigorously but fairly. . . ." When he had finished, Weston and Isadore both went over the lifeless prose. "Frank," Weston said finally, "you're drawing important distinctions to a prosecutor, but we're trying to show you as someone totally attuned to the 1970s. Our script is pungent, it's dramatic . . . and *there's no rebuttal*."

Burton Roberts then got in the act, wheedling and cajoling until the Chief finally agreed to the "You can't play politics" line on one condition: "I'll say it once but I never want to hear it again."

Never hear it again? Weston informed Hogan that the campaign slogan would be plastered on thousands of billboards all over Manhattan. More than 30,000 posters had already been ordered and paid for. Hogan groaned, then turned to face the cameras as he delivered Isadore's original script.

The cameras rolled through forty-seven consecutive takes. The shooting session droned on for five hours. Hogan sweated under the hot lights. His shirt wilted. His voice cracked.

On instant replay, he looked terrific.

On videotape, Frank S. Hogan, with his somber brow and glistening white hair, gloriously personified his own "Mr. Integrity" legend. The blue eyes drilled through the camera lens like lasers, riveting viewers with the sincerity of the message he himself had questioned. Hogan evoked all the Father Confessors of media history: Bishop Sheen, Senator Sam Ervin, Spencer Tracy, Dwight Eisenhower, Ed Sullivan . . . One glimpse at the TV monitor and Dick Weston knew the voters would lap it up.

"Super," he said.

The Frank Hogan bandwagon was ready to roll, but to get it rolling, Weston needed $100,000 in a hurry: the TV spot alone would cost that. It was urgent to buy the television time before vanden Heuvel gained greater momentum. Vanden Heuvel had the backing of several wealthy supporters—among them, Jackie Kennedy Onassis, prominent invest- ment bankers Bradley C. Drownie and John Jakobsen, and the can- didate's wife, heiress Jean Stein vanden Heuvel.

There was only $50,000 in Hogan's campaign chest, and the political clubs were no help to him. The *deus ex machina* arrived in the person of Governor Nelson Rockefeller, who had intervened in the Manhattan primary races in a vain attempt to forge a Republican-Liberal alliance behind Robert F. Wagner for Mayor. This attempt to restore New York City's past had stopped dead, but Rockefeller was still pledged to support Hogan on the "nostalgia ticket." Rockefeller *had* talked Hogan into the race. The Governor could not let him falter in the starting gate.

At Weston's suggestion, the Governor held a Hogan fund-raising sur- prise party at Rocky's sumptuous duplex on Fifth Avenue, overlooking Central Park. Hogan arrived early, tiptoeing among the Beautiful People who oohed and aaahed over Rockefeller's fabled art collection of French impressionists.

Rockefeller suddenly seized center stage in the living room. He plinked a fork against his cocktail glass, calling guests to attention. Conversation stopped. As everyone watched, Rockefeller sprang on top of an antique end table. From this expensive soapbox, the Governor pitched for con- tributions to "this fine community asset we have in the nonpartisan office of Frank Hogan." Rockefeller, never having known the taint of the word "money-grubber" that a man less endowed might have felt, was not shy about asking for money, even *begging* for it. He exhorted the crowd to yank out their checkbooks and fork over "a hundred grand" for a Hogan TV campaign.

While Rockefeller passed the hat, Hogan slunk off into a corner. The fund-raising itself was enough to embarrass him, but there was another discomfiting aspect to the evening. As he turned his back to the crowded room and walked toward a window, his eye was caught by a street scene below. A man stood picketing in front of the building, heckling Rockefeller's guests as they alighted from taxis and limousines.

"We are not selling Manhattan to the Governor!" the man shouted at each new arrival.

The man was William vanden Heuvel.

"And he calls himself a lawyer," Weston heard Hogan mutter in distaste.

Dignity was a luxury vanden Heuvel was less and less able to afford. After his initial windsprint into public popularity, vanden Heuvel now found himself slipping behind. Apprehension mounted in the rival camp a few weeks later when the Hogan TV commercial hit the screen and attracted viewers. At the same time, Hogan picked up solid support. The deans of ten law schools endorsed Hogan. The New York Bar Association rated him "highly qualified and preferred," dismissing vanden Heuvel as "not approved." The reason for nonapproval: vanden Heuvel had padded his résumé—listing himself as a "member" of Senator Jacob Javits' law firm. In actuality, he had been an associate of the firm, but not a "member," which in legal parlance means partner.

In subsequent radio and TV debates with Frank Hogan, the challenger fared poorly, contradicting himself about his involvement in the Pyles case. Hogan carped incessantly about the prison disturbances: "A great many members of my staff have a different philosophy than Mr. vanden Heuvel—they don't approve of a man who urges prison guards to defy the courts."

Vanden Heuvel's *coup de grace* was delivered in the New York *Times'* endorsement of Hogan:

"There can be little doubt that under normal circumstances, it would be time for the District Attorney—even one so eminent as Mr. Hogan—to retire, but we recognize the sincerity of his fear that the exacting standards of professional excellence, integrity and nonpartisanship which he made a hallmark of his office may be put in jeopardy.

"The campaign will give Manhattan voters an opportunity to decide whether age has diminished Mr. Hogan's demonstrated capacity to maintain these high standards, and, no less important, whether any rival on the ballot has the potential to match them.

"Whatever the result of the contest, it would be sensible to remove future choices from the political maelstrom by making the district attorneys as well as judges appointive."

Taking the last line of the editorial as his cue, Hogan seized the campaign opportunity to advance a bold proposal—perhaps the only worthwhile suggestion that emerged from the slugfest with vanden Heuvel. This was the season of Watergate. Former Attorney General John Mitchell had just been indicted on federal charges of conspiracy and perjury in accepting illegal contributions to the 1972 Nixon-Agnew campaign. Although Nixon kept insisting he wanted "an arm's-length relationship" between the Justice Department and the White House in the Watergate investigation, it was clear to Hogan—as well as to most lawyers—that a *prima facie* cover-up case had already been established against the President. As the scandal mushroomed, Hogan cautiously refrained from public comment.

In private, there was one aspect of the Watergate mess that reassured him, reaffirming his reputation for self-censure and guardianship of legal ethics: his most famous alumnus, former Attorney General and Secretary of State William P. Rogers, was one of the few members of Nixon's inner circle who remained untouched by the scandal that would eventually implicate more than 300 lawyers in charges brought before their respective state bar associations. ("Thank God I wasn't spattered by Watergate," Rogers told the author during the later Nixon impeachment hearings. "Frank Hogan would have been mortified.")

On May 16, 1973, Hogan gave a speech to a New York dinner meeting of the Association of Lawyers of the Criminal Courts. He addressed himself to the problems inherent in having partisan politics brought to bear on the proper administration of justice. His suggestion: "I propose that it is time we debated, as a people committed to a government of laws, the advisability of separating the prosecution function from cabinet responsibility in the national government. The question for sober, nonpartisan discussion is whether, in the long run, there should be fundamental change sufficient to ensure the total independence of the chief prosecutor of the United States. Absolute independence of the nation's chief prosecutor can be accomplished while preserving the Office of Attorney General, at cabinet level, as counsel to the government. The function of chief prosecutor presently residing in the Attorney General should be taken out of the office and vested in a new, permanent, statutory official, a Prosecutor General of the United States. He would be appointed for a fixed term, of six years, upon confirmation by the Senate.

The appointing authority would be the United States Supreme Court, as authorized by Article II, Section 2, of the Constitution. Under this proposal, the Federal Bureau of Investigation would also be under the authority of the Prosecutor General."

This speech, known as the "Watergate" speech, though he never mentioned the word, ended the formal phase of Hogan's campaigning. He remained sequestered in his office, getting the D.A.'s work done while his videotaped self did the vote-getting.

Election Night finally arrived, with Hogan down in the dumps: a last-minute poll showed the candidates running neck and neck. Were people going to vote for young vanden Heuvel in spite of the older man's prestigious support?

His eyes fixed on a television set, Hogan sat silently in an outer office of campaign headquarters, while Dick Weston took telephone calls from a cadre of assistant D.A.s spotted at polling places around the city. The first returns came in from a Little Italy district that had spawned the worst of the Mafia's killers in bygone days: Hogan led four to one.

"I've never seen anything like it," Weston said.

Thirty-five minutes after the polls closed, Frank S. Hogan stepped into the center of the balloon-decked headquarters to receive the crowd's cheers. With 940 of 955 districts reporting, the vote was Hogan 83,464, vanden Heuvel 57,677. Champagne corks popped. People hurled confetti. Someone pointed to a nearby stack of leftover campaign literature, and Hogan grinned playfully:

"We've learned a few tricks. Now what should we run for? Governor? President?"

The jubilance became official with a telephone call from vanden Heuvel, offering his congratulations. Hogan had to yell into the receiver to make himself heard above the pandemonium in the room. "I don't think the scars are too deep," he shouted apologetically. "I hope we didn't wound each other too badly."

Hogan strode to the rostrum and solemnly proclaimed his victory "a vindication for the nonpolitical composition and character of our office." Then he grinned. "It is also a vindication for a middle-aged man like myself." The throng of well-wishers cheered once more.

Dick Weston, his role at an end, reflected that in the psychological countdown of the campaign, he hadn't had time to meditate on what the political struggle signified, either to Hogan or himself. Had something useful been accomplished? Whatever the victory signified, Weston felt he

was an outsider, once more an interloper among all these diehard Hogan-
ites. But even as a "stepson," Weston had grown rather fond of Frank
Hogan during the campaign. Weston remembered one of their first dinner meetings together at the Tavern-on-the-Green in Central Park.

"Hogan was in a reminiscent mood that night, rambling on about all
the gangsters of the past, and he kept me spellbound for three hours.
When we got up to leave, he put on his gray fedora and you could just
see him in his younger days—Frank Hogan as Eliot Ness, rackets-
buster."

Although awed by this image, Weston drew back from an unpleasant
hubris in Frank Hogan, a disdain for electoral politics: "He simply did
not want to admit that he owed his office to people pulling a lever in a
polling booth. He felt the District Attorney should not be a constitu-
tionally elected office. That was all right for Mayors and Presidents, but
not for Frank Hogan. What bothered him on Election Night, I felt, was
that he owed his victory to me and other people like me—rather than to
his own record."

Having vanquished the first challenge in his thirty-two-year reign,
Hogan sailed happily into the office the next morning, to be met with
bad news: the campaign had run over its $150,000 budget and was now
$80,000 in debt.

"His reaction was so irrational that I feared for his health," Weston
later recalled. "Ordinarily, a winning candidate would schedule a fund-
raising testimonial dinner to cover the debt, and forget about it. But
Hogan freaked out. It seemed he had this image of having to take the
money out of his paycheck. He turned hostile to me, saying, 'I won by
such a large margin, I really didn't need you to build up this kind of
debt.' I was hurt. I felt like shouting at him, 'You ungrateful SOB! How
dare you say something like that!' But there was so much anger in his
voice, and he was trembling so badly, that I was afraid to say it, for fear of
bringing on a heart attack."

Hogan worried himself literally sick over the debt for the next few
weeks. He refused to hold a testimonial dinner and "go around with my
hat in my hand." He resolved to pay off the debt out of his own savings
account. Everybody agreed that this was unheard of, but Hogan stubbornly persisted. After thirty-seven years on the public payroll, at an annual salary that never rose above $41,000, he had accumulated a net
worth of $200,000. (The lion's share of his earnings and investments had
been donated to Columbia University.) His conversations on the subject

of the campaign debt became disjointed and irrational. Hogan seemed to be losing his grip.

In the midst of a July heatwave, the staff urged him to take a long weekend rest at Gurney's Inn, in Montauk, L.I. So he took Mary out to bask with him on the sand dunes, but he couldn't unwind. Hogan called the office three and four times a day; talking with his staff, he began to repeat himself, and to forget what had just been said to him.

When he returned to the office at the end of the month he was clearly not himself. He complained of headaches and memory dim-outs, lapsed in midspeech into nonsense syllables, and took to singing snippets of "Tommy Ladd," an Irish lullaby he had learned on his father's knee in Waterbury. Several times, he had to be driven home from the office early after a vomiting seizure or a fainting spell.

In the early-morning hours of August 11, he awakened with a coughing fit. When his wife tried to comfort him, he seemed not to know her. His face contorted, Hogan was rushed to the emergency room of St. Luke's Hospital by his brother Joseph, who drove down from his Connecticut home after a hysterical telephone call from Mrs. Hogan. A hospital resident diagnosed cerebral thrombosis, a blood clot in the brain. Paraphasia—the word-scrambling disorder—was characteristic of the stroke.

But Mrs. Hogan, seeing her husband this way, lapsed into irrationality herself, refusing to accept the medical diagnosis as anything more serious than "fatigue." She took up a bedside vigil, reminding hospital authorities that Mr. Hogan was a trustee of St. Luke's. As "Mrs. District Attorney," it was her wish that her husband's illness be kept secret.

She directed that Hogan's room be sealed off to all visitors. Hospital authorities acceded—posting security guards at the door and announcing to the press that the District Attorney was in "for rest and tests." Mrs. Hogan said she herself would issue future "bulletins" on her husband's health, through the D.A.'s office.

Frank Hogan was still the multi-party candidate for reelection on the November 1973 ballot. Under state law, his name could be withdrawn any time before August 23, the deadline for filing by petition candidates. Almost surely, vanden Heuvel would step forward again if the truth about Frank Hogan was known. But once the August 23 deadline had passed, Hogan's name could be withdrawn only in the event of his death.

It is still difficult to be sure of the precise motives for what happened after Hogan's attack. Mary Hogan, the increasingly introverted and grief-stricken wife, perhaps simply could not accept the idea that her husband of thirty-seven years was on his deathbed. She issued false and misleading "bulletins" on Hogan's condition almost daily, telling the public that the D.A. was undergoing "routine tests" as part of a pre-vacation physical examination. Hogan's office, through acting D.A. Alfred Scotti, reiterated that the District Attorney was suffering "fatigue" and was expected to be discharged "in a few days."

The August 23 deadline passed, eliminating vanden Heuvel's last chance. Hogan's condition worsened. X-rays detected a tiny "suspicious" speck on his lungs. On September 7, he underwent massive chest surgery for a cancerous left lung. The only announcement from Mrs. Hogan was that her husband's condition was "good." She added that he had "a high temperature."

While Hogan lay speechless, the bland bulletins continued to be issued by associates—Al Scotti and Burton Roberts among them—who visited his bedside. Later, Scotti would say he was merely passing along the denials of Mrs. Hogan.

The cover-up ended on September 17, when a hospital employee leaked photocopies of Hogan's medical records to the New York *Post*.

"The conclusion is inevitable that these deceits were designed to prevent the emergence of a petition candidate," the *Post* noted editorially, terming the result "a crude frustration of the democratic process."

"Obviously," the editorial continued, "the stricken Frank Hogan was not an accomplice in these maneuvers. But those who arranged the cover-up were cynically operating to keep control of his office . . . In the meantime, it is lamentable that Hogan's burdens have been compounded by intrigues beyond his control and wholly inconsistent with his character."

Hogan was discharged from St. Luke's on September 20, and for a few days in October, he was seen strolling on his wife's arm through Riverside Park. Mrs. Hogan said that her husband—reassured of victory in November—was steadily improving and anxious to get back to the office. In actuality, these daily strolls were pathetic evidence that Frank Hogan would not walk much longer.

One morning, his dedicated chauffeur and bodyguard, Detective Toby Fennell, approached the couple in Riverside Park. Affectionately, Toby leaned over, as he always did when he met the Boss' wife, to kiss Mrs. Hogan's cheek. At that, the D.A. feebly tilted *his* head forward, somehow expecting that the kiss had been meant for him.

"I think he recognizes you, Toby," Mrs. Hogan whispered. The body-guard turned and kissed Hogan's cheek, then opened his arms to him. Fennell could feel the old man's shoulderblades poking sharply through the loose flesh. As Fennell walked away, he felt he should turn around once more to see the Chief. Toby was startled by the sight: Hogan stood still, the light gone from his eyes, the life from his body; his hand was raised in a frail wave of goodbye.

The unprecedented ninth-term vote rolled in automatically for Hogan on November 4, but the victor, thin and immobile, in bed, already looked like a cadaver.

On December 26, his long-time friend Bernard Botein, former justice of the Appellate Division, was commissioned to read a formal statement of resignation. In a fifteen-minute press conference, Botein, his face heavy with melancholy, noted that Frank Hogan, "never a man to strain for a last hurrah," was bowing out for reasons of ill health. "To the members of his staff, past and present, he is and always will be their Chief," Botein asserted, "and if a tinge of hero worship is also evident, that's refreshing in these unheroic and cynical times."

Carried back into St. Luke's on December 27, Hogan remained semi-comatose for three months. Another malignant tumor was detected—in the vital center of the old man's brain.

There was one former associate whose love for Frank Hogan destined him to go now and stand for all the others. Justice Burton Roberts, *enfant terrible* of the Hogan years, stayed with him to the end. "Take my hand, fella," Roberts insisted, feigning the playful swagger that had always amused Hogan in the past. "You're the greatest! You hear me? *The greatest!*"

The District Attorney died in his sleep at 12:10 P.M., April 4, 1974, at the age of seventy-two.

The official tributes were led by Richard H. Kuh, the improbable figure whom the state's new governor, Malcolm Wilson, had appointed Hogan's successor (ignoring Hogan's last wish that Scotti succeed him). Sworn in as the new D.A., Kuh's first official word was a pledge to "carry on the tradition" of his predecessor.

"Frank Hogan was a complex person," Kuh eulogized at a memorial service. "A prosecutor for almost forty years, he had the compassion of a Darrow." First Assistant D.A. David Worgan added that Hogan "possessed a stunning awareness of the human dimension in things, of how public prosecution is so inevitably bound up in the pathos and frailty of human life." Justice Burton Roberts, consumed by heartache over the loss of his mentor, vowed: "If I sit on this Court until I am one hundred years of age, each day and every day that I adjourn court I shall note on the record that this Court stands adjourned in memory of Frank Hogan."

Chief Supreme Court Justice Warren Burger paid tribute to Frank Hogan, as did New York's Governor, the City's Mayor, and many of the nation's highest judges and prosecutors. On April 5, 1974, traffic patrolmen had to set up roadblocks on Park Avenue to make way for the crush of official limousines and dignitaries arriving at St. Ignatius Loyola Church to pay their final respects. The gray stone cathedral was filled. Among the honorary pallbearers were former Attorney General William P. Rogers, Governor Wilson, Mayor Abe Beame, Chief Judge Charles Breitel, and Police Commissioner Michael Codd. The high requiem mass and eulogy delivered by the Rev. Dr. Robert I. Gannon, former president of Fordham University, hearkened back to a saying by one of Hogan's favorite literary characters, Mr. Dooley (Finley Peter Dunne):

" 'Tis a good thing th' fun'ral sermons ar-re not composed in th' confissional."

"Shy and quiet," said Father Gannon, "he remained in the public eye for thirty-two years as the Chief, as 'Mr. District Attorney.' Of course, no one can prosecute so many racketeers, nobody can investigate so many dubious political situations, and not be criticized occasionally as being too strict or too lenient. But the longsuffering public, as well as the hundreds of lawyers who looked up to him, kept him on the pedestal year after year because he was a man of courage and integrity. A man who was devoting his life not to the winning of convictions, but to the protection of his fellow New Yorkers by the just application of the law. To his family, it may seem that he was taken too soon. But who knows? Life for so many of us can become such an anticlimax! For him, death was just a kindly usher who opened the door to eternity and beckoned to him to cross the threshhold."

Hogan's widow, Mary, and his brother Joe and sister Martha followed the rosewood coffin as it was carried to a waiting hearse. Hogan's body would be taken from his adopted New York City to Waterbury, Connecticut—and there buried in a cemetery near his birthplace.

An uninvited funeral guest filed out of the church along with the mourners. No stranger to the D.A.'s office, he was known in the 1960s as the Rev. A. Kendall Smith, a black civil-rights activist who stepped down from the pulpit to run as an unsuccessful independent candidate for City

Council. In 1967, the gadfly politician was found guilty of passing a worthless $50 check in a Washington, D.C., clothing store. The conviction capped a lengthy record of sit-in arrests and disorderly-conduct charges against the hyperemotional clergyman. The following year, police pegged him as an "outside agitator" at the Columbia-SDS riots. After 1968, the bearded minister showed up frequently at police stations, usually in handcuffs. He deteriorated into reckless drinking bouts and self-destructive troublemaking. On one blackout bender, he drew a gun and shot up an East Side bar and grill, wounding a beer-drinker in the rump.

On the day of Hogan's funeral, there was an outstanding arrest warrant against Smith. The D.A.'s squad spotted him in the crowd just as Hogan's coffin was borne into the street.

Shortly before the service began, Mrs. Hogan had slipped the detectives a telegram sent to her by the preacher:

"Having been New York County's most arrested and prosecuted human rights clergyman under the distinguished administration of Mr. Hogan, please understand and accept my sincere expression of sympathy to you. I pray that the administration of justice in New York County will now be void of injustice against those who are willing to be jailed and prosecuted for equality in New York. I do appreciate the last charges dismissed against me last year while I remained in exile. I hope Mr. Hogan's soul will find justice in God's eternal administration."

The detectives translated this message of condolence into one word of their own: "Troublemaker."

Following Smith out of the church, detectives were prepared to keep a wary eye on him—but were totally unprepared for what they did see. Smith had slipped behind the wheel of a rented limousine that was now parked in the funeral motorcade directly behind the hearse—between Hogan's casket and the undertaker's car bearing his widow. The detectives panicked: how the hell had this happened? What kind of an ugly scene was the preacher here to stir up?

They charged over, yanked open the limousine door and seized the fugitive by his preacher's collar. Pinning him against the car fender, they listened to Smith spitting and snarling curses against the "white Establishment"—and swearing up and down that he was only there "to pay my respects."

"We appreciate your sympathy," one of the detectives snapped as they frisked his pants legs. (In deference to the dignity of the occasion, they resisted the impulse to spread-eagle their prisoner, as they would ordinarily have done, over the hood of the nearest vehicle—in this case, the hearse.)

Smith's face reflected the hard life he had lived: it was a composite sketch of every indigent, every criminal, every prisoner—every marginal man—who had ever peered out of the Tombs. It was a face that Hogan's office underlings confronted almost daily in court—but one that he himself almost never saw.

Amid all the confusion, the pallbearers slipped Hogan's casket inside the hearse. Father Gannon uttered a hasty benediction. But his were not the last words recited over Hogan's departed soul. The next sentence spoken seemed more appropriate than any benediction or sprinkling of earth. They were the words Frank Hogan never heard spoken in life, although they underscored his magisterial power and set his corporate crime-fighting machine in motion.

They were the words of a detective as he scuffled with Smith over Hogan's hearse and snapped on the handcuffs.

"You're under arrest!"

By the time the hearse arrived at Hogan's final resting place in a Waterbury cemetery, detectives in New York learned that Smith had billed the limousine rental, without permission, to the National Council of Churches.

The Reverend A. Kendall Smith was carted off to the Tombs.

Frank Hogan was lowered to his grave.

INDEX